AF251743

Judaism
and
Psychoanalysis

BOOKS BY MORTIMER OSTOW, M.D.

Judaism and Psychoanalysis
The Psychodynamic Approach to Drug Therapy
Sexual Deviation: Psychoanalytic Insights
The Psychological Bases of War (with H. Z. Winnik and R. Moses)
The Psychology of Melancholy
Drugs in Psychoanalysis and Psychotherapy
The Need to Believe (with Ben Ami Scharfstein)
Diagnostic Electroencephalography (with H. Strauss and L. Greenstein)

Judaism and Psychoanalysis

Mortimer Ostow, M.D., Med. Sc. D.

KTAV PUBLISHING HOUSE, INC.
NEW YORK
1982

Library of Congress Cataloging in Publication Data
Main entry under title:

Judaism and psychoanalysis.

  Bibliography: p.
  Includes index.
  1. Judaism and psychoanalysis—Addresses, essays,
lectures. I. Ostow, Mortimer. [DNLM: 1. Judaism.
2. Psychoanalysis. 3. Religion and psychology.
WM 460.5.R3 085j]
BM538.P68J8   150.19′5   81-3700
ISBN 0-87068-713-1   AACR2

Contents

Preface

It was Mr. Bernard Scharfstein, of Ktav Publishing House, Inc., who suggested collecting a set of essays on the subject of Judaism and psychoanalysis. Checking the idea with a number of colleagues and friends, I found enough encouragement to undertake the project.

I have selected the papers assembled here with two criteria in mind. First, I required that each paper deal with the concepts, theories, and observations of authentic psychoanalysis or psychoanalytic psychiatry in the tradition of Sigmund Freud. Second, I required that each author write from sophisticated knowledge of both disciplines. The first essay, "Judaism and Psychoanalysis," was written specifically for this book, and was intended to serve as an introduction. Dr. Arlow's paper, "Unconscious Fantasy and Political Movements," was also prepared for this volume. The others are reprinted, having been published originally elsewhere, or were written for other purposes.

The individual essays are fairly diverse in content. Most assume some degree of familiarity, on the part of the reader, with psychoanalytic concepts and with Jewish history, Scripture, and post-Scriptural literature.

I have arranged the essays in a sequence that corresponds with the sequence of topics in the introductory essay. Although they are not related to each other in any systematic way, they do provide what I believe to be a fair sample of responsible thinking about the relation between Judaism and psychoanalysis.

I wish to thank Drs. Arlow, Bergmann, Lifton and Rubenstein, and Mrs. Edith Sillman for permitting me to use the material presented in this volume.

My friend and colleague, Dr. Gerson D. Cohen, Chancellor of The Jewish Theological Seminary of America has instructed, inspired guided and counseled me for many years, and I wish here to express my indebtedness and appreciation.

I should like to acknowledge my gratitude to my friends, Rabbi Edward T. Sandrow, who, until his recent death, served as rabbi in Cedarhurst, Rabbi Armond E. Cohen of Cleveland, and Rabbi Harry Halpern of Brooklyn, all of whom pioneered in applying psychoanalytic principles to the discipline of rabbinic counseling, and encouraged the previous Chancellor, Dr. Louis Finkelstein, to introduce rabbinic counseling into the curriculum of The Jewish Theological Seminary. Dr. Bernard Mandelbaum, President Emeritus of the Seminary, is to be credited with implementing the program during the period when he served as Dean of Students at the Rabbinical School and later as Provost of the Seminary.

Finally I should like respectfully and gratefully to recognize here the prescience and initiative of my father, Kalman I. Ostow, who established, at the Seminary, the Ostow Family Fund for Psychoanalytic Studies in Judaism, which sponsored the study on which "The Jewish Response to Crisis" is based.

Contributors

Mortimer Ostow, M.D., Med. Sc. D. Psychiatrist, psychoanalyst; Edward T. Sandrow Visiting Professor of Pastoral Psychiatry, Jewish Theological Seminary of America.

Jacob A. Arlow, M.D. Psychiatrist, psychoanalyst; past president of the American Psychoanalytic Association; Clinical Professor of Psychiatry, New York University College of Medicine; formerly Editor-in-Chief of the *Psychoanalytic Quarterly;* Faculty, New York Psychoanalytic Institute.

Martin S. Bergmann, Ph.D. Psychoanalyst; Faculty, New York Freudian Society; Chairman of the New York Group for the Psychoanalytic Study of the Effect of the Holocaust on the Second Generation.

Robert Jay Lifton, M.D. Professor of Psychiatry, Yale University.

Richard L. Rubenstein, M.H.L., Rabbi, (Jewish Theological Seminary); S.T.M., Ph.D. (Harvard); Distinguished Professor of Religion, Florida State University.

Leonard R. Sillman, M.D., Psychiatrist and psychoanalyst, 1914–1976.

Introduction

Judaism and Psychoanalysis

MORTIMER OSTOW

EDITOR'S COMMENT

This paper, written as an introduction to the volume, discusses the question of why Judaism and psychoanalysis are so often bracketed. It deals with the fact that both value knowledge, to the point of inviting mystical elaborations (esoteric knowledge) of their respective disciplines. It suggests that Jews were attracted to the discipline in its early years because both Jews and psychoanalysis were marginal. It discusses how psychoanalysis as a profession helps Jewish psychoanalysts to resolve their ambivalence toward their Jewishness. And it appraises the early applications of psychoanalytic theory to the study of Jewish history, culture, and Scriptures.

In a letter to his friend, the Reverend Oskar Pfister, written in 1918, Sigmund Freud asked, "Why was it that none of all the pious ever discovered psycho-analysis? Why did it have to wait for a completely godless Jew?" (Meng and Freud, p. 63). Freud's question was probably intended mischieviously and provocatively, but nevertheless it invites an answer. Why indeed was it an unbelieving Jew who discovered psychoanalysis, and Jews who embraced it? Was it just a fortuitous association, or is there a true connection between Jewishness and psychoanalysis?

Psychoanalysis is sometimes referred to as a Jewish science, as though there were something essentially Jewish about psychoanalysis. The association is entertained even though it is well known that Freud spared no opportunity to declare his rejection of the Jewish religion along with all other religions. In fact the only kind remarks he had for religion are expressed in the letters written to Pfister (1.c.). I shall consider in this essay four areas in which Judaism and psychoanalysis relate to each other. Both Judaism and psychoanalysis teach that salvation, though conceptualized differently, can be obtained by virtue of special knowledge. Judaism and psychoanalysis share marginality: Jews are considered socially marginal and psychoanalysis is considered academically marginal. Psychoanalysis offers an activity in which Jews struggling at the interface between the Jewish community and the non-Jewish world can express their conflicting needs. Psychoanalysis offers a new approach to the study of Jewish religion, ideas and behavior, an additional dimension of understanding.

THE POWER OF KNOWLEDGE

Pirke Avoth, a well-known, terse mishnaic statement of the ideal rabbinic ethos, stresses that direction and a sense of the meaning of life come from study and knowledge, as well as commitment and involvement in one's community. The ignorant man may be natively good but, the text tells us, he cannot achieve the kind of religious fulfillment that rabbinic tradition demands. The observant Jew prays three times a day for knowledge, understanding, and judgment. Though learning was not available to the masses, it was valued by them, and the learned were held in respect and awarded prestige. To be sure, the Hassidic movement attempted to substitute for learning, enthusiasm and commitment as requirements for piety, or at least to make them equally valid qualifications. However, in normative Judaism, religious fulfilment requires learning.

Psychoanalytic theory teaches that relief from neurosis can be achieved by acquiring knowledge about oneself. The specific information that is required is information that exists within the individual psyche, but that is not ordinarily retrievable without technical assistance, namely, the application of the psychoanalytic method. When one learns about impulses, affective reactions, and defensive maneuvers that one ordinarily conceals from oneself, and when one learns to detect them in their mental derivatives in conscious life, and when one learns about their origins in childhood, then one acquires some degree of control over them and some relief from neurosis.

Judaism and psychoanalysis therefore share the basic principle that one must acquire knowledge in order to obtain the benefits that each offers: leading a life of mitzvah and obtaining its rewards, in the first instance; and freedom from the disability and pain of mental illness, in the second. They both posit that special knowledge is a prerequisite for elitist status and for personal mastery over a crucial aspect of one's destiny.

The concept that knowledge leads to self-improvement, or, that in order to derive benefits from any discipline, one must master its use, can be applied to a very large number of areas of human endeavor. The fact that this principle applies to both Judaism and psychoanalysis is therefore not very remarkable.

However, there have been developments in both disciplines that extend the concept of the power of knowledge beyond the quality of instrumental utility. Recurrently in the history of Judaism, as well as in probably all other religions, men have aspired to the transcendent experience of the Divine as a way of escaping the frustrations and heartaches of daily life. When the pursuit of transcendent experience engaged groups rather than individuals, the major mystical movements ensued. In Judaism we know of rabbinic mysticism of the second and third centuries, that of the Zohar in the thirteenth century, Lurianic Kabbalism of the sixteenth century, and Hassidism of the eighteenth century and thereafter. Transcendence, in mystical states, is usually experienced and described as "knowledge." "Mysticism, according to its historical and psychological definitions, is the direct intuition or experience of God; and a mystic is a person who has, to a greater or lesser degree, such a direct experience—one whose religion and life are centered, not merely on an accepted belief or practice, but on that which he regards as first-hand personal knowledge" (Underhill, pp. 9 f.).

The Jewish mystic was always concerned with obtaining secret and esoteric knowledge. It was knowledge of esoteric meanings of the verses of Scripture, and knowledge of God. For him the acquisition and contemplation of this knowledge was the mystical experience (see Scholem, pp. 20 f.).

In psychoanalysis, as the discipline was laid down by Freud, the knowledge to be sought out was knowledge of one's unconscious conflicts, and their origins in traumatic childhood experience. The purpose of acquiring this knowledge was only to effect a cure of the patient's neurosis. However, Freud thought that the psychoanalytic method could also be applied to myths and other forms of literature, for the purpose of elucidating the early history of the group and its collective fantasies. He encouraged his students to study mythology (Ellenberger, p. 695), and he himself published *Totem and Taboo* (1913), a speculative essay in which he tried to reconstruct the history of human social and religious organization. Much later in his career he composed *Moses and Monotheism* (1939), a psychoanalytic contribution to an understanding of Judaism and Jews. These studies aimed, not at achieving a practical goal, such as the alleviation of illness, but at obtaining knowledge respecting the origins and basic nature of human society in the first instance, and the Jewish people in the second. This technique of psychoanalytically informed historical speculation aspired to the attainment of universal principles that one could think of as prevailing above and beyond any specific society that existed. The search for universal principles is a scientifically respectable activity, but the assumption that such overarching principles exist, and the pursuit of them, suggest the attitude of the mystic who pursues his vision of eternal and supernal verities, whether in a religious context or not.

A further step in the transition from a concern with instrumental knowledge to mysticism was taken by Jung. He shared Freud's interest in mythology, but pursued it much more intensively than other analysts. He moved away from Freud and arrived at theories of mental function that cannot be thought of as other than mystical. He spoke of a "collective unconscious," in which the unconscious of each individual participates. It has, as he described it, an independent existence and is represented in each individual by universal symbols and themes (Jung, 1934). Psychotherapy, as practiced by him, is intended not only to alleviate illness, but to educate people toward independence and moral freedom; it aims to promote human relationships between individuals and inner cohesion within society (Jung, 1966).

The fact that mystical elaborations have developed in both Judaism and psychoanalysis raises the question of whether these elaborations have built upon mystical inclinations present in the respective normative disciplines, but not generally recognized or acknowledged. Kadushin speaks of "normal mysticism" in Jewish life, that is, the experience of God in the absence of sensory perception of Him, making everyday phenomena and situations significant, and conferring a mystical consciousness of a relationship to God.*

Few psychoanalysts would acknowledge that any element of mysticism colors the normative practice of their profession. Yet I think some case could be made for the proposition that it does. The analytic patient unconsciously experiences his analyst as a repre-

---

*Bakan suggests that in the discipline of psychoanalysis, Freud presents a secularized version of Jewish mysticism. I see little merit in this hypothesis. Whatever mystical element contributed to the creation of psychoanalysis, cannot be distinguished from the mysticism of many other scientists, including some of the greatest (e.g. Newton and Einstein) who, in their scientific endeavors, sought to elucidate what they considered to be the ultimate unity of the universe. This conviction of unity, the Christian *unio mystica* or the Jewish *d'vekuth*, overcomes the sense of alienation. Also, there is nothing in whatever mysticism inheres in psychoanalysis to warrant associating it more closely with Jewish mysticism than with Christian or secular mysticism.

sentation of a parental figure remembered from his infancy and childhood. This phenomenon is called transference. During the analysis, his feelings toward the analyst vary, as children's feelings towards their parents vary, depending upon external circumstances and the degree of gratification or frustration that they experience. There are periods, however, in many or most analyses when the patient yearns to be close to, and intimate with, to know and to merge with the parents and the parents' representation, the analyst. Such wishes are normal childhood wishes, and they are reactivated in adult mental illness, but also in transference. When an illusion of merging develops, the transference acquires a mystical quality. It creates the impression of reunion with a parental object, the precursor of the image of God; it is private; it is extremely gratifying; it is associated with an alteration in the perception of reality; and it is almost not susceptible of communication. Both patient and analyst approach the treatment with the conviction that the knowledge to be acquired will liberate the former from inner restraints. It is secret knowledge, unknown to the public, to the analyst, and to the patient. It is esoteric in the sense that it can be acquired only by a special kind of revelation. It is not merely that the data must be elicited by a special technique, but once they are elicited and conveyed back to the patient by interpretation or reconstruction, he responds affectively. It is the experience of hearing from an omniscient parental representative the reconstruction of a forgotten portion of one's life, responding to the formulation with strong affect, and understanding how the underlying pattern influences one's current behavior and feeling, that constitutes the experience of revelation.

The patient's attitude toward acquiring the liberating insight suggests the Gnostic principle that learning the names of the existing demons, and techniques for overpowering or evading them, will permit the soul to ascend to the *pleroma*, the fullness of God's life (Scholem, pp. 49 f.)

The analyst, of course, will contend that he is conducting what is only a technical procedure, based upon scientific principles. He will probably not deny that the patient, looking for relief from anguish, will expect the revelation to relieve him, and may attribute magical powers to having been granted the revelation by a parental and—in fantasy, omniscient—figure. Does the analyst too attribute magical powers to these revelations? A strictly scientific, objective analyst may not. Analysts who are not always completely and absolutely scientific might unconsciously invest these revelations with magical powers of cure. We all find it difficult to appraise our abilities and our work objectively, and as our moods change, our evaluation of these fluctuates between overestimation and underestimation. When the analyst overestimates his abilities, he exaggerates the therapeutic power of the revelations that he provides.

Every modern analyst was once a patient; his training requires that he himself participate in the psychoanalytic process as analysand. In that role, he himself experienced the magical power of revelation. It is true that theoretically no analysis is complete unless the transference is analyzed, that is, unless the figure of the analyst is freed of the magical, unrealistic aura with which the transference endows it. But no one who has heard an analyst speak of his own training analyst will believe that the idealization has been completely undone. I believe that it is reasonable to conclude that to some analysts and many patients, the analytic process is seen consciously as a technical procedure, but unconsciously as something which, at times, approaches or suggests a mystical experience.

The feature of both Judaism and psychoanalysis that comes first to mind when one thinks of them together is the principle that the meaning of a matter is not exhausted in its appearance or literal text, but that true knowledge, essential aspects of meaning, can be obtained only by a process of interpretation or exegesis.

Biblical exegesis in Judaism occupied its teachers, thinkers, theologians, and philosophers from the centuries before the destruction of the second Temple until recent centuries. If day-to-day law, ritual observance, ethics, morality, standards, and values were to be based upon the Pentateuch, it became necessary to infer them from the crisp and spare verses of the latter. The Written Law had to be complemented by the Oral Law. Also, since the circumstances of Jewish life changed from time to time and from place to place, interpretations had to be altered, varied, and replaced.

Further, changes in the trends of Jewish thought and practice, occasioned by social forces and by the cultural preoccupations of host populations, could not be made without the sanction implied by their being based upon traditional sources. Making such changes required reinterpretation of these sources. The art of interpretation therefore became highly developed in Judaism. A number of varieties of interpretational modes were conventionally recognized. First, one ascertained the plain meaning of the text *(p'shat)*. Second, one could find in the text, or at least read into it, hints of alternative, implied meanings *(remez)*. For example, one could treat a word of the text as an abbreviation for a phrase (i.e., as an acronym) or as a combination of words *(notarikon)*. Third, one could abstract from the text a homiletic meaning *(d'rash)*. Fourth, the mystics of the various generations each read into the text an esoteric meaning *(sod)* that supported their own view of the immediate experience of God and its consequences. In medieval times, the term *pardes*, an acronym *(prds)*, was employed to designate this collection of technics. They were used for hermeneutic as well as exegetical purposes. Three sets of hermeneutic principles are available for the Talmudic exegesis of the Pentateuch (Kadushin; Moore). The word *pilpul* designates an exercise of exegetical disputation aimed toward extracting the most accurate interpretation of the text. Dating back to the Talmudic period, it was continued by students of the yeshivoth thereafter. It was originally intended as a serious method for arriving at truth, but in later centuries it sometimes deteriorated to the exhibition of disputational skill. For this reason, the term is sometimes applied pejoratively to scholastic hair-splitting and inconsequential argumentation.

The psychoanalytic process requires the examination of material presented by the patient for its hidden meanings. The material may consist of accounts of what the patient did, or is doing, or plans to do; fantasies, dreams, prose or poetic compositions, or any other products of his mental function. The assumption is that when carefully examined in a suitable atmosphere, the material will reveal, beneath its surface meaning, impulses, defenses against them or derivatives of them, childhood memories, intentions, fears or worries which the patient resists knowing and which he excludes from his consciousness. The examination can be compared with the process of exegesis. Just as the rabbis of the Talmud devised principles of Biblical exegesis, so Freud devised psychoanalytic interpretative techniques. For example, when an individual's behavior seems inconsistent with his declared intentions, the former can be taken as a more reliable indication of his unconscious intentions. When he makes an error in speech or writing that has a meaning that seems inappropriate, it probably betrays unconscious intention. When a number of independent items are mentioned in sequence or apparently at random, if a unifying theme can be found, the latter is probably troubling the individual at that moment. Excessively strong denial of a thought suggests unconscious acceptance of it. Some nonhuman images, appearing for example in dreams, often symbolize humans, or structures of the human body. When specific behavior patterns repeat during an individual's life, it is likely that they were established first during childhood, either as a repetition of some experience, usually at the hands of the parents, or as a rejection of it. Symptoms of illness can all be understood as expressing the conflicts involved in the process of illness or the history of the illness. In many or most instances, psychoanalytic experience with these principles of exegesis complies with expectations, so that most analysts will agree on the interpretation of a given piece of material. In other instances, the clues are so faint or so atypical that different analysts will offer different interpretations.

Although these two procedures, Biblical exegesis and psychoanalytic interpretation, proceed from different assumptions, and are applied to different materials, and are pursued with different purposes, nevertheless they resemble each other in that both infer concealed meaning from manifest text, by the application of a set of rules.

In a letter addressed to Freud in 1908, Abraham wrote, "Some days ago a small paragraph in *Jokes* strangely attracted me. When I looked at it more closely, I found that, in the technique of apposition and in its full structure, it was completely Talmudic" (Abraham and Freud, p. 36). This similarity helps to create the impression of an affinity between Judaism and psychoanalysis.

MARGINALITY

When one thinks of the connection between Judaism and psychoanalysis, one considers also the fact that at its beginnings, the psychoanalytic movement was composed almost exclusively of Jews, with but few exceptions. Now, the proportion of Jews among psychoanalysts is considerably lower. Names that seem recognizably Jewish to me in the rosters of the various national components of the International Psycho-Analytical Association constitute barely one-half of the names in the American Psychoanalytic Association; one-third to one-quarter of those listed in Britain; one-fourth of those in Argentina; one-fifth of those in Canada, France, and Belgium; between one-fifth and one-tenth of those of other South American countries; and a somewhat lower proportion of the names in other countries of Western Europe. Of course in every country, the proportion of Jews among psychoanalysts very greatly exceeds the proportion of Jews in the total population.

The psychoanalytic movement began in Central Europe at the end of a century of progressive emancipation of European Jewry, country by country. In fact, the end of the nineteenth century saw the beginnings of a reaction to emancipation and an intensification of anti-Semitic agitation. Freud himself was eleven years old at the time of the emancipation in Austria-Hungary, 1867. The emancipation was a legal move but, in itself, it did little toward overcoming anti-Semitism. Hints in the early literature of psychoanalysis, and published correspondence, reveal that anti-Semitism was a constant concern among the first generation of psychoanalysts. All but a few of the twenty-nine references to "Jews" in the index of the Standard Edition of the *Complete Psychological Works of Sigmund Freud* are references to prejudice or anti-Semitism. Faced with newly available opportunities to play a role in general society, commerce, the arts, intellectual and professional life, and simultaneously faced with pockets of anti-Semitism, many Jews responded in either of two ways. First, as a marginal people they embraced marginal occupations, and second, many of those who did not convert tried to express their Jewishness in universalist, humanistic interests and activities. Both of these tendencies converged in the creation of the psychoanalytic movement.

The Jews were *marginal* in the sense that though no longer legally disabled, they still were kept outside the central social and industrial institutions of society. As a consequence, they had to find for themselves openings in vocations where there was room for them, and where they were acceptable. Of course they remained in occupations in which they had traditionally engaged, that is, finance, trading, and commerce. But they were drawn also to occupations in which individual talent rather than family connections made for success, such as creative arts, professions, and academia. These occupations attracted them because they conferred a higher social status and because they embodied the traditional Jewish value of intellectual achievement. Having little rooting in the old traditions of the host country, they were not inhibited from trying to get ahead by embracing what was modern and what was novel, so that they favored not merely marginal occupations, but specifically avant-garde occupations. They were the "modernists" of Vienna and Berlin. Peter Gay (1978) points out that they were not the only modernists, nor were they all modernists. However they were well represented among the modernists. (For a fuller discussion of Jewish occupations, see Kuznets.)

Political emancipation for the Jews did not mean true redemption from inferior status. The exposure to greater opportunity than before aroused more extravagant hopes for social advancement. A few Jews hoped to achieve first-class status by converting as well as assimilating. That is why Freud (1925) wrote: "My parents were Jews, and I have remained a Jew myself." Most, like Freud, disdained conversion and tried to express their Jewishness in universalist and humanistic terms. That is, they openly rejected what Christians—and under their influence, many Jews—called the priestly and ritual, particularist ways of being Jews, and proclaimed their loyalty to prophetic ideals of social justice and charity in the general community.

Yehezkel Kaufmann (1930, Vol. III, Part 2, Book 1, pp. 248 et passim) observed that though many Jews embraced the opportunity for cultural and national assimilation, and though many rejected the Jewish religion, by and large the Jewish community did not opt for conversion.

In Freud's 1926 address to B'nai B'rith (1941) he spoke of his attraction to Jewry as consisting of several components: a clear consciousness of inner *identity*, the safe privacy of a common mental construction, freedom from intellectual restriction, and a readiness to join the opposition. His interest in Jewry, he says, lies in both a common identity, and a readiness to stand up to a common enemy. His concern with anti-Semitism and with the correctness of his posture toward it is expressed in many writings (e.g., Freud, 1900, pp. 196 f.). But he was also concerned with what Jewishness really was. It is evident that his interest in Jewish jokes arose from a desire to ascertain what a Jew is really like. Freud (1905) observed that the jokes that he quoted demonstrate that Jews are unusually inclined toward self-criticism; that they think of the Jewish community in democratic terms so that the community frequently seems undisciplined; that they are religiously obligated to care for poor fellow Jews; that they are pessimistically cynical; and that they do not hesitate to attack their own religious beliefs.

Freud's use of the term *identity* here is its first use in psychoanalytic literature. Put differently, psychoanalytic interest in identity began with the question of Jewish identity. Indeed, Erik Erikson, who developed the concept further, acknowledges that the issue of his own Jewish origins stimulated his interest in identity (see Coles, p. 180).

Freud's opus on *Moses and Monotheism* can be seen as an effort to ascertain how much of what is specifically Jewish history and character can be understood to be determined by the paradigm of the Oedipus complex. An extended discussion of Freud's attitude toward his Jewishness will be found in Bergmann's paper.

Freud obviously saw that Jewishness places the Jew outside of the general community, or at least, at its margins.

Rothman and Isenberg attribute to Freud's awareness of his Jewish marginality the intention not merely to find an acceptable social position and professional role. They propose also that the new discipline, by establishing a universalistic psychology, "denied the reality of culture and of cultural differences." There are three ways to escape from marginality, they note. First, one may attempt to assimilate into the majority culture. Freud at times did consider religious conversion, but always rejected it. Second, one may attempt to undermine the dominant culture that delineates the margin. Third, one may attempt to transform oneself and one's group into a majority, as the Zionists did. Freud hesitated to adopt the Zionist ideology (Freud, 1926, p. 273).

The second option, subverting the cultural categories that define Jews as marginal, was offered by Charles Liebman as an explanation of the characteristic Jewish attachment to universalist ideas of a radical or liberal nature. Rothman and Isenberg, following Schorske, proposed that Freud's early flirtation with radical politics in his university years, and his ambition to adopt a legal and political career dedicated to social reform, were put aside in favor of "an attempt to resolve the dilemmas of the political liberal on the psychological level by attaining inner freedom." Psychoanalysis not only provided a professional haven for intellectual Jews who were eager to reject Jewish particularism. It became a revolutionary force undermining the religious European culture that determined the marginality of the Jews.

It may be its antagonism to prevailing institutions of cultural and political dominance that attracted and still attracts Jewish political liberals and radicals to the psychoanalytic profession, rather than simply the opportunity to escape into a universalist discipline. I find this suggestion of Rothman and Isenberg worth considering, for it seems evident that psychoanalysis has contributed much to the cultural revolution of the twentieth century.

WORKING AT THE INTERFACE

Joining the avant-garde movement of psychoanalysis provided a new professional occupation, in which the highest ideals of humanitarian service could be expressed, and it did not require conversion. One finds among the earliest analysts: rejection of religious ritual observance, high standards of personal behavior, and concern with anti-Semitism, the cause of their social marginality. These values prevailed in both personal and professional behavior.

Why did Freud and his early associates reject the Jewish religion so vigorously? Certainly the enlightenment, which affected both the Jewish and the Christian world, made the rejection possible. But the need to reject probably arose from the discomfort of Jewish marginality. Liebman suggests that Jewish attraction to liberal ideas was motivated by a wish to undermine cultural categories that defined Jews as marginal. But a border is defined by two domains. Many Jews resented not only the excluding culture, but also the culture that was excluded. Rejection of Jews by Gentiles challenged their self-esteem. The search for self-esteem and prestige, no less than economic pressures, caused many Jews to attempt to escape from their marginality. "A half-dozen duels," Theodor Herzl wrote, "would very much raise the social position of the Jews" (quoted in Schorske, p. 160). While the route of assimilation was chosen by some, as Kaufmann (1930) observed, it was rejected by most. But rejecting conversion did not mean making peace with Jewishness. The resulting ambivalence was resolved by Freud and his friends by concentrating their resentment upon the Jewish religion, while still professing attachment to the Jewish people and its prophetic ideals. Robert (1976), in a thoughtful and perceptive study, documents Freud's disparagement of his Jewish origins.

Alongside the rejection of religion and ritual, a few of the early analysts developed and maintained a positive interest in nonreligious Judaism, i.e., secular, cultural, Zionist, social and historical. Freud's participation in the Vienna B'nai Brith served as an example and model. According to Knoepfmacher he was joined in this activity by Bibring, Hitschman, Reik, and Sperling. Some analysts, during the first decades of the twentieth century, became active Zionists. A few joined the Blau-Weiss, a Jewish counterpart to the German youth movement, Wandervogel. Siegfried Bernfeld was an active organizer of Zionist youth and established a journal, *Jerubbaal*, to promote his program. Willi Hoffer, who was also active in Blau-Weiss, associated himself with some of Bernfeld's activities (see Hoffer, and Utley, 1979, *a* and *b*). Unfortunately the facts are not readily available. Max Eitingon went to Palestine in

1933 and was soon followed by other European analysts. Some went out of conviction, some out of expediency, and some out of both.

A number of analysts: Loewenstein (1951), Simmel (1946), Jones (1945), and Fenichel (1946), during and after World War II, wrote about anti-Semitism. Most of the explanations offered invoked either the scapegoat phenomenon, that is, anti-Semitism is the result of projection and displacement, or the Oedipus complex, in which the Jew is seen as a representation of the punitive father or the rebellious son. Other than writing about anti-Semitism, these men undertook no action on behalf of the Jewish community as such. Of course, vigorous efforts were made by American and British analysts to rescue European colleagues before and during the War, and to help them to become established again. Paul Friedman (1948) visited internment camps in Cyprus in 1948, and kibbutzim where refugees had been absorbed, and wrote about the condition and needs of children and adults, with the eye of a psychoanalyst and the heart of a Jew. In the 1950's and 1960's in Europe, Israel, and the United States, descriptions of the psychic effects of the concentration-camp and survivor experience appeared in the literature: e.g., Krystal, Niederland, Bettelheim, and Chodoff (see also Krystal and Niederland). The fact that most victims were Jews was acknowledged, but no one commented on the significance of the Holocaust as an example of Jewish destiny, and what it means to the Jew as a Jew, with respect to both the victims and the survivors. Klein and Last in Israel, however, have studied the effect of the Holocaust on self-esteem among Jewish children in both Israel and the United States. Neubauer and Bettelheim and others have studied children raised in kibbutzim.

One could argue that the psychoanalytic movement, at least in its early years, can be seen as a kind of cultic association within Judaism. It was composed almost exclusively of Jews. The Jews were self-conscious, and therefore encouraged and cherished non-Jewish members. In fact, it was in order to overcome the evident Jewishness of the movement that Freud promoted Jung's candidacy for presidency of the International Psycho-Analytical Association. Intolerance of other religions characterizes religious sects. The psychoanalytic movement rejected conventional religion as invalid and unworthy for any purpose other than as the object of psychoanalytic study. As recently as thirty years ago, religious belief or affiliation was considered by psychoanalysts sufficient indication of the existence of neurosis.

The structure of the early psychoanalytic community suggests that of a cult, or at least, a dissident sect, secular if not almost religious. Freud was the leader and no questioning of his authority or wisdom could be accepted. Central features of psychoanalytic doctrine could not be questioned. Following the defection of some of the prominent early analysts, Adler, Stekel, and Jung, Ernest Jones (1955) proposed to Freud the formation of a secret "Old Guard." "It would give him," Jones said (l.c., p. 152), "the assurance that only a stable body of firm friends could, it would be a comfort in the event of further dissensions, and it should be possible for us to be of practical assistance by replying to criticisms and providing him with necessary literature, illustrations for his work drawn from our own experience, and the like. There would be only one definite obligation undertaken among us: namely, that if anyone wished to depart from any of the fundamental tenets of psychoanalytic theory, e.g. the concept of repression, of the unconscious, of infantile sexuality, etc., he would promise not to do so publicly before discussing his views with the rest. The whole idea of such a group had of course its pre-history in my mind: stories of Charlemagne's paladins from boyhood and many secret societies from literature."

The members of this "committee," which, after 1919, numbered six members beside Freud, demonstrated their unity and commitment to each other by each wearing a ring carrying on it a Greek intaglio, the latter provided by Freud.

Like dissident sects, while replacing the central dogmas of the parent group with its own dogma, the early psychoanalytic group nevertheless retained other characteristics of the parent group. It was proud of those qualities that Freud considered essentially Jewish, namely, to use Freud's words, a "common mental construction," freedom from intellectual restriction, and dispensing with the approval of the "compact majority." It may be, too, that its essential humanitarianism, its respect for the physical and mental integrity of the individual person, is derived from Judaism. As I observed above, many of the early analysts, including Freud, participated in Jewish social, self-defense, and Zionist activities, while rejecting religion.

The corpus of Freud's writing was treated as a canon. Fritz Wittels wrote in 1924, "The trouble arises from the suppression of free criticism within the Society. Suppression makes people snappish. The members have metapsychological leanings and I'm afraid they are inclined to stray into scholastic paths. . . . Freud is treated as a demi-god, or even as a god. No criticism of his utterances is permitted. Sadger tells us that Freud's *Three Contributions to the Theory of Sex* is the psychoanalytic Bible. This is no mere figure of speech. The faithful disciples regard one another's books as of no account. They recognize no authority but Freud's; they rarely read or quote one another. When they quote it is from the Master, that they may give the pure milk of the Word. The medical element has passed into the background. The philosophers hold sway." Jones (l.c.) reported that Rank insisted on publishing Freud's collected works "partly for pietistic and partly for commercial reasons."

As the movement grew and accepted many non-Jewish students and members, especially after Freud's death and World War II, it lost its cultic quality. Central authority weakened and disappeared. The condition of subscribing to fixed dogma was bypassed. A number of classical beliefs are being challenged, modified, or replaced—not always to advantage. The movement abandoned aloofness and sought affiliation with and, implicitly, approval by medical associations. The disdain for religion and the religious was muted. Members of Catholic religious orders and observant Jews have been accepted into and graduated from psychoanalytic institutes.

It may well be that a general, vaguely apprehended understanding that the early psychoanalytic movement suggested a dissident cult within Judaism contributed to the widespread impression that Judaism and psychoanalysis were closely linked.

That Freud saw Jewishness as especially congenial to psychoanalysis is indicated in the following quotations from letters to Abraham (written in 1908). "Please be tolerant and do not forget that it is really easier for you than it is for Jung to follow my ideas, for in the first place you are completely independent, and then you are closer to my intellectual constitution because of racial kinship, while he, as a Christian and a pastor's son, finds his way to me only against great inner resistances. His association with us is the more valuable for that. I nearly said it was only by his appearance on the scene that psychoanalysis escaped the danger of becoming a Jewish national affair" (see Abraham and Freud, p. 34).

Two months later Freud wrote with respect to the same matter, "On the whole it is easier for us Jews, as we lack the mystical element" (l.c., p. 46).

That Freud saw the attitude of non-Jews toward psychoanalysis as resembling their attitude toward Jews, he explained in another letter shortly thereafter. "I nurse a suspicion that the suppressed anti-Semitism of the Swiss that spares me is deflected in reinforced form upon you. But I think that we as Jews, if we wish to join in, must develop a bit of masochism, be ready to suffer some wrong. Otherwise there is no hitting it off. Rest assured, that if my name were Oberhuber, in spite of everything my innovations would have met with far less resistance" (l.c., p. 46).

With the passing of the cultic quality and especially during the past fifteen years or so, many Jewish psychoanalysts have begun to assert their interest in what happens to Jews above and beyond problems created by anti-Semitism. There are a number of reasons for this change in addition to the relaxation of cultic restrictions. The Jews of this country have acquired a sense of pride, paradoxically, as a result of the enormous sacrifice of Jews in the Holocaust, and the success of the State of Israel and the heroism of its people. Pluralism has become respectable in the United States. We have a number of areas in which Jews can be active as Jews, other than religion, which is still anathema to most psychoanalysts. Jewish analysts have begun to participate in fund-raising for the Jewish community, as analysts. A group of psychoanalysts, under the leadership of Judith Kestenberg, Milton Jucovy, and Martin Bergmann, have begun a study of the influence of the survivor experience on survivors and on their children. The most notable achievement of all has been the establishment of the Freud Chair at the Hebrew University, under the vigorous leadership and inspiration of Martin Wangh. Joseph Sandler has become the first Freud Professor of Psychoanalysis at the Hebrew University.

PSYCHOANALYTIC STUDIES OF JUDAISM

The essays in this book—with one exception, Bergmann's essay on Freud's Jewishness—exemplify a fourth connection between Judaism and psychoanalysis, namely, psychoanalytic studies of Judaism and of Jews. Similar studies were published by the early analysts, but I shall try to demonstrate the limitations of their studies, and the origin of these limitations not only in the primitive state of the psychoanalytic discipline at the time and the ignorance of the students, but also in their ambivalence.

Freud's studies of Judaism and Jews betray his ambivalence, well described below by Bergmann, and by Robert (l.c.). He implied in his psychoanalytic works that though he was familiar with classical Rome and Greece, their literature and language, he knew almost nothing about Jewish literature and language, and little about Jewish history. To some extent this may have been a posture. When his father returned to him, on the occasion of his thirty-fifth birthday, the Phillipson Bible (in Hebrew and German) that Freud had studied and discarded as a child, and that his father had preserved "like the fragments of the broken Tablets," he accompanied it with a message in Hebrew, which he evidently expected his son to understand. We know that as a member of the Vienna B'nai Brith, Freud not only attended regularly for many years, but also actively served on its program committee (Knoepfmacher). Bergmann observes that in the analysis of one of his dreams, Freud mentions having seen a play the preceding evening, *The New Ghetto*, but omits mention of the name of its author, Theodor Herzl (see also Simon, p. 274, and Falk, p. 10). Bergmann questions Jones' simple explanation that Freud was unfamiliar with the term "menorah" because of "his unfamiliarity with synagogues." Nobody with Freud's background, with whatever religious education he was offered, or accepted, living in the Jewish community in Vienna, regularly attending meetings of B'nai Brith, could have been unfamiliar with the menorah, or its name. If nowhere else, he encountered it at Jewish cemeteries.

Falk (p. 15) too expresses skepticism of Freud's denial of his knowledge of things Jewish. Rainey has reconstructed what was probably the curriculum of Freud's Jewish studies. Gerson D. Cohen has inspected this material, has examined the texts that Freud studied in his youth, and the references that he provided for *Moses and Monotheism*, and he informs me that in his opinion, Freud learned a great deal about Judaism and Jewish history as well as the Hebrew language in his youth, and had learned even more by the time he wrote *Moses and Monotheism*. However, Freud mentions in a number of places (e.g., 1925), that he was ignorant of the "Hebrew language and literature."

When he finally left Vienna for London in 1938, Freud compared himself to Johanan ben Zakkai (Jones, 1957, p. 221). "After the destruction of the Temple in Jerusalem by Titus," Freud observed, "Johanan ben Zakkai asked for permission to open a school at Jabneh, for the study of the Torah. We are going to do the same. We are, after all, used to persecution by our history, tradition and some of us by personal experience." The Roman and Greek metaphors of his early life had given way to Jewish metaphors.

Yet it is clear that Freud was interested in studying the Jewish people and understanding their characteristic qualities. We have already mentioned one such project, namely, approaching the study of Jews through their humor. In the introduction to the Hebrew edition of *Totem and Taboo* (1930), he said: "If the question were put to him: 'Since you have abandoned all these common characteristics of your countrymen, what is there left to you that is Jewish?' He would reply: 'A very great deal, and probably its very essence.' He could not now express that essence clearly in words; but someday, no doubt, it will become accessible to the scientific mind." The same wish to understand is expressed in the following excerpt from a letter to Arnold Zweig written in 1932: "How strange this tragically mad land you have visited must have seemed to you. . . . Palestine has never produced anything but religious, sacred frenzies, presumptuous attempts to overcome the outer world of appearance, by means of the inner world of wishful thinking. And we hail from there; our forebears lived there for perhaps half or perhaps a whole millennium and it is impossible to say what heritage from this land we have taken out into our blood and nerves. Oh, life could be very interesting if we only knew and understood more about it."

His major effort to understand Jews and Judaism is presented in *Moses and Monotheism*, commented on below by Bergmann. It seems likely that his attempt to understand Jewishness reflected one aspect of his attempt to understand himself, that is, his self-analysis.

Freud applied the methods of interpretation that he had learned from working with patients, in order to obtain insight into his own personality. It is clear, from his published writings about his self-analysis, that he succeeded in reconstructing the Oedipus complex, but there is no explicit evidence of his having achieved insight into the complexities of the residua of his earliest conflicting feelings toward his mother. Having become familiar with the Oedipus complex in both his self-analysis and in his analyses of neurotic patients, Freud explored the applicability of the Oedipus paradigm to human affairs in general. He took a special interest in establishing the relation between Oedipus complex and group psychology and explored also its relevance to the organization of the religious community (Freud, 1915, 1921). Finally in 1939, he published his summarizing composition, *Moses and Monotheism*, which can be interpreted as the answer to the question: What can we learn about the nature of the Jewish people from the Oedipal paradigm? (Dr. Gerson D. Cohen (1981) discerned an esoteric message in *Moses and Monotheism* alongside the familiar exoteric thesis. The message is a vigorous rebuttal of anti-Jewish accusations and an equally vigorous assertion of the virtues and strengths of the Jews.)

Because of his interest in applying psychoanalytic insight to problems of society, Freud encouraged his students to investigate the possibility of a psychoanalytic type of analysis of mythology. Many did so and achieved some striking results. Jung, in fact, made the study of mythology a point of departure for his own psychology. He took classical myths as clues to a transcendent, omnipresent, and eternal psychologic reality, from which each individual psyche springs and with which it remains in contact.

A number of analysts chose Jewish "mythology" as their subject. Of these, the most prolific was Theodor Reik. He wrote on the "origins" of the Kol Nidre Prayer (1931), the Shofar (1931), and the "prayer shawl and phylacteries of the Jew" (1951), among other Jewish religious topics (1951). Most of the early Jewish psychoanalysts who wrote about Jewish "mythology" applied psychoanalytic principles to a fragmentary knowledge of Judaism that they had picked up in their youth. Their childhood impressions were occasionally supplemented by reference to the works of historians, theologians, and other commentators.

The earliest analysts, in their discussions in the Vienna Psychoanalytic Society, spoke of Jews in fairly derogatory stereotypes (Nunberg and Federn, 1961, 1967). Only Freud made a positive comment (l.c. Vol. III, p. 273).

Abraham (1920), in a paper entitled "The Day of Atonement," wrote about Jewish matters with an air of authority though he commited there a number of errors.

Reik, on the other hand, quotes from many legitimate authorities whom he had apparently read with care, and also from fairly impressive sources. I assume that Hebrew texts were either read in published translation or that appropriate passages were translated for him, for from his spelling errors, it would seem that he was not too familiar with the Hebrew language. Yet in his case also, one feels that he is looking at an alien population through the eyes of a kindly but objective and remote scientist. For all of his erudition he too commits serious errors. For example, in *Mystery on the Mountain* (1959) he gives ten days as the age for ritual circumcision. In a book published as late as 1941 he makes the following surprising statement (p. 397, n.): "There is a strange silence among the Jewish people about their suffering. Jehovah did not enable them to say what they endure. None of the great poets expressed their complaints and denunciations. It is as if they accepted and acknowledged suffering as an unchangeable part of their destiny. Their lips are sealed and their voice mute" (Reik, 1941). Granted that the Crusade Chronicles and the works of consolation that followed the

Spanish Expulsion are not widely known (though a good German translation of the former was available by the end of the nineteenth century), no one who is at all familiar with Jewish liturgy, the Tisha B'Av service, the Book of Lamentations, the Midrash on Lamentations, or even the Sabbath Av Harachamim, or Psalm 137, would make such a statement.

What was the intention of these early psychoanalytic explorations into Jewish practices? It would probably not be valid to assume that all the investigators harbored the same motives, and we do not have much autobiographical data to go by. From the evident ambivalence of these early psychoanalysts to their religious background, and from the way they handled the materials, I would guess that their investigations served at least three purposes. First, they served to demonstrate the validity of the psychoanalytic method and psychoanalytic theories in yet another sphere of human behavior. Second, not only was the psychoanalytic approach valid, but it took the measure of the Jewish religion; it exposed its irrationality and limitations. If discipline A can "explain" discipline B, and not vice versa, then discipline A has "triumphed over" B. The psychoanalytic "analysis" of Judaism can be seen as a kind of intellectual imperialism. Third, beneath the critical, derogatory attitude, there may well have been concealed an affectionate and appreciative one. For example, even in the minutes of the Vienna Psychoanalytic Society, Freud is quoted as having said in 1911, "The old Jewish religion has rendered great service in the restriction of perverted sexuality, by guiding all libidinal currents into the bed of propagation" (Vol. III, p. 273). Herman Nunberg has told me that in his later years, Freud's comments about religion were much milder and considerably less derogatory than the comments of his earlier years.

But there is an even more positive purpose, at least in the case of Reik (1931). He seems to have shared with Freud the idea that the psychoanalytic study of the earliest legendary experiences of the Jewish people, as these are reflected in its Scriptures, will tell us something about the nature of the Jewish people, the secrets of its survival, and the personality of the Jews living now. "Every student of the development of Judaism is irresistibly impelled to face the weighty question: What harmonious or discordant psychological forces, acting now as heretofore in their religion as in their national history, invisibly dominate the devleopment of the Jewish people? Their history of suffering, their existence under abnormal conditions of life, and the mystery of their persistence must be of the greatest interest to the psychoanalyst, since it becomes more and more evident that the psychology of consciousness is not able to give us a sufficient explanation. He would feel, as he becomes absorbed in the history of the unique culture of Judaism, that dynamic processes of an unconscious nature, processes which have not hitherto been considered, have taken and are still taking, a great and important share in its development" (p. 23).

What did Reik learn? Reik learned what he expected to learn, namely, that wherever one looks in Jewish Scripture or religious practice, one finds the Oedipus complex and conflict between fathers and sons, as well as between God and the people, and between leaders and followers. The Kol Nidre expresses a compromise between a rebellious repudiation of the covenant with God and remorse for doing so. The sound of the Shofar represents the triumphal identification of the leader with the totem bull or calf god, and at the same time suggests the sound of an animal being slaughtered. It frightens the worshipper so that he will not be tempted to repeat the act. *Tallith* and *t'fillin* symbolize the wearing of the skin of the slaughtered totem animal.

In his last work on this subject, *Mystery on the Mountain*, written considerably later (1959), Reik recapitulates various of his earlier studies, but from a broader perspective. He also introduces at least two new ideas of some interest. The first is his proposal that what happened at Mount Sinai was an initiation rite, in which the people of Israel were inducted into a covenant with the god to whom Moses was introducing them. In developing these themes, he compares this covenant with group puberty rites and initiations of cohorts of young people into ancient, secret societies. He shows that in such rites, the initiate is subjected to frightening sounds and sights. The experience of fright, he says, encourages the cohesiveness of the group. The sounds and sights that accompanied the theophany at Mount Sinai, and the threats implied in the preparatory precautions, served similarly to unify the group into a single religious community.

I find two things of interest in these ideas, though the argument does not persuade me. First, the suggestion, valid or not, moves one step beyond Freud in the attempt to establish an analytical psychology of the group rather than the individual. Reik is saying that when adolescents are exposed to a frightening experience in the presence of contemporaries, they are impelled, presumably defensively, to associate into a coherent group with these others. Secondly, and more generally, this hypothesis reminds me of certain observations to the effect that noxious stimuli exhibited by a parent or other powerful figure, not only fail to induce aversion, but even facilitate attachment. Such phenomena have been observed in the laboratories. Harlow and Harlow separated a group of infant monkeys from their mothers, and exposed them to unfriendly and even traumatizing mechanical models. They found that the monkey infants clung more tightly to these models the more abrasive they were. A discussion of the subject of infantile attachment paradoxically intensified by maltreatment appears in a recent review by Rajecki, Lamb, and Obmescher.

What is even more interesting about these generalizations is that they explain a number of puzzling clinical phenomena. Children raised by hostile mothers tend, in general, to cling tightly to them and to fail to mature to independence. Even adults tyrannized by others—for example, in a hostage-terrorist situation, or in a "brain washing" interrogation—tend to develop feelings of affection, compliance, and respect for their captors. This fact serves as the basis for occasional reports, exaggerated in fictional accounts, of perverse attachments of Jews to their Nazi persecutors, and possibly for their legendary reluctance to accept emancipation from Egyptian slavery.

Reik's hypothesis and all these observations suggest that in certain circumstances, especially when the subject is exposed to an overwhelmingly more powerful adversary, the experience of a frightening threat generates or facilitates affectionate bonds between the individual and the group that shares the experience with him, and between the individual and the powerful adversary—

fraternal bonds in the former instance, and a submissive attachment in the latter. It is to this principle that I attribute the efficacy of a common practice in group life, namely, the practice of recurrently recalling to the group past traumata and past threats to its existence. Such public recollecting—for example, in the ritual of the Passover Seder—powerfully strengthens group ties. These group memories, based upon actual or purely fantasied events, are shaped into legends which are preserved and cherished by groups as aids to maintaining cohesion.

Certainly one cannot attribute the need for community to this ritual intimidation ceremony. The former seems basic and probably biological. Yet the prevalence of the puberty ritual suggests that it performs an essential function. Most psychoanalysts, following Freud, interpret the puberty ritual as a relic of castration presumed to have been "carried out by a jealous and cruel father upon growing boys" (Freud, 1933). However, in *Civilization and Its Discontents* (Freud, 1930), Freud suggests that puberty and initiation rites help the youth to detach himself from his immediate family, and to transfer loyalty and obedience to the group and to its leaders. Reik's view, and the general hypothesis that intimidation binds, would support this suggestion.

The second new idea that Reik introduces in *Mystery on the Mountain* is that the truly novel religious contribution of the Jews was not simply the proposition that there is one rather than a multiplicity of gods, but that the spiritualization of the concept of a deity was accompanied by the internalization of what he called "a collective superego." The superego is composed of the sum of the moral and ethical demands imposed upon the child by his father, and on the people by its god. To the adult these demands are no longer recurrently imposed by an external authority *ad hoc*, but are incorporated into the psyche, where they can exercise supervision and guidance with the authority that the father once exerted over the child. What was novel about the Jewish God, Reik says, was not that he reigned alone, but that he was perceived as the author of, and the authority behind, the collective superego that Moses created for the Jewish people.

I find some important shortcomings in these early psychoanalytic studies of Judaism. It is true that by calling attention to the Oedipal paradigm, so easily visible in the mythology of almost all religions, and relating it to the unconscious determinants of the symptomatology of patients with neurosis, Freud, Reik, and their colleagues established the universality of these elements of human behavior. This was no small achievement for the early days of psychoanalysis, that is, the second and third decades of this century, and for its first attempts to become a general psychology.

My reservations fall into two categories, those relating to the method from the psychoanalytic point of view, and those relating to the treatment of Judaism. With respect to the former, I see the following problems. While the basic theories of psychoanalysis were derived from clinical experience with patients, these sociologic essays were contrived by applying to data of social behavior the theories derived from individual illness. Primary theories based upon clinical observation are one step away from the data. Secondary theories derived from the application of the primary theories to group behavior are two or more steps away, and they compel less conviction. In none of these studies have I seen any effort to confirm inferences by reference to clinical data. Nunberg studied the meaning of circumcision not by simply applying the Oedipus paradigm to anthropologic data, but by examining the productions of patients confronted with a circumcision experience. And he arrived at entirely new formulations.

For a number of years I have been scrutinizing carefully, analytic material offered by Jewish patients on the occasions of Jewish festivals. Themes of child sacrifice, infanticide, castration, and so on, occur only infrequently. Much more commonly one encounters themes of family unity and dissension, and attempts to overcome sibling rivalry. Perhaps the former set of themes is more deeply repressed, and feelings of guilt and anxiety about death are partially controlled by the religious service itself, so that little escapes into the analytic sessions.

All of the psychoanalytic studies of Judaism seem to assume that from currently prevalent rituals and myths, one can infer the history of the beginnings of the group, and that from that history, one can account for at least some of the characteristics of the group visible in all of its subsequent history, including the present. I do not find these assumptions at all persuasive. It seems to me that group myths and legends reflect the universals of group organization, and especially those significant at the time they were promulgated and recorded, and those significant at the time they are recollected and celebrated (see Arlow's papers). The assumption that the history of the formation of the group will account for its subsequent characteristics is based upon the clinical observation that the child's earliest experiences strongly influence his personality and subsequent behavior. In the first place, the correlation between infantile experience and subsequent personality and behavior, while highly significant, is far from complete. Even in those instances in which we see infantile trauma represented in subsequent behavior, we will require more than knowledge of the trauma to predict whether it will be represented as an inoperative fantasy, as a neurotic symptom, as a personality characteristic, or as a sublimated activity. For example, an early experience with the death of a sibling could induce neurotic guilt, inhibition about succeeding, obsessive fears of dying, or, on the other hand, a need to help others or a wish to become a successful physician or medical scientist. Second, there is no evidence that what is true of the individual is true also of the group.

I also find fault with the fact that the material selected for psychoanalytic study in these early efforts is selected to confirm one point of view, the Oedipal paradigm. Material relating to maternal deities, for example, is all but ignored, though their cults played an important role in the societies from which our society and its religions arose. (See Rubenstein's essay below.)

From the point of view of Judaism, I have already mentioned two reservations, that is, poor scholarship, and prejudice on the part of the writer. Let me detail some of the serious errors and oversights that I detect. In many of these studies, the institution of Jewish monotheism is considered. The problem is that the authors do not understand the uniqueness of Jewish monotheism. Jewish monotheism is certainly not the fact that Jews have one rather than many gods. Nor is it that the God is invisible. These characteristics prevail in other religious systems. The unusual insights of Yehezkel

Kaufmann (1960) inform us convincingly that what was and is unique about Jewish monotheism is that its God is not subject to limitations and influences imposed upon Him by a pre-existing cosmos. The Jewish God does not arise out of, or have to contend with, a primordial cosmic essence that determines and limits His powers. He alone possesses absolute control of all elements of the universe, and does not share that control with other deities or other influences that might exist in what Kaufmann calls a "metadivine realm" (*hawaya al elohith*).

I suspect that Reik was groping for this insight when, in *Mystery on the Mountain*, he asserted that it was the collective superego rather than the oneness of God that characterized Jewish monotheism, but he did not really arrive at Kaufmann's formulation. One might say in defense of the psychoanalytic writers that Kaufmann's work became available in English only in 1960, after all of these studies were written. But that excuses only the writers' lack of information; it does not lend validity to their unsupported inferences. (Sillman's paper, reproduced below, is not invalidated.) To be fair, Kaufmann's sweeping generalizations are not fully credited by all students of Jewish history. And probably the doctrines actually held by the monotheists and the pagans overlapped to an appreciable degree, at least preconsciously or unconsciously, if not consciously. Yet the conceptual distinctions that he introduced are so cogent and so illuminating that it seems impossible to discuss the issue without considering them.

What is especially interesting is that Kaufmann's understanding of the difference between monotheism and paganism permits a psychoanalytic statement of the fundamental and psychologic distinction between them. Kaufmann (l.c.) says, "Yet all these embodiments involve one idea which is the distinguishing mark of pagan thought; the idea that there exists a realm of being prior to the gods and above them, upon which the gods depend, and whose decrees they must obey. Deity belongs to and is derived from, a primordial realm" (p. 21). "The god is thus a personal embodiment of one of the seminal forces of the primordial realm. His nature and destiny are determined by the nature of this force. The multiplicity of pagan gods stems from the manifold powers and 'seeds' of the primordial realm, each of which is conceived as a self-contained divine entity. Water, sky, light, darkness, life, death, and the like—all derive from the primordial realm; this sets the natural and eternal bounds to the dominion of each pagan deity. It is not the plurality of gods per se, then, that expresses the essence of polytheism, but rather the notion of many independent power entities all on a par with one another, and all rooted in the primordial realm" (pp. 22 f.).

"There are two realms; that of the divine powers, another of the metadivine. Even the gods are depicted as calling upon metadivine forces to surmount their own predestined limitations. Pagan man feels himself subject to and in need of both realms. He prays to the gods to enlist their aid, but, conscious that the gods themselves are specific embodiments of a more generalized power, and learning from his myths that they call upon forces outside themselves, the pagan employs magic also, hoping thereby to activate the forces of the metadivine" (pp. 23 f.).

Of the Israelite religion he says (l.c.): "The basic idea of Israelite religion is that God is supreme over all. There is no realm above or beside him to limit his absolute sovereignty. He is utterly distinct from, and other than, the world; he is subject to no laws, no compulsions, or powers that transcend him. He is, in short, non-mythological. This is the essence of Israelite religion, and that which sets it apart from all forms of paganism" (p. 60).

"The store of biblical legends lacks the fundamental myth of paganism; the theogony. All theogonic motifs are similarly absent. Israel's God has no pedigree, fathers no generations; he neither inherits nor bequeaths his authority. He does not die and is not resurrected. He has no sexual qualities or desires and shows no need or dependence upon powers outside himself" (pp. 60 f.).

In psychoanalytic terminology, this contrast can be restated as follows. The pagan peoples his cosmos with a collection of fantasy creatures whom he considers deities. Upon scrutiny, these deities seem to represent idealized composites of the world in which he lives, namely, mothers, fathers, sons, daughters, brothers, sisters, husbands, wives, as individuals, as couples, as groups. These gods can be described as projections of images which each individual contains within his own psychic apparatus, specifically, that part that is accessible to consciousness, which we call the *ego*. We all maintain in our egos images of the individuals with whom we have related or do relate significantly. With these images we review the past, scrutinize the present, and plan the future. In a sense we really do not live within a world of people; we live within a world of images.

When we are affected by the feeling that we live in an inhospitable cosmos, the dangers of which seem to threaten to overwhelm not only us, individually, but our community as well, we tend to project out into this empty, inhospitable cosmos the familiar figures from our respective egos. We populate the cosmos with allies to fill what is perceived as a threatening void.

The images that are projected out as deities do not faithfully reflect the literal qualities of the individuals they represent; their qualities are exaggerated. The images of mother, for example, that appear in the child's dreams and fantasies, are those of a fairy godmother or a witch, depending upon whether she is being seen as a gratifying or a frustrating person. In this sense, the divine cosmic images too are stereotyped.

They are stereotyped in another sense as well. When an individual projects his own personal fantasies, unless he is psychotic, he does not attribute the quality of reality to these images. However, when he learns that he shares certain fantasies, and the images that they contain, with the other members of his community, he and they together impress the stamp of reality upon them. In order to secure this group sanction, therefore, individuals share their projected images within the members of the community, so that the images become stereotypes. It is these caricatures and shared images which people the cosmos for each pagan group, and constitute its deities.

Now another interesting thing happens. It is not simply that a pantheon of static images is projected out. Again, as in dreams and fantasies, the common wishes, impulses, needs, and fears of the individual are attributed to these deities, as are the actions that commonly issue from these motivational elements. So that what emerges is a group fantasy, that the group is surrounded by a divine community of gods who behave toward each other as humans do. The group resides within a familiar community of celestial creatures. It is no longer alone. The characteristic behavior of the gods not only makes them more familiar and representative, but also more real and more immediate. The accounts of the gods' relations with and behavior toward each other form the collection of myths of the local religion. The cultic rituals of the religion permit its members to feel that they are participating in the life of the gods, and thereby achieving whatever purposes are served thereby. For example, the common death and rebirth rituals of many religions reassure the human worshipper that he too is participating in, encouraging, and enjoying the fruits of the death and rebirth experience.

Kaufmann (1960) emphasizes the primordial stuff that antecedes and limits the gods. I suspect that this concept of a primordial matrix out of which the gods emerge, and of which they are composed, represents the psychic structure, the ego itself, within which the images are formed, and from which they are projected out into the celestial universe. Both theogony and mythology characterize every pagan religious system. The theogony represents the psychic creation of a fantasized cosmic population, while the mythology symbolizes and explains the attitudes, affects, and motivational tendencies associated with each of the projected ego images.

By contrast, the God of Jewish monotheism, as Kaufmann (l.c.) observes, arose from no primordial pre-existing matrix, does not generate other deities, does not behave as humans do, does not share their feelings or motives, does not relate to or contend with other deities, is not limited by his nature or origin. He is concerned only with the loyalty and obedience of his people. He is pleased with them when they behave properly and displeased with them when they misbehave. No mythology surrounds him. Worship signals that the worshipper accepts God's dominion, not that he participates in God's experiences in any way. The God of Jewish monotheism then can be described as a projection of the *superego*. The latter incorporates ideals of moral and ethical behavior, a system of rewards and punishments, and the principle that one's impulses must be subdued in deference to God's demands. It was this idea to which I believe Reik was reaching (1959).

"The progress in spirituality which made the Sinai experience the decisive turn of the human adventure is the establishment of the collective super-ego, of an inner standard within the people created by the introduction of Yahweh into the formation of the ego. This new agency is the greatest achievement of Moses—not monotheism. The greatest contribution of the Jews to human culture is the creation of an invisible deity and of its successor and heir in the form of a collective super-ego" (Reik, 1959, p. 169).

I would not say that Moses created a collective superego. He replaced the pantheon of ego projections with a single God who represents to each individual his own superego. Individuals share the God whom they worship, but that does not mean that He is perceived identically by each.

The sense of familiarity and comfort in the cosmos is achieved no longer by participating in the lives of celestial representatives of limited humans, but by controlling one's behavior so as to command the favor of an omnipotent and omniscient solitary, divine Father and Judge.

Of course, classical Jewish literature, Scriptural as well as rabbinic, contains many accounts of typical intrafamily loves and hates, conforming to the family dynamics so familiar to the psychoanalyst. These differ from pagan accounts in that these are *legends* rather than *myths*. This difference between legend and myth is usually overlooked, and the two terms are usually used interchangeably (as they are in this book) to designate non-factual accounts of events that are affectively significant to the community that holds and transmits them, events usually assumed to have taken place early in its history. According to the *Oxford English Dictionary*, myth deals with supernatural figures, while legend contains a nucleus of fact. In pagan religions, it is the gods who engage in struggles, whereas in Jewish tradition, it is human ancestors.

Some of our ancestors appear in legend as consistently righteous, others are primarily wicked, but most as exhibiting both virtues and failings. Many of these ancestors are obviously presented as ideals with whom the individual, and especially the child, is encouraged to identify. That they have faults, and at times engage in unworthy activities, makes them seem less remote from us; the images are not so ideal that they are unnatural. Never in Jewish classical literature is the human-divine boundary transgressed. While humans are encouraged to *imitate* God (e.g. Lev. 19:2), they must never *identify* with Him. The Jewish past is peopled by legendary ancestral figures who provide us with ideals and who encourage us to believe that Israel is a timeless community. But neither they, some of whom have had communication with God, nor we, are ever free of God's dominion or exempt from his commandments. The myths and legends of the pagan world include some figures who cross the human-divine boundary; the gods mate; they generate a hybrid progeny; some gods are incarnated in human form; some humans achieve apotheosis. In the pagan world, humans and gods do not escape fate, and they are both limited by the inherent properties of the primordial matter from which they are derived, but they are not subject to the control of the single, dominant, omniscient and omnipotent God. In the pagan world the gods reflect human frailties; in the Jewish world, God rewards the overcoming of these frailties and punishes succumbing to them. I am suggesting that these differences reflect the different origins within the individual psyche of the images that are projected out: ego images in the case of pagan gods; the superego in the case of the Jewish god. Ego images and their behavior reflect reality; superego images establish ideals.

In most of the psychoanalytic studies of mythology, and especially Jewish mythology, one encounters the genetic fallacy. Specifically, the author reveals the pagan "origin" of current religious practice. That "origin" and the accompanying psychodynamic conflicts are taken as the "explanation" of the religious practice. It is implied that since the "origins" are so primitive, current practice is equally unworthy, an exercise, if not in psychopathology, then certainly in primitive, magical thinking. It is true that in ancient Israel some few pagan practices persisted in folk usage. But Kaufmann (1960) infers that these were minor residues, not encroaching to any serious extent on Israelite religion, and, except for a few brief, locally limited episodes, not associated with an organized cult. The prophetic denunciation of pagan practice gives an exaggerated view of its prevalence and importance.

"The biblical cult, like the other aspects of biblical religion, is a composite creation with roots lying in the pagan pre-history of Israel. Scholars have endeavored to analyze the ancient materials and have found rites embodying magical, animistic, and demonistic notions. But here especially pagan analogues are apt to mislead. For the pagan religions of the ancient Near East combined very disparate elements in the course of a gradual and organic evolution. Beliefs and practices grew old and fell out of fashion without ever becoming rejected. Polytheism is capable of sustaining its most ancient roots and branches without ever lopping them off as withered members. Biblical religion, however, repudiates worship of gods other than YHWH, forbids the worship of the dead, spirits, and animals. It broke with the old religion; hence its relationship to ancient elements preserved in it was different. All was reformed and brought into harmony with the new idea. The cult laws of the Bible had no mythological or magic background—that is the heart of the transformation. This was not the product of artificial reworking, consciously and rationally undertaken by the priesthood of a certain age. It is the result of an organic development of Israelite religion through the course of generations" (pp. 101 f.).

"Examination of the thousand-year struggle of the biblical writers against idolatry indicates that already in the time of the judges and the early kings there was no battle with the fundamental idea of paganism, with myth. The pagan idea, the mythological-magical world view of paganism, no longer existed in Israel. The biblical struggle with idolatry restricts itself entirely to the area of cult and ritual. This is decisive proof that from the earliest times Israel was no longer a genuinely pagan people" (p. 147).

The point that relates to our interest is that one learns considerably less about Jews and Judaism from the characteristics of their pagan precursors than from what they did with their pagan heritage. It is difficult to know which characteristics of the Jews have been accounted for by the psychoanalysts' studies of Jewish origins. Freud (1939) expressed interest in learning the secret of the Jews' self-confidence and optimism, which accounts for their resistance to extermination. He attributed these to their having been chosen by Moses (pp. 105 f.). He also thought that a pervasive sense of guilt could be accounted for as a reaction to murderous hostility toward the father. The sense of guilt, in turn, gave rise to unusually stringent ethical ideals which he saw as "characteristic . . . obsessional neurotic reaction-formations" (p. 134 f.).

I find these conclusions not persuasive. The thesis that Jewish self-confidence is attributable to the choice of the Jews by Moses is not demonstrated. Jewish self-confidence, I believe, is to be understood as a response of the Jewish people to its vulnerability and its repeated defeats. The doctrine of the election of Israel rationalizes that self-confidence and encourages it. It tends to sustain morale when morale is threatened.

One can question whether feelings of guilt are more characteristic of Jews than others, if one makes allowance for Jewish tragedy. Misfortune creates a feeling of guilt. This is a common clinical observation. The feeling of guilt seems to arise from a sense of helplessness and recedes when the helplessness recedes. It is this mechanism that accounts for the guilt frequently encountered in Jewish thought and writing. Where tragedy is absent in Jewish history, guilt does not appear. The author of Deuteronomy understood well that prosperity engenders arrogance and rebellion, the opposite of guilt. Verse 15 of Chapter 32 reads:

> Jeshurun grew fat and kicked;
> You have become fat, and gross, and layered over;
> And he abandoned the God who created him,
> And despised the Rock of his salvation.

Freud holds the Prophets responsible for creating an exaggerated sense of guilt, while inspection of the Scripture tells us that their concern was that there was too little guilt in Israel. Kaufmann (1960) explains prophetic denunciation as required for theodicy, that is, to justify God for having permitted Israel's misfortunes. Freud suggests that it was the same consideration, theodicy, that participated in the creation of the sense of guilt. I cannot believe that a profound affective state can be generated just to rationalize a belief. The feeling of guilt was induced simply by the experience of catastrophe.

The "moral masochism" that accounts for the hypertrophied ethical development can be directly traced to the guilt induced by misfortune. Reik, in *Mystery on the Mountain* says, "Whoever wants to understand the religion of Israel, and whoever wants to inquire into the mystery of Jewish destiny or the particular features of Jewish character, has to take Exodus and Sinai as the ultimate point of departure. . . . As it is impossible for a psychologist to understand a person's character and vicissitudes without exploring his childhood, thus it is unfeasible to comprehend the nature and destiny of the Jewish people without exploring the early phases of their history, of their emergence on the scene, and of their formative years 'when Israel was a child' . . . Without understanding the significance of the Exodus-Sinai as the most important event, the solidarity of the Jews will always remain a puzzle" (pp. 30 f.). The promise of that understanding is never fulfilled in Reik's book. The "solidarity" of the Jews is explained by his hypothesis that the theophany at Mount Sinai was really an initiation ritual. But the hypothesis is merely stated, not proven.

These psychoanalytic studies of Judaism seem to assume a fairly continuous transmission of personality characteristics from ancient times until the present. Freud (1939) speaks of "psychical precipitates of the primeval period" that "become inherited property which, in each fresh generation, called not for acquisition but only for awakening" (1939, p. 132). He rejects Jung's idea of a collective unconscious, which to me, carries mystical overtones. I suspect that it was this mystical aura that made it unacceptable to Freud, though as I mentioned above, the rationalization by a "psychical precipitate" does not remove the mystical flavor from Freud's assumption. Yehudah Halevi (1905) spoke of a divine essence, a divine seed, and a divine influence, that passed from generation to generation of Jews, an equally mystical concept. This is a concept which appeals to Jews. It makes them feel close to their ancestors and members of a more coherent community. But that there is any truth to it, and if so, what specific truth there is, must yet be established. In the words of Robert Alter: "Clearly, there are recurring conceptual themes in the bible and also certain suggested, if uneven lines of continuity between the biblical world and the successive historical stages of Jewish life. What should be avoided at all costs is to reintroduce ethnic stereotypes into serious intellectual discussion by constructing in the name of semiotic analysis a monolithic Hebrew mind that dominates the actions of Jews from Leviticus to the Likud. The Jewish historical experience for nearly three and a half millennia has surely exhibited more then a single consistent strategy for ordering reality: indeed, the persistent polyphony of Jewish culture may ultimately be one of the secrets of this peculiar people's survival" (p. 52).

The psychoanalytic studies of Judaism by Freud and his early followers seem to me flawed. To a certain extent we can attribute these flaws to ignorance of the subject matter and to the primitive state of psychoanalysis at the time of their composition. To a much greater extent, it seems to me, we must see them as reflecting the ambivalence of the authors to their own religion, culture, and people. Every individual will choose from his cultural milieu certain components that give him especial pleasure, while ignoring those that do not. However, when we see not merely indifference but unnecessarily strong criticism, we naturally suspect ambivalence.

At the time that these writers became analysts, the training analysis had not yet been instituted as a requirement for the practice of the discipline. As a result, the early analysts, while brilliant and insightful, nevertheless were partially blinded by unanalyzed complexes and prejudices. Ambivalence to Judaism was one of these problematic complexes. Further, since these patriarchs of analysis were the earliest to conduct training analyses, their Jewish students too were left with unanalyzed ambivalence in this area, so that, identifying with their training analysts, Jewish psychoanalysts until recent years, to a greater extent than other Jewish professionals, have distanced themselves from Judaism.

To return now to Freud's question to Pfister, psychoanalysis was discovered and embraced by godless Jews precisely because as Jews they were marginal in the Gentile world; and since it was their

Jewishness that made them marginal, they rejected what they considered the particularistic beliefs and rituals of their religion, but adhered to its tradition of intellectuality and its universalistic ideals of social justice. Psychoanalysis attempts to show that it is the mental life of the individual that determines human history, and that the perception of external reality is what is effective, rather than the reality itself. In the words of Lionel Trilling, "We must, I think recognize how open and available to the general culture the individual has become, how little protected he is by countervailing cultural forces, how unified and demanding our free culture has become. And if we do recognize this, we can begin to see why we may think of Freud's emphasis on biology as being a liberating idea. It is a resistance to and a modification of the cultural omnipotence. We reflect that somewhere in the child, somewhere in the adult, there is a hard, irreducible, stubborn core of biological urgency, and biological necessity, and biological *reason*, which culture cannot reach and which reserves the right, which sooner or later it will exercise, to judge the culture and resist and revise it. It seems to me that whenever we become aware of how entirely we are involved in our culture and how entirely controlled by it we believe ourselves to be, destined and fated and foreordained by it, there must come to us a certain sense of liberation when we remember our biological selves." Psychoanalysis complemented the political emancipation of the Jews with cultural emancipation.

I do not wish to imply that I see no possibility that psychoanalytic studies can illuminate Jewish history, Jewish thought, or Jewish personal behavior. I can see great possibilities for the study of Jewish materials by the psychoanalytic method, with the result that Judaism, Jews, and Jewishness will be better illuminated, and that a psychoanalytic theory of social behavior will be developed. However, these studies must be considerably better than the classical studies to which I have referred. If possible, they should be based upon actual clinical experience, the mental state of the individual reflecting the significance of his participation in the group. Of course that could be possible only for current states of mind. The psychoanalytic sophistication of the investigators should be matched by their sophistication in handling the Jewish materials. They must see Jewish behavior as determined not merely by ancient history, but by subsequent history and current experiences. The investigators must keep in mind that the production of a written statement at any point in history responds to a need of that time, even though the statement may deal with a previous one.

Richard Rubenstein, in his book, *The Religious Imagination* (1968), approaches this kind of psychoanalytic study of Judaism. (See Rubenstein's contribution below.) To illustrate what I consider a useful psychoanalytic approach to Judaism, let me quote his penultimate paragraph: "The Aggadah riveted the attention of the Jew where it belonged. It helped the Jew to formulate a conception of his place in the cosmos, his obligations to his peers and to his God, the meaning of his precarious historical situation, the irrational psychic conflicts which threatened his personal and social order, and the nature of things hoped for in a broken and tragic world. Without the precise terminology of contemporary depth psychology, the Jew is helped to cope with such psychic dilemmas as his archaic oral strivings, his awesomely ambivalent feelings toward the mother, his fear of the need to identify with the father, as well as his conflicts at every level of psychosexual development" (p. 183).

I have tried in this volume to assemble a few essays which, I believe, conform to the foregoing criteria to some degree, and I hope that this material may inspire others to broaden the psychoanalytic study of Judaism.

REFERENCES

Abraham, H. C., and Freud, E. L. (1965). *A Psychoanalytic Dialogue: The Letters of Sigmund Freud and Karl Abraham, 1907–1926*. Translated by B. Marsh and H. C. Abraham. New York: Basic Books.

Abraham, K. (1920). "The Day of Atonement: Some Observations on Reik's *Problems of a Psychology of Religion.*" In *Clinical Papers and Essays on Psychoanalysis*. Edited by H. Abraham, translated by H. Abraham and D. R. Ellison. New York: Basic Books, 1955.

Alter, R. (1979). "A New Theory of Kashruth." *Commentary,* Volume 68, pp. 46–52.

Bakan, D. (1958). *Sigmund Freud and the Jewish Mystical Tradition*. New York: Schocken Books.

Bettelheim, D. (1979). *Surviving and Other Essays*. New York: Knopf.

Chodoff, P. (1963). "Late Effects of the Concentration Camp Syndrome." *Archives of General Psychiatry*, Volume 8, pp. 11–32.

Cohen, Gerson D. (1981) Mss. in preparation.

Coles, R. (1970). *Erik H. Erikson and the Growth of His Work*. Boston: Little, Brown.

Ellenberger, H. S. (1970). *The Discovery of the Unconscious*. New York: Basic Books.

Falk, A. (1977). "Freud and Herzl." *Midstream*, January, pp. 3–24.

Fenichel, O. (1946). "Elements of a Psychoanalytic Theory of Anti-Semitism." In *Anti-Semitism, A Social Disease*. Edited by E. Simmel. New York: International Universities Press, pp. 11–32.

Freud, E. L. (1970). *The Letters of Sigmund Freud and Arnold Zweig*. Translated by E. N. W. Robson-Scott. New York: Harcourt, Brace & World, p. 40.

Freud, S. (1900). *The Interpretation of Dreams* (first part). Standard Edition, Volume 4, pp. x–338.

———— (1905). *Jokes and Their Relation to the Unconscious*. Standard Edition, Volume 8, pp. 3–247.

———— (1913). *Totem and Taboo*. Standard Edition, Volume 13, pp. vii–161.

———— (1921). *Group Psychology and the Analysis of the Ego*. Standard Edition, Volume 18, pp. 67–143.

———— (1930). *Civilization and Its Discontents*. Standard Edition, Volume 21, p. 103.

———— (1933). *New Introductory Lectures*. Standard Edition, Volume 22, p. 80.

———— (1939). *Moses and Monotheism*. Standard Edition, Volume 23, pp. 3–137.

———— (1941). *Address to the Society of B'nai Brith*. Standard Edition, Volume 20, pp. 271–274.

Friedman, P. (1948). "The Road Back for the DP's." *Commentary*. Volume 6, pp. 502–510.

Gay, P. (1978). *Freud, Jews and Other Germans*. New York: Oxford.

Halevi, Y. (1905). *The Kuzari*. New York: Schocken Books, 1964.

Harlow, H. F., and Harlow, M. K. (1971). "Psychopathology in Monkeys." In *Experimental Psycho-Pathology*. Edited by H. D. Kimmel. New York: Academic Press.

Hoffer, W. (1965). "Siegfried Bernfeld and *Jerubbaal:* An Episode in the Jewish Youth Movement." *Leo Baeck Institute Yearbook*, Volume 10, pp. 150–167.

Jones, E. (1945). "The Psychology of the Jewish Question." In *Essays in Applied Psychoanalysis*. London: Hogarth, pp. 284–300.

———— (1955). *The Life and Works of Sigmund Freud*, Volume 2. New York: Basic Books.

Jung, C. G. (1934), *Archetypes and the Collective Unconscious*. Translated by R. F. C. Hull. Collected Works, Volume 9, Part I, Bollingen Series XX. New York, Princeton University, 1959.

———— (1966). "General Problems of Psychotherapy." In *Psychotherapy Today*. Translated by R. F. C. Hull. Collected Works, Volume 16, Bollingen Series XX, pp. 94–110. New York: Princeton University, 1966.

Kadushin, M. (1952). *The Rabbinic Mind*. New York: Jewish Theological Seminary of America.

Kaufmann, Y. (1930). *Gola ve-Nekar*. Tel Aviv: Dvir.

———— (1960). *The Religion of Israel*. Translated and abridged by Moshe Greenberg. University of Chicago Press.

Klein, H., and Last, U. (1974). "Cognitive and Emotional Aspects of the Attitudes of American and Israeli Youth Towards the Victims of the Holocaust." *Israel Annals of Psychiatry*, pp. 111–131.

Knoepfmacher, H. (1979). "Sigmund Freud and the B'nai B'rith." *Journal of the American Psychoanalytic Association*, Volume 27, pp. 441–449.

Krystal, H. (1968), ed. *Massive Psychic Trauma*. New York: International Universities Press.

Krystal, H. and Niederland, W. G. (1968). "Clinical Observations on the Survivor Syndrome." In H. Krystal, ed., *Massive Psychic Trauma*. New York: International Universities Press, pp. 327–348.

Kuznets, S. (1960). "Economic Structure and Life of the Jews." In *The Jews, Their History, Culture and Religion*, by Louis Finkelstein, 3d Edition. New York: Harper.

Liebman, C. (1972). *The Ambivalent American Jew*. Philadelphia: Jewish Publication Society.

Loewenstein, R. H. (1951). *Christians and Jews: A Psychoanalytic Study*. Translated by V. Damman. New York: International Universities Press.

Meng, H., and Freud, E. L. (1963). *Psychoanalysis and Faith: The Letters of Sigmund Freud and Oskar Pfister*. Translated by Eric Mosbacher. New York: Basic Books.

Moore, G. F. (1954). *Judaism in the First Centuries of the Christian Era: The Age of the Tannaim*. Cambridge: Harvard University.

Neubauer, P. (1965). *Children in Collectives*. Springfield, Ill.: Charles C. Thomas.

Niederland, W. G. (1968*a*). "The Psychiatric Evaluation of Emotional Disorders in Survivors of Nazi Persecution." In *Massive Psychic Trauma*. Edited by H. Krystal. New York: International Universities Press, pp. 8–22.

———— (1968*b*). "An Interpretation of the Psychological Stresses and Defenses in Concentration Camp Life and the Late After Effects." In *Massive Psychic Trauma*. Edited by H. Krystal. New York: International Universities Press, pp. 60–70.

Nunberg, H. (1949). *Problems of Bisexuality as Reflected in Circumcision*. London: Imago Publishing Co.

————, and Federn, E. (1962, 1967, 1974, 1975). *Minutes of the Vienna Psychoanalytic Society*. 4 Volumes, New York: International Universities Press.

Rainey, R. M. (1971). "Freud as Student of Religion: On the Background and Development of His Thought." Ph.D. Thesis, Columbia University, Faculty of Philosophy.

Rajecki, D. W., Lamb, M. E., and Obmescher, P. (1978). "Toward a General Theory of Infantile Attachment: A Comparative Review of Aspects of the Social Bond." *Behavioral and Brain Sciences*. Volume I, No. 3, pp. 417–464.

Reik, T. (1931). *Ritual: Psychoanalytic Studies*. Translated by Douglas Bryan. American ed., 1946, London: Hogarth Press, New York: Farrar, Strauss.

———— (1941). *Masochism in Modern Man*. Translated by M. H. Beigel and G. M. Kurth. New York: Grove Press.

———— (1951). *Dogma and Compulsion: Psychoanalytic Studies of Religion and Myths*. New York: International Universities Press.

——— (1959). *Mystery on the Mountain.* New York: Harper and Brothers.

Robert, M. (1976). *From Oedipus to Moses: Freud's Jewish Identity.* Garden City, N.Y.: Anchor Books.

Rothman, S., and Isenberg, P. (1974). "Freud and Jewish Marginality." *Encounter,* pp. 46–54.

Rubenstein, R. (1968). *The Religious Imagination.* Indianapolis: Bobbs-Merrill.

Scholem, G. G. (1961). *Major Trends in Jewish Mysticism.* New York: Schocken.

Schorske, C. (1973). "Politics and Patricide in Freud's Interpretation of Dreams." *American Historical Review,* April, pp. 328–347.

Simmel, E. (1946). "Anti-Semitism and Mass Psychopathology." In E. Simmel, ed., *Anti-Semitism as Social Disease.* New York: International Universities Press, pp. 33–78.

Simon, E. (1957). "Sigmund Freud, the Jew." *Leo Baeck Institute Yearbook,* Volume 2, pp. 270–305.

Smith, W. R. (1889). *The Religion of the Semites.* Fifth printing. New York: Meridian Books, 1956.

Trilling, L. (1955), *Freud and the Crisis of Our Culture* Boston: Beacon Press.

Underhill, E. (1964). *The Mystics of the Church.* New York: Schocken.

Utley, Phillip L. (1979*a*) "Siegfried Bernfeld's Jewish Order of Youth, 1914–1922." *The Leo Baeck Institute Yearbook,* 349–368, No. 24, London.

——— (1979*b*) "Radical Youth: Generational Conflict" in the *Anfang Movement, 1912–January 1914* 208–228. History of Education Quarterly.

Wittels, F. (1924). *Sigmund Freud: His Personality, His Teaching and His School.* Translated from the German. New York: Dodd, Mead & Co. Quoted by G. Zilboorg, in *Sigmund Freud: His Exploration of the Mind of Man.* New York: Charles Scribner & Sons, 1951, pp. 4 f.

Psychoanalytic Exegesis

The Consecration of the Prophet

Jacob A. Arlow

EDITOR'S COMMENT

This paper is reprinted from *The Psychoanalytic Quarterly*, Vol. 23, pages 374–397, 1951. It is an excellent example of the kind of understanding that classical psychoanalysis can contribute to the study of Scriptural text. Arlow is not only one of the leading theoreticians and clinicians in contemporary psychoanalysis, but, as the essay indicates, he is familiar, in the original Hebrew, with the material that he discusses, with its historical background and with its social and religious significance.

Unlike the early analysts, Arlow does not attempt to construct a virtual pseudohistory from a text. He has selected examples of one of the few types of subjective psychic experience that one finds in the Jewish Bible, and he discusses its psychodynamic meaning. The psychodynamic hypotheses he suggests are based upon classical psychoanalytic "exegetic" technic. He examines the words and phrases of a Biblical text exactly as the analyst examines the words and phrases of the text of a dream presented by a patient. Using symbolic equivalents, inference by association of words and ideas, and inference from indirect allusions, the author extracts meanings from the text that are not conveyed explicitly. The reader familiar with classical religious exegesis of the Biblical text will see the resemblance.

The essay tells us something about the state of mind of those who became the classical prophets of Israel. Arlow also begins to consider, in this essay, the nature of the relation between the prophet and his followers, and the prophet's role in providing group ideals and common purposes.

Reading this essay thirty years after it was written, I believe that one can go somewhat further in the analysis of the material.

The experience that Arlow describes is typical not only of what he calls the consecration of the prophet, but of the hysterical trance state in general. Vivid hallucinatory experiences of this kind are encountered in the literature of many religions, and they encourage the subject to believe that he has had the privilege of receiving the special favor of his god, of having been granted a new and direct revelation, and of having been elected for a special destiny. (Interestingly, the mysticism of post-

Biblical Judaism focuses not so much on the subjective trance state as on religious fantasies and on altering one's view of daily life so that one sees in the most mundane acts, spiritual significance not visible to others.) Not every trance state leads to a career of prophecy, but many people who have become religious leaders describe such experiences of initiation. (See, for example, Evelyn Underhill's *The Mystics of the Church* [New York: Schocken, 1964].)

Arlow describes the sense of invigoration, narcissistic grandiosity, and the confidence in one's leadership that issues from such mystical revelations, and he compares the post-revelation state to a hypomanic state. In another essay I suggest that Nathan of Gaza might have been functioning as a hypomanic personality. He was known as the "prophet" of Shabbatai Zevi. Scholem (in *Sabbatai Sevi, the Mystical Messiah*, translated by R. J. Z. Werblowsky [Princeton: Princeton University Press, 1973, Bollingen Series XCIII]) notes that Nathan's prophetic awakening began with mystical visions of God (pp. 204 f). Trance states, however, are characteristic of no one mental illness or personality type, though in modern terminology, we should consider them a hysterical type of phenomenon. The subject feels that the trance—which he experienced as personal revelation—created in him a state of illumination and the readiness to prophesy. The psychoanalyst might interpret the mystical experience as a manifestation of an inner change rather than its cause.

We should also take note of the prophet's withdrawal from emotional involvement with his community that Arlow describes. The prophet usually sets himself against the community, criticizes and threatens it, and points to his revelation as authority to do so. Jonah clearly regrets the remission of the sentence he had pronounced on Nineveh. Similarly, the community that the prophet threatens, resents him and often seeks to destroy him. Although Arlow says that the prophet speaks to the needs of the people, in most instances his prophecy comes to be valued only years or generations later, when people feel the need to be reunited with God by accepting rebuke and criticism. It is unusual for him to be appreciated by his contemporaries.

The prophet withdraws his love from his community and redirects it to God. By submitting to God in love, as Arlow suggests, he acquires God's authority to set himself over his fellow men, to criticize, to scold, to threaten and condemn them. The situation will be seen somewhat differently depending upon whether one believes that the prophet was responding to an external divine influence or that his contact with divinity was an illusion. In the former instance the initiative is God's. The prophet obeys God and carries the message to the people. In the latter instance, the illusory submission to and identification with God are explained as defensive responses to the rejection of human society. The prophet's need to reject society derives from some conflict between them, and this conflict starts the process in motion.

Finally, I should like to make a point about the ego state of the subject of the trance. Arlow notes the recurrent imagery of fire and brilliance, and he offers symbolic interpretations. I agree with his interpretations, but it is important also to note that mystical trances, as well as trances associated with pathology, such as the trances of acute schizophrenia or hysteria, those associated with certain forms of epilepsy, and those induced by hallucinogenic drugs, usually make reference to a fairly constant collection of sensory experiences: brightness or cloudiness, noisiness or silence, awareness of bodily functions, synaesthesias, hallucinations of scintillation and shimmering (often interpreted as water, mist, or jewels), feelings of strangeness and weirdness, familiarity and unfamiliarity, illusions of largeness or smallness, a sense of literal or figurative elevation, and the impression of "seeing a light" literally or figuratively (see *Mysticism: Spiritual Quest or Psychic Disorder?*, Group for the Advancement of Psychiatry, Vol. IX, Publication No. 97 [New York, 1976], Chapter 8). While each of these components of the trance state may have personal symbolic meaning to the subject, they are all characteristics of the state itself, and, I believe, reflect specifically the function of the temporal lobe of the brain, which becomes especially active at that moment (see Ostow, "Antinomianism, Mysticism and Psychosis," in *Psychodelic Drugs*, edited by R. E. Hicks and P. J. Fink [New York: Grune & Stratton, 1969]).

Recorded in the Old Testament are several passages of vivid imagery and terrifying magnificence portraying the consecration[1] of the prophets. The occasion is usually an intensely dramatic experience, signalized by supernatural portents, accompanied by auditory and visual hallucinations; a commingling of passive abnegation with ecstatic grandeur in which the prophet, having humiliated himself and proclaimed his unworthiness, accepts, as it were, the awful burden of prophecy. Revelations of this nature are most striking in the instances of Moses, Samuel, Isaiah, Jeremiah, and Ezekiel.[2]

Since it represents a special psychological experience in exceptional types of individuals whose influence upon the moral history of Western civilization is paramount, the consecration of the prophet would in any event excite the interest of psychoanalysts. Variations of such experiences in attenuated or distorted forms, moreover, have been known in every age. Prophetic experience is an important element in the heritage of civilization.[3]

Freud's study of Moses[4] approached the problem from an interest in demonstrating the historical recurrence of certain unconscious forces, persistently vital in the mythology of a race and representing, he felt, a prehistoric truth whose effects linger to this very day. The intrapsychic struggles of the individual prophet and the manner in which the prophetic calling represented a solution of these conflicts he did not discuss.

Because of the methodological difficulties inherent in such a study it is essential that its scope and nature be clearly defined.[5] In certain instances, as of Moses and Ezekiel, grave doubts have been cast as to whether these prophets ever existed. Almost everything we know about the prophets is derived from their writings or from books about them or ascribed to them. These documents have been demonstrated by critical scholarship to be quite frequently of composite authorship. Fortunately, the records of the consecrations of Samuel, Isaiah, Jeremiah, and Ezekiel are fairly well-integrated literary units and appear to have suffered relatively less from contradictory distortions and additions than do other sections of the Old Testament; however, no unequivocal stand can be maintained concerning their textual accuracy.

Whether or not the prophets ever existed as historical persons, and whether or not the documents connected with them are authentic, it cannot be disputed that the prophets and their teachings exerted a profound influence upon the imagination and the moral development of the Hebrew people, who enshrined them as their heroes, canonized their writings, and accepted their words as revelations of God's will. The prophet served as a model of consummate devotion to and identification with the cause of righteousness experienced by the prophet as the will or the voice of God.

Not a psychoanalytic study of individual prophets, this is the study of a composite, a type of person motivated chiefly by the conviction that his spoken words were the words of God. This is clearly the Hebrew version of prophecy. The Hebrew word for prophet, *nabi*, is of obscure origin but it does not carry the implication of prediction. This element, according to many authorities, was introduced as a result of a misunderstanding of the term used to translate the word *nabi* from the Hebrew into Greek.[6] The central theme of the Book of Jonah, for example, is the prophet's prediction of the imminent destruction of Nineveh which did not materialize. What is paramount in this example is the exhortation to turn from evil and to repent, rather than a forecast of the future. Martin Buber[7] states, 'The biblical *nabi* conception is seen most clearly in the passage, Exodus, VII:1, in which it is used as a simile of the relationship between two people who are to each other exactly what the *elohim* . . ., God, and the *nabi*, its herald, are to each other. "See", says God to Moses, "I give you to pharaoh for an *elohim* [God] and Aaron, your brother, shall be your *nabi*".' A similar passage, Exodus, IV:16, parallels this relationship of Moses and Aaron in which God says, 'He shall be thy spokesman unto the people: and he shall be, even he [Aaron] shall be to thee instead of a mouth, and thou [Moses] shalt be to him instead of God [*elohim*]'. According to Buber, '. . . to be the *nabi* of an *elohim* [God] means to be his mouth'. This use of the term *nabi* makes it clear that in the

Old Testament prophecy was understood to mean speaking in the name of God.

Why the prophet's preachment proved so apt a solution to the trying problems of his people in those critical moments of historical travail remains in the province of the historian. More intriguing is how the prophet was able to transcend the limitations and the comprehension of his contemporaries to perceive the path his countrymen were ready to follow.

Prophets exist in every age as outstanding personalities distinguished by missionary zeal with attributes of leadership and dedication to a cause. Inspiration is regularly ascribed to prophets, either by their own declaration or by attribution. The impression is created that they operate in response to some force beyond their own persons.[8]

In the cultural milieu of the Old Testament this relationship was stated explicitly by the Hebrew prophet. He regarded himself as a mere instrumentality in the service of a greater cause, a timeless, omnipotent, irresistible force before which all other considerations, including current vicissitudes of his community and the fortunes of the prophet himself, paled into nothingness. Lawgivers or reformers might call for enlightenment and betterment, but the prophet thundered for redemption and salvation. His inner turmoil was intense and ceaseless. In moving poetic language, employing every device of cadence and imagery, he transcended the barrier of reason and played on the unconscious emotions of his listeners, exhorting them to participate in his exultation and to share with him his vision of glory. In this respect he fulfilled the social function of the artist,[9] not only in his message but in his entire life; his stage was the national scene. Specific to the prophet, however, is his peculiar relationship to his mission or his peculiar relationship to his God for whose ministry he has been consecrated. For this mission the prophet left the land of his fathers, the comforts of home, the ties of friends, wife, and children, prepared to withstand, without complaint, all manner of trials and humiliation and to surrender even life itself in the pursuit of his calling. The lives of the prophets lead one to suspect that suffering and death were sometimes sought as fulfilments of their destinies.

This utter subjugation to the will of God results in a peculiar combination of meekness and grandeur. Toward his master, the prophet is the massive 'rod of his wrath' but in so doing he is permitted to share in God's omnipotence. He exhorts the multitudes, berates kings and high priests, and proclaims God's will. This ambivalent attitude appears clearly in the consecration of Jeremiah. After having been informed by the Lord that he was selected to proclaim his message throughout the world, Jeremiah states, 'Ah, Lord God! behold, I cannot speak: for I am a child'; whereupon '. . . the Lord put forth his hand, and touched my mouth. And the Lord said unto me, Behold, I have put my words in thy mouth. . . . I have this day set thee over the nations and over the kingdoms, to root out, and to pull down, and to destroy, and to throw down, to build, and to plant.'[10]

Of the personal lives of the prophets we usually learn little. God's service alone gives meaning to their lives. The poignant foibles of human relationships, the joys and sorrows which bind his fellow men in ties of affection, the prophet has put behind him. Such ties as he does maintain are recorded only in terms of his dedication: thus Hosea, at God's command, chooses a harlot for a wife in order to illustrate the parable of redemption through love; Isaiah gives his children names to dramatize the events of his calling. To the prophets, ordinary human relations have become meaningless and insignificant; they are emotionally impoverished. Feeling is withdrawn from all other relationships and reinvested in a special relationship with God. There exist no other attachments to compete with the prophet's love for God or to subvert it. His entire life is inexorably centered in his mission. The prophet is sacred (*ka-dosh*), that is, set aside or separated from the rest of humanity. This is the price of consecration. From that moment the prophet's existence has no other meaning.

That such withdrawal of object libido characterizes the creative efforts of artists is well known. This element in the constitution of the poet and the prophet is clearly and beautifully expressed in the first and third stanzas of O'Shaughnessy's Ode.[11]

> We are the music-makers,
> And we are the dreamers of dreams,

> Wandering by lone sea-breakers,
>   And sitting by desolate streams;
> World-losers and world-forsakers,
>   On whom the pale moon gleams.
> Yet we are the movers and shakers
>   Of the world forever, it seems.
>
> We, in the ages lying
>   In the buried past of the earth,
> Built Nineveh with our sighing,
>   And Babel itself with our mirth;
> And o'erthrew them with prophesying
>   To the old of the new world's worth;
> For each age is a dream that is dying,
>   Or one that is coming to birth.

In the phrases, 'lone sea-breakers' and 'desolate streams', one perceives the projection of the poet's mood onto objects in the external world which the poet consciously experiences as the sources of his inspiration.[12] In 'world-losers' and 'world-forsakers', the withdrawal of cathexis from the external world is evident.

If the essence of prophecy is an all-encompassing labor of love for God, we may ask, from what elements in the preprophetic personality might such world-shaking powers be derived? What are its precursors? Do there exist earlier human relations which may serve as models for the devotion of the prophet to his God? The answer to these questions becomes apparent almost at once. In Judaeo-Christian tradition, God is experienced in terms of the father.[13] From the earliest period when he was conceived of as an irascible warrior who contended with the archetypal Behemoth and the primordial Leviathan to his later moral elevation as the benevolent ruler of the universe, God is uniformly a masculine deity. That the prophet Jeremiah identified God with his father is stated in the passage in which God says, 'Before I formed thee in thy mother's womb, I knew thee'.[14]

It was Freud who demonstrated the origin of the male god from the attitude of the son toward his father. The experiences and fantasies which center in this relationship reach a climax of intensity in the oedipus conflict. Before the resolution of this conflict, which is so momentous in shaping the personality of the boy, assumes its definitive character, many emotional crises must be endured and mastered. In the eyes of the child the image of the father looms as a giant, possessed of insuperable physical prowess and limitless magical knowledge. He seems an autocrat who can punish parricidal wishes with unspeakable mutilation and yet can bestow all measure of blessing upon those who gain his favor. This is the image after which the little boy must model himself if he is to achieve man's estate. It is an image toward which he has variously felt hatred and love, scorn and envy, withdrawal in angry defiance, reconciliation in submissive love. To emulate the father he must master the anxiety connected with the fear of retaliation for competitive aggression. Clinical analytic experience demonstrates how frequently this goal is not reached. According to Freud,[15] in the monotheistic religion of the Old Testament as in the patriarchal family, this conflict in the son is decided in favor of the father.

One form of resolving these conflicting anxieties and wishes deserves special mention. This is the plight of the son who, overcome by fear and guilt, surrenders his active, aggressive, masculine strivings and, by becoming passive, masochistic and, as it were, feminine, seeks reunion and reconciliation with a loving and forgiving father. This early relationship with the father governs subsequent relations with older men in authority and male competitors. These unresolved conflicts remain repressed, ready to burst forth with overwhelming intensity to the ego should some event disrupt the mechanism of defense.

In the course of uncomplicated development, the image of the prohibitive and threatening father is incorporated into the personality as the nucleus of the superego. In regressive mental states the direction of this process may be reversed, and the relationship to one's own superego may once again be experienced as a relationship with an external object. A similar transformation takes place in the origin of the masculine deity. The reprojection of the superego to a graven image, or to some anthropomorphic heavenly figure or, in a deanthropomorphized form, in pantheistic moral philosophy, is what is subjectively experienced as God. The vicissitudes of the process are many and complex, but its essence remains unchanged.

The feeling for God is derived from the feeling for the father. Upon this emotional basis is founded the relationship between the prophet and his God.

The dynamic instability of a personality is to a large extent determined by the persistence of ambivalent attitudes. This is particularly true in the case of the prophets. Impressive as the prophet and his unswerving devotion to God may be, his attitude toward authority is steeped in ambivalence, if not outright rebellion.

The intense ambivalence toward the father is portrayed in a most straightforward fashion in the consecration of the prophet Samuel.[16] The simplicity of this experience may be accounted for by the fact that it took place when Samuel was still a young child. This is the only instance of prophetic revelation in childhood recorded in the Old Testament. It is also the only experience which Samuel had in which he both heard and saw God.

From the time of his weaning Samuel had been dedicated by his mother to the service of God. For this purpose she had entrusted her son to the kindly and indulgent Eli, the aged priest whom thereafter Samuel served. To the child Samuel, ministering to Eli and ministering to God would be synonymous, as Eli from that time, for all practical and emotional purposes, filled for Samuel the role of a father. In the text he refers to Samuel as 'my son'.

In Eli's household Samuel was at a disadvantage. His natural aspirations, reinforced by his mother's hopes for him, were to succeed to Eli's position. This wish was thwarted by the fact that he was not of the clan of the priests nor even of the tribe of Levi. Toward Eli's sons, Samuel would have felt inferior, handicapped in the competition for the father's affection by the knowledge that he was an outsider. Eli's sons were a disappointment to their father because of their arrogance and licentiousness.[17] Samuel tried to overcome the natural advantage of blood ties which Hophni and Phineas enjoyed by offering himself to Eli as a different and better son, fashioning himself in obedience and humility according to Eli's ideals. The presence of this worthy lad in his household must have afforded the aged Eli some measure of surcease from the painful awareness of his own sons' abominable behavior.

The consecration of Samuel occurred as a hallucinatory experience during the interval between waking and sleep when the mind slowly divests itself of the impediments of logical thinking. The emotional setting for Samuel's consecration is set forth explicitly in the Bible: 'And it had come to pass at that time, when Eli was laid down in his place, and his eyes began to wax dim, that he could not see'. Samuel knew that the death of his beloved guardian was imminent. Lying on his couch, oppressed by this knowledge, Samuel could have realized that the death of his master would signalize his own defeat. The knavish Hophni and Phineas would succeed to the priesthood while his position would be rendered most insignificant. This jealousy of his rivals would have been compounded with anger at the gentle Eli who never could summon up enough forcefulness to make his usurping sons desist from their abominations. Engaged in such thoughts, Samuel's feelings may be assumed to have surged to heights of hitherto unattainable intensity. At this point his inner feelings seemed to have become external realities: he began to hallucinate. He heard his name being called and thought it was the voice of Eli.

That the hallucinatory God is Eli is evident from the fact that Samuel cannot distinguish between their voices. The identification of God with Eli was, in any event, an easy substitution since the name Eli in Hebrew is practically the equivalent in sound to 'My God'. Throughout this section, Eli and God are addressed by Samuel in precisely the same terms.

In his revelation from God, Samuel's instinctual wishes are fulfilled. God decrees annihilation for Eli's sons, Samuel is to succeed to the pre-eminent position in Israel, and Eli is to be punished for his vacillation. This is Samuel's victory. What he could not get from Eli, God gives him in his revelation.

Plagued by feelings of guilt for the hostility toward his rivals as well as the rebuke to Eli in his vision, Samuel '. . . feared to show Eli the vision'. At Eli's insistence he unburdens himself of his revelation. What follows proves that Samuel's wishes were no empty illusions. They were based upon a correct intuitive perception of Eli's feelings. That is why Eli, who was no prophet and never had a vision, was able to confirm Samuel's revelation and could say, 'It was the Lord. His will be done.' For in the previous chapter[18] Eli had, in fact, searched his conscience, in the words of 'a man of God', had weighed his sons in the balance, had concluded that they warranted destruction and that he deserved to share their fate.

More dramatic is the consecration of Isaiah, the son of Amoz, which is recorded in the sixth chapter of the Book of Isaiah. In a passage of great beauty and sublimity, we are afforded perhaps the best opportunity for insight into the prophetic experience of consecration.

> In the year that king Uzziah died I saw also the Lord sitting upon a throne, high and lifted up, and his train filled the temple.
>
> Above it stood the seraphim: each one had six wings; with twain he covered his face, and with twain he covered his feet, and with twain he did fly.
>
> And one cried unto another, and said, Holy, holy, holy, is the Lord of hosts: the whole earth is full of his glory.
>
> And the posts of the door moved at the voice of him that cried, and the house was filled with smoke.
>
> Then said I, Woe is me! for I am undone; because I am a man of unclean lips, and I dwell in the midst of a people of unclean lips: for mine eyes have seen the King, the Lord of hosts.
>
> Then flew one of the seraphim unto me, having a live coal in his hand, which he had taken with the tongs from off the altar:
>
> And he laid it upon my mouth, and said, Lo, this hath touched thy lips; and thine iniquity is taken away, and thy sin purged.
>
> Also I heard the voice of the Lord, saying, Whom shall I send, and who will go for us? Then said I, Here am I; send me.
>
> And he said, Go, and tell this people, Hear ye indeed, but understand not; and see ye indeed, but perceive not.
>
> Make the heart of this people fat, and make their ears heavy, and shut their eyes; lest they see with their eyes, and hear with their ears, and understand with their heart, and convert, and be healed.
>
> Then said I, Lord, how long? And he answered, Until the cities be wasted without inhabitant, and the houses without man, and the land be utterly desolate.
>
> And the Lord have removed men far away, and there be a great forsaking in the midst of the land.

> But yet in it shall be a tenth, and it shall return, and shall be eaten:
> as a teil tree, and as an oak, whose substance is in them, when they
> cast their leaves: so the holy seed shall be the substance thereof.

This hallucinatory incident portrays graphically the prophet's agony of dedication.

The event which led to this consecration was the death of a king, Uzziah. Uzziah's reign had been long, prosperous, and successful, and with the exception of one dereliction, he had walked in the way of the God of Israel, a most uncommon path for the corrupt court of Judah. Throughout this passage, Isaiah's conception of God is in terms of a monarch. He refers to God as a king and sees him seated on a throne surrounded by fiery courtiers. Uzziah was a great military leader,[19] outstanding in the days of Judah's declining powers. He conquered the Philistines and the Arabians and exacted tribute from the Ammonites so that 'his renown spread abroad, even to Egypt'; moreover, 'Uzziah had a host of fighting men, that went out to war by bands'. His army numbered two thousand six hundred officers and three hundred seven thousand five hundred men. In the desert he built outposts, and Jerusalem he fortified with ingenious military machines. Isaiah, furthermore, had applied for the ministry like a courtier volunteering for an ambassadorship, a scene which Isaiah surely must have witnessed during his attendance at court.

Since Uzziah had reigned for fifty-two years, and since Isaiah continued to prophesy during the reigns of the three succeeding kings of Judah, it is a certainty that Uzziah had been king at the time of Isaiah's birth and throughout the formative years of the prophet's personality. Those who recall the universal grief and felt the very personal emotion which was occasioned by the death of President Roosevelt will readily understand how deeply stirred the patriotic Isaiah might have been by the death of the good king. Precisely how Isaiah felt toward the recently deceased monarch we cannot know, but the image of the king or president is usually identified with the image of the father. For Isaiah, this identification was accentuated by the fact that the prophet, according to most authorities, was of noble if not of royal lineage. Mourning for the king is reconstructed as reactivating in Isaiah conflicting feelings connected with his father. The passions that swept through Isaiah are expressed in the line, 'And the posts of the door moved at the voice of him that cried, and the house was filled with smoke.' This might well represent a projection of the prophet's ecstatic bodily shuddering and the clouding of his consciousness.

That the prophet should assert he had seen the Lord face to face is in itself remarkable. The taboo of forbidden or aggressive looking was strong and explicit in ancient Israelite tradition. God said to Moses, 'No man may see me and live.' For the crime of forbidden looking, Adam and Eve were expelled from paradise, and Noah condemned Ham and his descendants to eternal servitude. This taboo has survived into modern orthodox Jewish lore, where there exists a superstition that looking at the hands of the priests in the act of bestowing the triple blessing will be punished with instantaneous blindness. The strength of this scoptophilic taboo must be related to the most basic of all taboos, the prohibition against incest. The taboos of scoptophilia and of incest are expressed in the Bible in identical terms, *Gi-looy ar-ah-yoth*, namely, the uncovering of nakedness. The conflict over looking at God is expressed in Isaiah's vision symbolically in relation to God's surrogates, the seraphim, who are described as covering their faces and their feet with their wings.

Psychoanalytically, the face and feet are found in dreams and hallucinations to be symbols of male nakedness. Kent,[20] the eminent biblical scholar, translates the 'feet' in this passage as 'loins,' explaining that 'feet' is introduced as a euphemism. It is also striking that the medieval Jewish biblical commentator, Rashi, in commenting on this passage, states that the seraphim did so, 'in order not to appear before their creator in their total nakedness.'

Isaiah's exclamation of guilt, 'I am a man of unclean lips . . . for mine eyes have seen the King, Lord of Hosts,' is puzzling. Since his aggression is visual, it would seem more correct for him to have imputed uncleanliness to his eyes, in which case the 'live coal' should have been applied there instead of to his lips in accordance with the *lex talionis*. We conclude that aggressive looking and speaking are equated and that Isaiah had at one time felt guilty of both. The Mosaic code provided the death penalty for those who raised their voices in curses against their parents.[21] So strong was the taboo against blasphemy that 'to curse God' is rarely found in the Bible.[22] The taboo against saying the Tetragrammaton, Yahweh, is probably derived from this prohibition. This connection between looking and irreverence is by no means fortuitous. Fenichel,[23] in commenting on the prohibition against looking at God's face, states that this prohibition is directed at the aggressive wish to become like God through an act of scoptophilic introjection. If we add to this Bornstein's[24] observation that the inhibition of looking at people's faces results from the displacement upward of the wish to stare at their genitals, it is probable that the wish to see God's face must, in part, be related to genital competition with the father. That other wishes may enter into this conflict one cannot doubt.

In the application to his lips of the burning coal, Isaiah indicated his wish to renounce forever all aggressive, masculine, competitive strivings with the image of God the Father. The organ of aggression having been purged of its rebellious sinfulness, it is now placed at God's disposal for the execution of his mission. By this submission he is reunited with God and, as his emissary, he now shares in his omnipotence. The auditory elements in this experience are striking. What Isakower[25] indicated about the spoken word in the hallucinatory experience of dreaming would apply very well to the prophet's hallucination of consecration: the voice of the Lord represents the projection of the prophet's superego. Through the introjection of the word of God, the prophet's ego is united with the superego. The prophet is identified with the God-Father image. Isaiah proclaims

> Hear, O heavens, and give ear O earth
> For the Lord hath spoken.

The subjective awareness of his loss of emotional ties with other objects in the real world finds expression, again through the mechanism of projection, in the statement, 'Until the cities be wasted without inhabitant, and the houses without man, and the land be utterly desolate.' This corresponds to the well-known delusion of the world coming to an end, a delusion which very frequently announces the onset of schizophrenia. This delusion, Freud[26] demonstrated, signalizes awareness of a change in the libidinal economy of the individual: a withdrawal of libidinal cathexis from the external world of objects and its reinvestment in the ego. In this instance this process was initiated by the withdrawal of libido from the highly cathected object, the recently deceased king, a paternal superego figure. What resulted was a regression from love to incorporation, from object relation to identification, from object libido to narcissism. It is essentially an incorporation of a superego figure, a fusion of ego and superego cathexes. This structural reorganization of the personality corresponds to the psychopathology which Freud,[27] Abraham,[28] Lewin,[29] and others have indicated characterizes the hypomanic state.[30] In this heightened narcissism, analogous to hypomania, the prophet embarks upon his mission. Freed from doubt or ambivalence, exuding conviction and certainty, he pursues his mission with unswerving devotion, heedless of the wishes of kings or the importunities of commoners. This narcissistic regression, achieved through the reorganization of the psychic structure of the prophet, ensures the success of his ministry. The aura of omnipotence exerts a fascinating effect upon dependent individuals passively seeking salvation.[31] In periods of catastrophe the number of such persons is ostensibly much greater than in more stable eras. In this fashion the prophet gathers about him disciples who are ready to follow him blindly, who find in him the lost omnipotence of their childhood.

For these reasons the prophet's influence may extend through the centuries. In every generation individuals with similar conflicts may find, through identification with the prophet, a model for the resolution of their own conflicts. Like the prophet's disciples, individuals in all generations seek adherence to prophetic, seemingly omnipotent figures who infuse in them a sense of certainty and safety against the torments of guilt and ambivalence. In this fashion, the prophet is an auxiliary superego in the struggle against one's own ambivalence, a phenomenon frequently encountered in the analysis of obsessional patients.

An analysis of the vision of Isaiah's consecration would be incomplete without reference to the promise of restoration contained in God's message. In spite of the forecast of utter annihilation, God does not withdraw his love entirely: a 'holy seed' survives. Grasping this tenuous libidinal tie, the prophet begins his quest for salvation. The nation, whose utter and fitting devastation he had visioned, he now seeks to restore to greater glory. This promise gives his life a new and exalted meaning. His new interest in mankind is intensified with wondrous significance.

A comparison with Freud's[32] analysis of the Schreber case is unavoidable, especially since Messianic delusions occasionally characterize attacks of paranoia. Freud demonstrated that the delusion of persecution is an attempt to restore the libidinal ties which have been abandoned. 'Such a reconstruction after the catastrophe is more or less successful but never wholly so. . . . [The world which] the paranoiac builds up again is not more splendid than before . . . but at least he can once more live in it.' In contrast to the delusion of the paranoiac, the mission of the prophet successfully restores libidinal ties and may, indeed, build up a world more splendid than before.

Oral incorporation, only an intimation in the consecrations of Isaiah and Jeremiah, is the central theme of the consecration of the prophet Ezekiel. Exactly what event initiated the psychic processes which led to his experience of consecration we do not know. It must, however, have been some very specific incident, for the precise day of the event is recorded. Because of the frequency of his hallucinatory experiences and the vividness of their details, Ezekiel has been said to be psychotic by many authors. Such long-range diagnosis is hazardous and not particularly illuminating.

The Book of the Prophet Ezekiel is introduced with most detailed descriptions of the presence of God and of the train of his attendants. The mystical symbology of these chapters continues to baffle the interpretative efforts of biblical scholars, and has been a rich source of esoteric speculation for the cabalists.

Most pronounced in his vision is the impression which the element fire made upon the prophet. His awareness of a fiery presence reappears several times.

And I looked, and, behold, a whirlwind came out of the north, a great cloud, and a fire infolding itself, and a brightness was about it. . . .[33]

As for the likeness of the living creatures, their appearance was like burning coals of fire, and like the appearance of lamps: it went up and down among the living creatures; and the fire was bright, and out of the fire went forth lightning.[34]

. . . above the firmament that was over their heads was the likeness of a throne, as the appearance of a sapphire stone: and upon the likeness of the throne was the likeness as the appearance of a man above upon it.

And I saw as the color of amber, as the appearance of fire round about within it, from the appearance of his loins even upward, and from the appearance of his loins even downward, I saw as it were the appearance of fire, and it had brightness round about.

As the appearance of the bow that is in the cloud in the day of rain, so was the appearance of the brightness round about. This was the appearance of the likeness of the glory of the Lord. And when I saw it, I fell upon my face, and I heard a voice of one that spake.[35]

This bears a resemblance to a repetitive dream wish, recurring in various editions, with increasing transparency, the final version having a nightmarish quality. The symbol, fire, is ascribed to the entire cloud which encompasses God and his attendants. (In the vision of Isaiah, fire is associated with God's surrogates, the angels and the holy creatures.) The entire body of Jehovah is invested with fiery brilliance, but finally it is upon the 'appearance of his loins even downward' that the eyes of the prophet focus. When this scoptophilic crescendo reaches its phallic climax, the prophet is completely overwhelmed, falls upon his face, and begins to hear the voice of God speaking.

The introjection of Jehovah and the divine phallus first conceived in visual terms continues at the auditory and oral levels.

And [Jehovah] said unto me, Son of man, stand upon thy feet, and I will speak unto thee.

And the spirit entered into me when he spake unto me, and set me upon my feet, that I heard him that spake unto me.

> And he said unto me, Son of man, I send thee to the children of
> Israel, to a rebellious nation that hath rebelled against me. . . .[36]
>
> But thou, son of man, hear what I say unto thee; Be not thou
> rebellious like that rebellious house: open thy mouth, and eat that I
> give thee.
>
> And when I looked, behold, a hand was sent unto me; and, lo, a
> roll of a book was therein;
>
> And he spread it before me; and it was written within and without:
> and there was written therein lamentations, and mourning, and woe.
> Moreover he said unto me, Son of man, eat that thou findest; eat this
> roll, and go speak unto the house of Israel.
>
> So I opened my mouth, and he caused me to eat that roll.
>
> And he said unto me, Son of man, cause thy belly to eat, and fill
> thy bowels with this roll that I give thee. Then did I eat it; and it was
> in my mouth as honey for sweetness.
>
> And he said unto me, Son of man, go, get thee unto the house of
> Israel, and speak with my words unto them.[37]

The Hebrew word for 'caused me to eat' almost carries the
connotation of a coercive act. In the original Hebrew the word for
stomach is synonymous with the word for womb and is indeed the
same word which occurs in Jeremiah's vision when Jehovah says,

> Before I formed thee in thy mother's womb,
> I knew thee.

Ezekiel's concentration on God's loins is expressed by the prophet
in terms reminiscent of a fellatio-impregnation fantasy. The fiery
phallus of the vision has been transformed at this point into the roll
which tastes like honey. This symbolism is in accord with Freud's
interpretation of the Prometheus myth in which the hollow fennel
stalk is equated with the penis, and the fire, through representation
by its opposite, with water.[38]

This association by the opposite is also explicit in the passage from
Ezekiel,

> . . . from the appearance of his loins even upward, and from the
> appearance of his loins even downward, I saw as it were the appear-
> ance of fire, and it had brightness round about.

> As the appearance of the bow that is in the cloud in the day of rain,
> so was the appearance of the brightness round about.

In this fashion, God's word was literally ingested by the prophet. It has been demonstrated by many authors[39] that words written or spoken may represent feces in the unconscious. In his study of unconscious factors in reading, Strachey[40] refers to the printed word as 'the author's thoughts, fertilizing and precious . . . [equated with] the father's penis or feces'. In a footnote he refers to Ezekiel's vision as a fantasy of fecal impregnation by the word of God. This form of impregnation brings to mind Jones's[41] essay on the Madonna's conception through the ear. Jones interpreted this famous myth as a displacement upwards of a fantasy of anal gaseous fertilization in which the reception of divine speech represented the introjection of the father's flatus. The prophet states, 'and the spirit entered into me when he spake unto me'. The Hebrew word *Ru-akh* means spirit, wind, and breath.

The introjection of God through the various orifices of the body demonstrates the symbolic equivalence of phallus-fire-speech-breath-flatus-feces. The coprophagic fantasy is particularly striking in Ezekiel. One of the first missions assigned to him was to symbolize the coming of famine and national pollution by storing various grains in one vessel for a long period of time and then eating them baked in the form of a cake mixed with human dung. As a result of Ezekiel's protestations cow dung is substituted for 'dung that cometh out of man', a very insignificant displacement of the coprophagic impulse.[42] This incident illustrates very clearly how the sublimation of prophecy permits the emergence of and indulgence in perverse, pregenital forms of sexuality.[43] Similar illustrations can be culled from the lives of the other prophets. That Ezekiel's incorporation of God's word was an identification with Jehovah is evident. After receiving God's message Ezekiel is told to go to the people of Israel and speak to them in God's name in the first person, introducing his message with the phrase, 'Thus saith Jehovah'.

The withdrawal of object libido from the external world during consecration was experienced by Ezekiel not only psychically but also physically. The revelation of God's presence culminated in the command to withdraw from the world, to lock himself up in his house and to utter a word to no person. Only after a period of isolation did Ezekiel emerge to proclaim his message.

During the exercise of his calling, the prophet speaks to the people in the same tenor as his conscience (God) has spoken to him. Isaiah, who reproached himself for having been a bad son, states, 'I have nourished and brought up children [sons], and they have rebelled against me'.[44] This neatly condenses the idea of God, father, and king. In the pursuit of his ministry, what had been an exclusively intrapsychic relationship between the prophet and his superego is now replaced by a relationship between the prophet and his people. In this way the prophet restores his object relationships but on a new and different plane in the exercise of his mission.

The shift in emphasis from the exclusively intrapsychic relationship between the prophet and the superego to a relationship between the prophet and his people accounts for contradictory attitudes taken by the prophets. Thus Moses, for example, when identified with God, behaves as superego and berates the erring nation. When identified with the nation, he suffers their torments, very much as does the ego in depression, and he implores God (the superego) to be lenient with the nation.[45]

Without a mission, a prophet could have no existence. He would be living in an emotionally depopulated world. His mission fulfilled, Moses had to die just as the children of Israel stood at the threshold of the Promised Land. In the legend of the death of Moses, he retired in lone splendor to the top of Mount Nebo, and no creature in heaven or earth could be found to do God's bidding and bring the soul of Moses aloft. Finally God himself drew the soul of Moses out of his body with a kiss.[46] His mission having been completed, no emotional ties bound Moses to his fellow men; he was reunited in love with God, the father.

SUMMARY

The consecration of the prophet is a temporary schizophrenoid abandonment of reality and withdrawal of object libido. The schizophrenic tries in vain to re-establish these ties by involving his fellow men in the distorted relations of his delusions. The prophet, however, through his mission, succeeds in re-establishing the emotional bonds with the world of reality because his message truly corresponds to a deep emotional reality waiting to be stirred in the soul of his contemporaries. The apocalyptic dream of Isaiah of an era of universal peace, when 'nation shall not lift up sword against nation',[47] is a true representation of the aspirations of humanity.

In accepting the vision of the prophet, the nation completes the process his consecration. The people install him in the office of their collective ego ideal. The universal selection of the prophet or his memory as the collective ego ideal gives unity and cohesion to the group.[48] In this sense the prophet symbolizes a stage in the historical evolution of the moral conscience of his people. Only the historical test of mass acceptance and the course of history itself validate the truth of the prophet's vision, and this is what distinguishes the true prophet from the false prophet. The true prophet is one who correctly divines and expresses the emergent, but still inarticulate dreams and aspirations of his people. In this respect prophecy is like great art and both survive for the same reason.

> For each age is a dream that is dying,
> Or one that is coming to birth.

At the threshold of the ages stands the prophet, midwife of humanity's dreams.

NOTES

[1]The term consecration here differs from the special sense in which it occurs in ecclesiastical literature. No definite term covers directly the phenomena of revelation, religious ecstasy, and dedication. The experience of 'receiving the call', which occurs frequently in the lives of many clergymen and converts, is only one aspect of the prophet's consecration, and it does not approach the dramatic intensity and supernatural proportions which the prophets described. The word consecration is derived from the Latin, *sacer*, meaning to set aside, designate as something special. This is perhaps the outstanding element of the experiences studied in this essay.

[2]These experiences are recorded in the following passages in the Old Testament to which the reader is referred: Exodus, III: 2 to 18; IV, 1 to 12; I Samuel, III; Isaiah, VI; Jeremiah, I; Ezekiel, I to III: 12.

[3]The prophesying by oracles during ecstatic trances is analogous to only part of the prophetic experience as it is observed in the Old Testament. It is not an essential element of the Hebrew version of prophecy. This distinction is developed below in part. For a further discussion of the differences, one is referred to Buber, Martin: Symbolical Existence in Judaism. In: *Hasidism*. New York: Philosophical Library, 1948, p. 118, and Ahad Ha' Am: *Selected Essays*. Philadelphia: Jewish Publication Society of America, 1912, pp. 125 and 306. Personality structure must in any event be viewed within the historical and cultural context of the age in which it occurs. Although the prophets were undoubtedly regarded by their contemporaries as different, they were not necessarily regarded as pathological or insane. With the advance of science, later ages have taken an increasingly sceptical attitude toward the phenomenon of divine or supernatural revelation. Yet even in our age, the attitude of society toward such problems is rather ambivalent. Individuals who profess experiences of communication with divine or supernatural agencies ordinarily escape commitment, and are not necessarily regarded as pathological provided they do not enter into too violent conflict with the social order, and/or if they manage to gather about them sufficient followers to constitute a sect. The founders of the Mormon Church and Father Divine are only two examples. One also observes the reluctance of official church hierarchies to recognize contemporary miracles except when the element of mass belief becomes evident.

[4]Freud: *Moses and Monotheism*. New York: Alfred A. Knopf, 1939.

[5]Loewenstein, Rudolph M., in his article, Historical and Cultural Roots of Anti-Semitism (In: *Psychoanalysis and the Social Sciences*, Vol. I, New York: International Universities Press, Inc., 1947), has outlined the various methods by which psychoanalytic theory has been applied to historical problems.

[6]Elmsie, William A. L.: *Encyclopaedia Britannica*, 1947, Vol. XVIII, p. 586.

[7]Buber, Martin: *Op. cit.*

[8]Kris, Ernst: *On Inspiration*. Int. J. Psa., XX, 1939.

[9]Sachs, Hanns: *The Creative Unconscious*, especially the essay, The Community of Daydreams. Cambridge, Mass.: Sci-Art Publishers, 1942.

[10]Jeremiah, I: 6 to 10.

[11]O'Shaughnessy, Arthur: Ode: We are the music-makers. In: *Modern American and British Poetry*. New York: Harcourt Brace & Co., 1923.

[12]Kris, Ernst: *Op. cit.*

[13]Freud: *Totem and Taboo*. In: *The Basic Writings of Sigmund Freud*. New York: The Modern Library, 1938.

[14]Jeremiah, I: 5.

[15]Freud: *Totem and Taboo. Op. cit.*

[16]The inclusion of Samuel among the prophets requires a note of explanation. As far as recorded scripture is concerned, he does not attain the stature of the other prophets discussed

in this paper. He shares with them, however, the position of a historical model of a pre-eminent moral figure whose words were taken by him and the nation as the words of God. It is in this sense that the prophetic figure is understood throughout this study.

[17]The Hebrew version charges specifically that 'They lay with the women who did service at the door of the meeting tent'. This charge is not found in the Greek version. If this passage is a later addition, as many scholars indicate, it would represent how some unknown scribe interpreted the meaning of the rebelliousness of Hophni and Phineas and the loyalty of Samuel.

[18]I Samuel, II: 27 to 32.

[19]II Chronicles, XXVI.

[20]Kent, Charles Foster: The Sermons, Epistles and Apocalypses of Israel's Prophets. In: *Student's Old Testament*. New York: Charles Scribner's Sons, 1925, p. 107.

[21]Exodus, XXI: 17.

[22]See, for example, Job, II: 9

[23]Fenichel, Otto: *The Scoptophilic Instinct and Identification*. Int. J. Psa., XVIII, 1937.

[24]Bornstein, Berta: *Zur Psychogenese der Pseudodebilität*. Int. Ztschr. f. Psa., XVI, 1930.

[25]Isakower, Otto: *On the Exceptional Position of the Auditive Sphere*. Int. J. Psa., XX, 1939. Also, contribution to the panel on *Dream Theory and Interpretation* at the midwinter meeting of the American Psychoanalytic Association, December 1948.

[26]Freud: *Psychoanalytic Notes Upon an Autobiographical Account of a Case of Paranoia*. Coll. Papers, III, p. 456.

[27]Freud: *Group Psychology and the Analysis of the Ego*. London: Hogarth Press, 1940.

[28]Abraham, Karl: Development of the Libido. In: *Selected Papers on Psychoanalysis*. London: Hogarth Press, 1942.

[29]Lewin, Bertram D.: *Analysis and Structure of a Transient Hypomania*. Psychoanalytic Quarterly, I, 1932, p. 43.

[30]Subsequent variations between elation and depression in the prophet's mood would reflect the shift from harmony to discord, between the ego and the superego. The brief 'prophetic' experiences of Saul, first king of Israel, clearly illustrate this point. Saul prophesied on only two occasions. Both occasions were critical turning points in the relation between Saul and Samuel. Samuel at the time represented the pre-eminent moral figure in Israel. Immediately after Samuel had invested him with the kingship Saul, in a state of elation, fell into a trance and began to 'prophesy.' Later, when it became clear to Saul that Samuel had deposed him and had gone over to the camp of David, Saul fell to the ground in grief and mourning, tore at his clothes, and 'prophesied' for the second time. The first instance of Saul's prophetic experience is comparable to a transient mania; the second, to a depression. In the first instance there was harmony between Saul and the superego figure; in the second, discord.

[31]Freud: *Group Psychology and the Analysis of the Ego. Op. cit.* See also: Olden, Christine: *About the Fascinating Effect of the Narcissistic Personality*. American Imago, II, 1941.

[32]Freud: *A Case of Paranoia. Op. cit.*

[33]Ezekiel, I: 4.

[34]Ezekiel, I: 13.

[35]Ezekiel, I: 26 to 28. The fiery glow about the superego figure brings to mind the study of Greenacre, Phyllis: *Vision, Headache and the Halo*. Psychoanalytic Quarterly, XVI, 1947.

[36]Ezekiel, II: 1 to 3.

[37]Ezekiel, II: 8 to 10, and Ezekiel, III: 1 to 4.

[38]Freud: *The Acquisition of Power Over Fire*. Int. J. Psa., XIII, 1932.

[39]*Cf.* Ferenczi, Sandor: Obscene Words. In: *Contributions to Psychoanalysis*. Boston: Richard C. Badger, 1916. Strachey, James: *Some Unconscious Factors in Reading*. In5. J. Psa., XI, 1930. Spring, William J.: *Words and Masses: A Pictorial Contribution to the Psychology of Stammering*. Psychoanalytic Quarterly, IV, 1935.

[40]Strachey, James: *Op. cit.*

[41]Jones, Ernest: The Madonna's Conception Through the Ear. In: *Essays in Applied Psychoanalysis.* London: International Psychoanalytic Press, 1923.

[42]Ezekiel, IV: 9 to 12.

[43]For this suggestion I am indebted to Dr. Ernst Kris.

[44]Isaiah, I: 2.

[45]By identifying with the prophet, individual members of the group may dramatize their own conflicted relationship with the ideals and authority of the group.

[46]Midrash—Deuteronomy.

[47]Isaiah, II: 4.

[48]Freud: *Group Psychology and the Analysis of the Ego. Op. cit.*

*The Meaning of Anxiety in
Rabbinic Judaism*

Richard L. Rubenstein

Professor Rubenstein approaches the psychoanalytic study of Judaism from the point of view of a theologian who has mastered a good deal of classical psychoanalytic literature and theory. This essay is Chapter 5 of his 1968 book, *The Religious Imagination: A Study in Psychoanalysis and Jewish Theology* (New York: Bobbs-Merrill). His concern is not simply an academic exercise in the confrontation of one discipline with the other, but rather to deepen the understanding of how rabbinic Judaism prepares the modern Jew to cope with his situation. As he says (p. 42), "Were it not for the fact that the experiences of the rabbis and their community in the face of Roman hostility and Christian rivalry were paradigmatic of the Jewish situation in the Western world since that time, their very special perspective would have ceased to command the authority they retain before the Jewish people."

The material that he studies is principally the body of Jewish literature called the Aggadah, "which consists of legends, myths, and folklore of the rabbis of the Talmudic period . . . the non-legal part of Jewish religious study, exegesis, and speculation." The Aggadah, based on traditional exegesis, can be examined by classical methods of psychoanalytic exegesis, and when that is done, we learn about the true concerns of the rabbis, and therefore, the true concerns of Jews who take the religion of the rabbis seriously. To a very large extent, these concerns apply to the Jews of today.

The Religious Imagination, while respectful of classical psychoanalysis, protests that what analysts have hitherto written about Judaism was inaccurate because of their limited knowledge of the subject, and that, by emphasizing the Oedipal paradigm, they offered little more than a caricature of the religion.

I believe that most readers of this book would find *The Religious Imagination* of interest. I have selected Chapter 5 to include in this collection because it introduces into the psychoanalytic study of Judaism a theme that is important, probably universal, namely, the conflict between the wish for and fear of incorporation by the archaic mother and her contemporary representatives. In today's world, the practicing psychoanalyst sees far fewer neurotics than patients with personality disorder. In classical neurosis, characterized by phobias, hysterical symptoms, or obsessions or compulsions, the Oedipal paradigm determines the pattern of the illness; in personality disorder, it is ambivalence toward the archaic mother. It is especially interesting, therefore, that Professor Rubenstein can demonstrate representations of this ambivalence in Aggadic material. He goes one step further: he suggests that Jewish monotheistic religion may have been welcomed because it offers as God, a relatively benign father image in place of a more terrifying, more archaic mother figure. This exchange of benign father for terrifying mother image may occur more often in neurosis and personality disorder than most analysts suspect.

The phenomenon of anxiety has been of increasing interest to philosophers, psychologists and theologians from the time of publication of *The Concept of Dread* by Søren Kierkegaard.[1] A thinker's understanding of the nature of anxiety has often served to illuminate his fundamental point of view. This was especially true of Sigmund Freud. Castration anxiety was the anxiety par excellence for Freud.[2] There was considerable development in Freud's conception of anxiety. As Rollo May has suggested, the trend in Freud's understanding of castration anxiety was toward an increasingly symbolic interpretation. May emphasizes that, in Freud's thought, anxiety has its ultimate source "in the fear of premature loss of or separation from the mother (or mother's love)." This conception is applicable to castration anxiety. Fear of castration is fear of the loss of that organ with which one would return to the mother or mother-surrogate.[3] Freud's conception of anxiety was particularly relevant to the psychoanalytic interpretation of Judaism. From the perspective of many psychoanalysts, fear of the Lord in Judaism is ultimately fear of the castrating father.[4]

Freud's interpretation of anxiety differed from Tillich's and Heidegger's. The latter regarded *Urangst*, man's primordial apprehension of the nothingness that forever threatens to envelop him, as primary and irreducible.[5] Freud held that, more often than not, fear of death is a covert form of castration anxiety. He argued that since we have no proper concept of death or nothingness, men are really anxious lest they lose their masculine power when they imagine that they fear death.[6]

Freud maintained that all men unconsciously desire to rid themselves of fathers and parental surrogates. Since the ultimate motive for antipaternal hostility is return to the mother, men are beset by anxiety lest their temptation entail punitive retaliation against the offending male organ. Men internalize their image of the father as the superego or objectify it as God in order to avoid this misfortune. They thus commence a lifelong servitude to one of the earliest objects of their own envy. The temptation which leads to superego formation is sexual. As a result, the deepest unconscious anxiety is said to be that any behavioral deviance will lead to castration.[7]

The importance of castration anxiety has often been stressed in the psychoanalytic interpretation of Judaism.[8] Pyschoanalysts have tended to interpret circumcision as symbolic castration.[9] The centrality of circumcision in Judaism is said to have had the effect of greatly reinforcing the castration anxiety of both Jew and gentile.[10]

The tendency to reduce Jewish religious deviance to sexual offense is very old and historically rooted. Insofar as the metaphor of the primal crime is applicable, Freud regarded religion as the result of the desire of the brothers of the primal horde to prevent a repetition of the murderous and deicidal deed. There was a consistent tendency in biblical Judaism to regard idolatry and rebellion against God as forms of sexual sin. The prophets insistently inveighed against those who went "awhoring" after other gods. Sins which were interpreted as sexual offenses engendered the fear of sexual retaliation. This was heightened by the fact that rabbinic Judaism explicitly accepted the measure-for-measure principle, the idea that punitive retaliation is directed against the offending organ.[11]

There are relatively few explicit instances of punitive castration invented or cited by the rabbis in the Aggadah. Nevertheless, they can be found. The most explicit traditions in which the sinner is thus punished concern the biblical characters Potiphar and the couple Zimri and Cozbi.

According to the rabbis, Potiphar hardly deserved a better wife than the one he possessed. They regarded him as a homosexual who purchased Joseph for his own purposes. In retaliation, they maintain, God castrated him. The tradition that he was castrated is dependent upon their interpretation of the biblical word *saris* as "castrate" or "eunuch." Scripture refers to him as "Potiphar, a *saris* of Pharaoh."[12] Usually, *saris* is translated as "officer." It can be translated as "eunuch" or "castrate." The story of his misfortune is given in the Aggadah:

"A *saris* of Pharaoh." This indicates that he was castrated, thus teaching that he [Potiphar] purchased him [Joseph] for the purpose of sexual abuse whereupon the Holy One, blessed be He, emasculated him . . . Hence it was written, "For the Lord loveth justice and forsaketh not His saints,"[13] which is actually written "His saint"[14] and refers to Joseph: "They are preserved forever: but the seed of the wicked shall be cut off"[15]—[meaning]—that God emasculated him.[16]

This legend takes an ambiguous biblical tale and assimilates it to one in which God Himself causes the sinner to be castrated. The verse "The seed of the wicked shall be cut off" would normally mean that the wicked shall fail of progeny. The rabbis take it to mean that they shall fail through punitive castration.

Even if the rabbis were correct in interpreting *saris* as eunuch, nothing in the Bible suggests that God castrated Potiphar in retaliation for his homosexual designs on Joseph. This detail originates in the rabbinic imagination. In most rabbinic sources God Himself castrates Potiphar. An agent does the deed on God's behalf in one tradition.[17]

Castration is also explicit in the legends concerning Zimri and Cozbi. According to Scripture, immediately after Israel's idolatry with Baal Peor, Phinehas, the priest and nephew of Moses, sought to avenge the Lord by punishing the chief sinners. Among the offenders were Zimri the son of Salu, a prince of the house of Simeon, and Cozbi, his idolatrous Midianite paramour. In the biblical account, Phinehas thrust his javelin at the couple in such a way that it went through the man and the "belly" of the offending woman. The plague sent by God against the entire camp of Israel was thus stayed.[18]

This tale reflects one of the most difficult problems of ancient Israel: the attraction of the more permissive non-Israelite cults and the consequent difficulties inherent in the interdict against intermarriage. The biblical story is terse and demands homiletic embellishment. As the rabbis retell the story, Cozbi is no longer merely the foreign paramour of Zimri. She is the daughter of Balak, the Midianite king, who, on the advice of Balaam, is prepared to prostitute his own daughter in order to bring about the downfall of Moses. Zimri demands that Cozbi surrender herself to him. She replies that her father commanded her to yield only to Moses, Israel's greatest man. Zimri thereupon seizes her hair and declares that he is greater than Moses. This introduces a hint of sexual rivalry between the leader and a rebellious member of his flock. After a time, Phinehas went out to punish the couple. There are a number of variations in the rabbinic description of what transpired. One is stated on the authority of Rabbi Johanan:

> Six miracles were wrought for Phinehas: Zimri should have withdrawn from Cozbi, but did not; he should have cried out [for help] but didn't; *[Phinehas] succeeded in driving his spear exactly through the sex organs of the man and the woman:* an angel came and lifted up the lintel; an angel came and wrought destruction among the people.[19]
> (italics mine)

In another source, Phinehas pierces both offenders while they lie coupled together. Rabbi Johanan's six miracles became twelve.[20] The new tradition may represent a later stage in the development of the story. In the embellished legend the couple are kept locked in intercourse long after they would normally have separated. The spear enters Cozbi's belly so that it catches Zimri's genitals. God did this so that no one would think that Phinehas had acted out of motives of personal hatred. The locked couple did not slide down when the spear was held aloft. Their sinful conduct was thus apparent to all. Finally, God preserved their spirits alive while they were suspended. This prevented Phinehas the priest from being ritually defiled as he held the spear. Had the couple perished Phinehas would have been under a priestly prohibition against touching the corpses.[21]

There is also a vast overestimation of Zimri's sexual capacities in related traditions:

> R. Nahman said . . . That wicked man [i.e., Zimri] cohabited four hundred and twenty-four times that day, and Phinehas waited for his strength to weaken . . . In a Baraitha we learnt: Sixty [times] until he became like an addled egg, whilst she became like a furrow filled with water. R. Kahana said: And her seat was a *beth seah* (i.e., she became very bloated). R. Joseph learned: Her womb was open a cubit.[22]

Apart from the specific issue of castration anxiety, the Zimri-Cozbi stories are interesting because of the association of unbridled sexuality and rebellion against authority figures in this rabbinic fantasy. This element is present in the Bible. It is greatly sharpened in the legends. The punitive elements are also greatly emphasized by the rabbis.

On the basis of psychoanalytic insight, it may be surmised that the biblical "belly" is a euphemism for genitals. This is made explicit in the Aggadah. Here again it is to be noted that the Aggadah frequently retells a story so that the primary process meaning is restored in contrast to that in the often rationalized and censored biblical source. The rabbinic myths restore an unconscious dimension. This is in all probability the result of rabbinic free association on the biblical text.

Another element in this legend related to castration anxiety is the hint at the idea of the *vagina dentata*. Phinehas'* inability to withdraw from the sexual posture is explicitly stated, as we have seen, in one of the traditions.

The rabbis also inserted an explicit reference to castration in the tale of the ten plagues God bestowed upon the Egyptians. The Bible says very little concerning the discomfiting of the Egyptians by the frogs. In the legends, the frogs are pictured as leaping at the genitals of the Egyptian noblemen and ripping them off:

> This was one of the nine occasions when the Holy One, blessed be He, gave the frail mastery over the tough. Whenever a frog would come and declare: "I am the emissary of the Holy One, blessed be He," the marble [of the Egyptian nobles' houses] would split open forthwith, and the frog would get up into the house. With reference to this, it is said: "The frog which destroyed them,"[23] that is, wrung their privy parts.[24]

The reference to punitive castration is explicit. The frogs act only as God's agents. There is no warrant for this in Scripture.

The final legend in which the rabbis added the idea of punitive castration to a biblical tale was the one about Ham's castration of Noah. In the Bible, Ham merely uncovers the nakedness of his father.[25] In the rabbinic traditions, Ham desires to prevent his father from cohabiting with his mother. He castrates Noah.[26] Usually, the rabbis interpreted Noah's misfortune as God's retali-

---

*The sentence should read: Zimri's inability. . . . M.O.

ation for failing expeditiously to fulfill the commandment that he be fruitful and multiply.[27] There is also a related tradition that Noah was sexually incapacitated when he left the ark.[28] In both traditions, a sin of phallic omission is taken as the reason for divinely inflicted castration.

To the best of my knowledge, there are few, if any, other traditions in the vast corpus of legends known as the Aggadah in which castration is an actual punishment of a sinner. I have attempted diligently to search out all of the relevant traditions concerning sin and punishment in rabbinic legend. I have examined thousand of such legends. I know of no other *explicit* reference to the punitive castration of the sinner. There is one other legend in which God appears explicitly as a castrator. According to one rabbinic tradition God castrated the primeval monster Leviathan in order to prevent its fantastic ability to multiply from rendering the world uninhabitable.[29] There is, however, no punitive element.

In addition to explicit legends concerning punitive castration, there are many in which castration is hinted at in thinly disguised form. In the psychoanalytic description of the onset of the castration complex, the child's masturbatory activity is accompanied by the fear that the organ will be punished measure for measure. At the primary process level of mental functioning, thought and deed are equivalent. The deviant is said to fear measure-for-measure retaliation for his guilty wishes. The measure-for-measure principle is the principle of punitive equity in the unconscious. It was also the principle operative in the Aggadah.

The measure-for-measure principle was regarded as the fundamental principle of punitive equity in both the legal (Halakah) and the mythic (Aggadah) parts of rabbinic literature. It is explicitly enunciated in the Mishnah, the definitive codification of Jewish religious law compiled in Palestine in the early part of the third century: "In the measure with which a man measures, it is meted out to him."[30]

The most interesting application of the measure-for-measure principle in this source is that of the *sotah*, the woman suspected of adultery who is compelled to submit to the biblical test of drinking the bitter waters:

She bedecked herself for transgression—the Almighty brought her to shame; she laid herself bare for transgression—the Almighty likewise laid her bare; she began transgression with the thigh first—therefore the thigh shall suffer first and afterward the belly; *neither shall ought else of the body go free.*[31] (italics mine)

The conception of punitive retaliation against the offending organ is explicit. Although nothing is said about masculine sexual offenses, there is a clear implication that offenses committed with the male organ would be punished by castration. The application of the talion principle is widespread in rabbinic thought. Many rabbinic comments on the plagues visited upon the Egyptians and other offenders attempt to justify a particular punishment by asserting that it was peculiarly appropriate because of the nature of the offense committed.

This tendency is especially visible in the Mekilta. A number of examples are given to illustrate the statement "For with the very thing which the Egyptians planned to destroy Israel, He [God] destroyed them."[32] The Nile was made bloody because Jewish women were prohibited by the Egyptians from purifying themselves after their menstrual periods.[33] The frogs were a punishment because the Egyptians forced the Jews to handle ritually impure reptiles.[34] The Egyptian first-born were slain because of Egyptian violence against the Israelite first-born and the crime of parricide.[35] The rabbis assimilated the biblical stories of the ten plagues to their own conception of punitive equity. These stories project the rabbinic unconscious more graphically than most. The rabbis invented the details that have been discussed. They never doubted the talion principle, the fundamental presupposition of castration anxiety.

No evaluation of the significance of castration anxiety in the Aggadah would be complete without reference to those legends in which punitive violence is visited upon female sinners. The afflictions visited upon Eve and her daughters have already been alluded to.[36] These traditions express the extent to which genital violence against both sexes was regarded in rabbinic fantasy as the appropriate retribution for sexual sin.

There are a number of other traditions which hint at castration. Already noted are the traditions in which the serpent was originally a manlike creature whose appendages were cut off in retaliation for his designs against Eve.[37] His serpentine form is the result of punitive mutilation. Nothing is explicitly said about castration. Nevertheless, it is difficult to regard the serpent's mutilation in any other way.

The Joseph legends corroborate the view that mutilation of the appendages was regarded as equivalent to castration in the rabbinic imagination. According to the rabbis, Joseph came perilously close to succumbing to Potiphar's wife. In one tradition, he avoided intercourse by digging his hands into the ground and allowing his semen to pass harmlessly out of his body through his fingers.[38] Here the fingers are regarded as phallus-like appendages.

According to one well-known tradition, as Joseph was about to commit the act, he saw a vision of his father's face "and his blood was cooled."[39] There are variants in which he sees both parents.[40] This tradition parallels the psychoanalytic conception of the superego as the introjected image of parental authority.

Another legend suggests that Joseph tried to sin but proved impotent. Rabbi Samuel ben Nahman interpreted the verse "And it came to pass on a certain day, when he went into the house to do his work: and there was not a man of the house there within."[41] "R. Samuel b. Nahman said: 'To do his work' is meant literally, but that 'and there was not a man'—on examination he did not find himself a man, for R. Samuel said: 'The bow was drawn but it relaxed . . .' "[42]

In another tradition, Joseph attempts sexual intercourse but suffers premature ejaculation.[43] Thus, Joseph's intended offense is deterred either by the censoring vision of his parents or by impairment of his sexual capacity. Nothing in the Bible offers the slightest support for these legends. The Aggadah reflects the rabbis' feelings about Joseph's predicament.

Impotence and premature ejaculation are Joseph's misfortunes. They are temporary forms of deprivation of sexual capacity. From the psychoanalytic point of view, both are normally rooted in unconscious castration anxiety which impairs normal sexual functioning.[44] The Joseph traditions must be included among those which reflect castration anxiety without explicitly stating it.

The Aggadah also contains a number of traditions in which a sexual offense is punished by the impairment of the male organ's capacity to function. These include the parallel traditions in which Abimelech, the Philistine king, and Pharaoh take Sarah away from Abram for a night. In the Bible, God punishes Abimelech by closing up the wombs of all the members of his household.[45] In the rabbinic retelling, God closes up every single orifice of both the males and the females of the house of Abimelech. One rabbi adds that even the hens of his house did not lay eggs. This was functionally equivalent to castration. It is explicitly stated that the king's sexual capacity was impaired.[46] According to Rabbi Levi, an angel stood over Sarah the entire night she was with Abimelech, holding a whip (or a drawn sword in some variants). Whenever she ordered the angel to strike or to desist, he would obey.[47]

The Bible relates that Pharaoh was smitten with "plagues" for attempting to molest Sarah.[48] The rabbis asserted that Pharaoh's affliction was leprosy.[49] Leprosy is frequently mentioned as a punishment. Leprosy is functionally equivalent to castration. The fear of leprosy undoubtedly contains some elements of castration anxiety. The terminal stages of leprosy involve the spontaneous amputation of the appendages. Even before that, the leper is hardly capable of leading a meaningful sex life. Nevertheless, leprosy also reflects older and more decisive anxieties than castration. Leprosy attacks the skin, the oldest erogenous zone of the organism. Leprosy includes castration anxiety. It also reflects the oldest and most primal anxieties of the organism as well.[50] As a matter of fact, the frequent references in the Aggadah to leprosy go back beyond the Oedipal and the phallic stage to the pre-Oedipal stage. When I began this study, I was struck by the enormous number of tales of leprous punishment that the rabbis invented, but that have no explicit warrant in Scripture. I assumed that leprous retaliation must reflect castration anxiety in rabbinic Judaism. In one sense, I have never departed from this view. However, I no longer see how the evidence can be interpreted so that legends in which the sinner is punished by leprosy can be understood as reflecting *only* castration anxiety.

Leprosy seems functionally equivalent to castration in the legend of Pharaoh's attempted possession of Sarah. The Bible tells of Pharaoh's misfortune. The rabbis sharpen the element of functional impairment. Rabbi Simeon ben Lakish held that the plague with which Pharaoh had been smitten was *ra'athan*, a skin-boil disease.[51] This is identified by Margulies, an Israeli scholar responsible for the critical edition of the text, as leprosy.[52] In rabbinic times *ra'athan* was thought to have an especially debilitating effect on sexual capacity. One rabbi lists twenty-four different kinds of skin disease, all of which are worsened by sexual intercourse. *Ra'athan* was reputed to have the most injurious effects of all.[53] Another rabbi lists twenty-four such diseases and comments that *only ra'athan* is sexually injurious.[54] Pharaoh was punished by a particularly injurious type of skin disease which resulted in functional castration. Some rabbinic traditions maintain that all of the injuries which befell Pharaoh also were visited upon Abimelech.[55]

There is another type of impairment of sexual capacity in the Aggadah. The rabbis depicted Nebuchadnezzar as a rapacious libertine and homosexual. In one tradition, Nebuchadnezzar seeks to use Zedekiah, the captive Jewish king, homosexually. In retaliation, God causes Nebuchadnezzar's uncircumcised *membrum* to be extended to the length of three hundred cubits. It then wags about before all those present. Too much is functionally equivalent to too little.[56]

The Aggadah does contain a goodly number of traditions in which sexual offenses are punished by castration, often directly by God Himself. It also contains other traditions in which a functional equivalent of castration is suggested as the sinner's punishment and in which punitive genital violence is directed against female offenders. The Eve traditions hint, but do not explicitly assert, that women are castrates.[57] The special character of female existence is, in any event, regarded as punitive.

These tales were told and retold for centuries in the synagogue, the school, and everyday conversation. Incidentally, these stories made their way into Christian exegesis with surprising frequency. As a result, the rabbinic legends were not without decisive influence on the religious development of the Western world.[58] The telling of these tales reinforced the tendency to conform in sexual matters and heightened the anxiety lest noncomformity have dire consequences. Castration anxiety was projected into these traditions by the rabbis. It was self-reinforcing and self-perpetuating in rabbinic Judaism. It is impossible to avoid the conclusion that the Aggadah offers much evidence of the existence of castration anxiety and what could, for want of a better term, be regarded as a decidedly "phallic *Weltanschauung*," in rabbinic Judaism.

It would be misleading to rest content at this point. If anxiety is the reaction of the organism to the possibility of loss, castration anxiety in some form is inevitable among *all* men. Furthermore, any society which asserts masculine prerogatives probably intensifies castration anxiety. In such societies, castration means more than loss of sexual capacity. It means the loss of one's place within the social structure.

Those who stress the decisive character of the Oedipal project in the individual will probably regard castration anxiety as the most important source of anxiety in rabbinic Judaism. An examination of the rabbinic legends does not validate this view. On the contrary, the Aggadah reflects a far greater preponderance of pre-Oedipal as opposed to Oedipal strivings. I have cited the vast majority of traditions that contain an explicit or an implicit suggestion of punitive castration. They are numerically as well as psychologically overwhelmed by another body of punitive misfortunes.

Leprosy occurs far more frequently in the legends than does castration, either expressed or implied. Most of the leprosy traditions were invented by the rabbis. They do not occur in the Bible. Though leprosy attacks the genital organs, its central and primary attack is on the skin as such. The skin is the oldest erogenous zone. It is the first area of contact with the external environment as well as the first source of pleasure and pain. The ego is in a sense a psychic extension of the skin's relatedness to the external world. The erogeneity of the skin develops at the same time as oral eroticism, to which it is related. Even the later localizing of pleasures to special areas does not cancel out the skin's character as the primary source of erogenous feelings. An attack on the skin constitutes a threat to the organism's oldest source of contact with the external world. Leprosy is a disease which attacks the epidermis most vigorously and with greatest terror to the victim. In so doing, it represents one of the oldest and most feared threats against the organism. This fear was especially great in the ancient Middle East where leprosy was a frequent and ever-visible occurrence. By contrast, fear of castration, though admittedly important, represents a late and localized anxiety. Although the castrative element of leprosy is stressed in the tales concerning Pharaoh and Abimelech, this element is not present in most of the other leprosy traditions.

One of the most frequent sins for which leprosy is suggested as a punishment by the rabbis is verbal wrongdoing—the sins of the mouth.[59] At first glance, this seems like an inordinately severe punishment. Thus, the spies who returned from the Promised Land with a false report were, according to the rabbis, smitten with leprosy.[60] This accords with Scripture.[61] In one tradition, it is explicitly stated that the limbs of the spies dropped off as a result of leprosy.[62] The rabbis dwell upon the fact that the sin of the spies was a sin of the mouth. There are also traditions in which the tongues of the spies are elongated until they reach down to and penetrate the navel, whence the tongues are attacked by worms.[63] In other traditions, they die of croup, a disease affecting the larynx.[64] Even the serpent's scales are said to be leprous. They are God's punishment for a sin of the mouth. The serpent is regarded as guilty of having slandered God.[65]

There is a tradition in which an offender who sins with his mouth is depicted as punished by God's causing his limbs to fall off one by one, though no specific mention is made of leprosy. The tradition concerns Jephthah, the son of Gilead, who made a vow that were God to grant him victory, he would sacrifice "whatever cometh forth of the doors of my house to meet me . . ."[66] His daughter was the first to meet him and was sacrificed in fulfillment of the vow.[67]

The Aggadah relates that for this improper vow, limb after limb fell off his body and was buried separately.[68] Jephthah's punishment was derived from the verse "And he was buried in the cities of Gilead . . ."[69] The rabbis noted that Scripture had not said "*city* of Gilead," but "cities of Gilead." Since nothing in Scripture could be without meaningful intent, the rabbis concluded that Scripture's purpose was to teach that his limbs fell off and were buried in different places. In this tradition, spontaneous amputation is the punitive retaliation for a sin of the mouth.

The best known homilies in which a sinner is punished for verbal wrongdoing by leprosy are those concerning Miriam. In the biblical account, she is depicted as being smitten with leprosy following an incident in which she spoke ill of her brother Moses.[70] The Bible does not explicitly assert that her leprosy is the result of her failure to act with propriety. In rabbinic tradition, it was so regarded.[71]

In spite of the seeming severity of the rabbinic assertion that the sins of the mouth are punished by leprosy, the assertion does make psychological sense. What is most striking is the coincidence of the rabbinic assertion and the psychoanalytic conception that anxieties concerning the skin reflect archaic oral strivings. The sins of the mouth are punished by wounding the decisive erogenous zone, if such it can be called, of the archaic oral period. Leprosy is thus only secondarily a reflection of castration anxiety, although it undoubtedly is also that. Its persistence throughout the legends is consistent with the fact that the strivings of the oral stage are by no means less significant in the development of either the individual or the group than those of the later phallic stage.

Fear of damage to the skin surface is apparently more closely related to fear of incorporation than to castration anxiety. Leprosy is a kind of incorporation. There are other anxieties expressed in the Aggadah which are even more explicitly related to incorporation than is leprosy. However, fear of leprosy seems to form the bridge between the phallic and pre-phallic anxieties evident in rabbinic tradition. It contains elements of both castration and incorporation anxiety.

It is not entirely clear whether incorporation anxieties reflect oral or intrauterine regressive strivings.[72] The question is not of decisive importance for us. What is important is that incorporation occurs in the legends as the most feared punishment. It hardly matters whether such anxieties reflect oral or intrauterine regressive strivings. In either case, the traditions reflect fear of the pre-Oedipal mother rather than the father. This in turn calls into question the so-called dichotomy between matriarchal and patriarchal religions as well as the assertion, repeated to the point of tedium, that rabbinic Judaism reflects fear of a tyrannical, castrating Father in contrast to the more permissive and humane matriarchal religions in which the warm freedom of the Mothers reigned supreme. Apart from the fact that circumcision is not castration but an attempt to ward it off, the God of rabbinic and biblical Judaism demanded circumcision, while Cybele, the *Dea Syria*, demanded literal castration from her *galloi*, the priests who served her.[73] Submission to the Jewish Father God may very well have reflected a defense against a barely hidden greater fear of the pagan mother goddesses.

Intrauterine regressive strivings are evident in some of the Adam traditions, which interpret extrauterine existence as a punitive fall from paradisaical dimensions and perfections. As we have seen, there are traditions that before sinning, Adam knew not death, disease, or travail. After sinning, he was expelled from the garden and subjected to the infirmities of normal human existence.[74] Nothing is said about the womb. Nevertheless, the description of the effortless paradise in which Adam enjoys cosmic dimensions and almost omnipotent strength reflects the fact that every individual at one time experienced an environment utterly lacking in the stresses and limits of our daily preoccupations. The Adam legends treat this environment as a remembrance of things past. In most of the traditions, however, it is the feared end rather than the wistfully recalled beginning.

Many of the incorporation traditions originate in the Bible. This is true of the flood legends. In these legends, the offense is usually phallic. The punishment is drowning, a form of incorporation. The rabbis assert that God sent the flood only after the generation had been guilty of excessive masturbation and homosexuality. In some traditions, the waters of the flood are described as resembling hot semen.[75] The flood traditions are important psychological data. Given the biblical tale of the almost universal drowning of the race, the rabbis tended to assert that masturbation and pederasty were the cause.

There are also traditions in which the sinner is burned to death. Graham Greene calls our attention to the relationship between leprosy and burning in the title of his book *A Burned Out Case*. The leper whose disease is so far advanced that it can go no further is thus designated. Both burning and leprosy attack the skin. Both are related to incorporation. In rabbinic tradition, burning is the punishment most frequently associated with arrogance. Just as the arrogant man seeks to "go up" beyond his station, so his punishment is a "going up" he hardly desires.[76] The generation of the Flood, Korah and his rebellious band, and Dathan and Abiram are said to have been consumed by fire or a fiery substance in addition to having been incorporated in earth or water.[77]

There is a biblical tradition that Nadab and Abihu, the priestly sons of Aaron, offered a "strange fire before the Lord . . . and there went out fire from the Lord, and devoured them, and they died before the Lord."[78] According to one rabbinic interpretation, though fire descended and burned the brothers, it left their bodies intact: "The streams of fire issued from the Holy of Holies, branching off into four, and two entered into each of their nostrils and burned them."[79] Commenting on this statement, an anonymous authority states in the same source that they were burned but their garments remained intact.[80] Similar legends of the burning of the soul while leaving the body intact are found elsewhere in the legends. Rashi, a medieval commentator, maintained that this disaster befell Korah.[81] Rabbi Johanan, a Palestinian Amora, maintained that it overtook Doeg, after which his ashes were scattered in the synagogues and schools.[82]

Ferenczi had an interesting speculation concerning the dual identification of earth and water with the maternal principle in dreams, myth, and religion. He maintained that the identification of the maternal principle with water represented the situation of fetus *in utero*. The identification with the earth represented the later situation of the suckling child at the mother's breast. He maintained that there was also a phylogenetic parallel in the original oceanic home of the species and its later less suitable land habitat after the "catastrophe" which drove them from the water. For Ferenczi, fear of earth-incorporation would reflect anxieties arising from the child's fear of retaliation for his cannibalistic attempts to achieve reunion orally with his maternal environment. Fear of drowning would reflect even older anxieties.[83]

The sinner is incorporated by means of the opening up of the "mouth" of the earth in the legends concerning Korah, Dathan, and Abiram.[84] In spite of the extraordinary importance of the story of Korah's rebellion, castration is never suggested as a punishment of the rebels. The biblical and rabbinic use of the term "mouth of the earth" indicates that religious tradition employed the metaphors of incorporation and orality long before psychoanalytic theory gave the matter objectivity and precision.

The incorporation of the rebels was so complete that no trace remained. This is a haunting anticipation of the nameless obliteration of European Jewry in the twentieth century. R. Samuel ben Nahman commented on the verse "They and all that pertained to them went down alive into the pit."[85] He held that even a needle borrowed from another Israelite was drawn after them.[86] One tradition maintained that the clothes they had deposited in the laundry rolled after them and were swallowed up.[87] In another legend there is an archaic confusion of the verbal and the concrete. Even the names of the band disappeared (or flew up) from all the documents containing them.[88]

There is also a tradition that they were eternally burned in Gehinom "as one turns flesh in a pot."[89] This resembles the legend in which Balaam boils forever in semen.[90] In another legend the "enemies of Israel" (perhaps Jesus) boil eternally in excrement.[91] These fantasies may have been originally polemic in intent. This would by no means reduce their psychological relevance. In psychoanalytic terminology, the fantasy of Korah boiling like flesh in a pot reflects oral sadism. The image of the "enemies of Israel" boiling in excrement probably reflects both oral and anal sadism.

Incorporation through drowning is the principal punishment of the Egyptians when they attempt to overtake Israel at the Red Sea.[92]

The rabbis speculated on the divine attack on Moses at the inn, which Zipporah forestalled by circumcising their son and throwing his foreskin at Moses' feet, declaring that Moses was a "bridegroom of blood" unto her.[93] Many rabbinic interpretations of the incident suggest that its purpose was to stress the utter indispensability of circumcision. God's homicidal reaction to Moses for his failure to circumcise his son provided the rabbis with a homiletic defense against the two most important challenges to circumcision that confronted Judaism in the first centuries of the Christian era, the anticircumcision polemic of the rival Christian Church and the proscription of circumcision by the Emperor Hadrian shortly before the Judaeo-Roman war of 132-35 C.E.[94]

According to Rabbi Eleazar of Modi'im, Moses unwisely acceded to Jethro's demand that Moses' first son be raised as a pagan in exchange for the hand of his daughter Zipporah. In retaliation, the angel sought to slay him. This was deterred by Zipporah's quick action in circumcising the child.[95]

The same source contains a number of comments on the great value of circumcision. The burden of the remarks is that circumcision is so important that even the merits of Moses could not delay his punishment for neglecting it. Moses' hazard became an object lesson in the potential dangers involved in the neglect of circumcision.

An extremely interesting interpretation of the incident appears in late Babylonian and post-Talmudic sources. Rabbi Judah ben Bizna is quoted:

> When Moses was lax in the performance of circumcision, *Af* and *Hemah* came and swallowed him up, leaving nothing but his legs. Thereupon immediately "Zipporah took a sharp stone and cut off the foreskin of her son," straightway "He let him alone."[96]

The tradition that Moses was swallowed up to his feet seems to be a euphemism for his having been swallowed up to his penis. This is the opinion of an important medieval commentator, Rabbi Nissim ben Reuben of Gerona. He accepted the tradition of Rabbi Simon ben Gamaliel that the angel's anger was directed against the child rather than Moses. He maintained that Rabbi Judah ben Biznah's statement meant that the child was swallowed up so that "the place of circumcision" was the only visible part of his body.[97] Rabbi Samuel Edels (d. Posen, 1641) cited an opinion supporting Rabbi Nissim's contention. He argued that Zipporah could not have known that circumcision was the issue between Moses and God, were it not that the extent of Moses' incorporation had made this apparent. He also maintained that Moses rather than the child must have been swallowed, else Moses rather than Zipporah would have performed the circumcision.[98] The tradition that Moses was swallowed up to the tip of the penis is stated explicitly in *Midrash ha-Gadol* on Exodus as well as in *Sh'moth Rabbah*.[99] The rabbis reasoned that Moses was the victim because he would have performed the circumcision had he been able.

This legend contains both castrative and incorporative elements. It illustrates my contention that fear of incorporation is more decisive than castration anxiety.[100] In the Flood legends, a biblical tale of the incorporation of a sinful world by water elicited from the rabbis a catalog of phallic sins as the reason for the incorporation. Here a phallic omission, the failure to circumcise, leads to the swallowing of the sinner, an oral retaliation. Castration is not stressed. The swallowing of the victim *up to* the penis may well suggest an inversion which contains a definite idea of castration. The fundamental image remains one of incorporation.

Incorporative elements also predominate in the story of Absalom, the rebellious son of David. His fate is used as an illustration of the measure-for-measure principle. Scripture states that Absalom took unto himself ten of his father's concubines. He was slain by ten young men of Joab's troop. There is no explicit association of the two episodes.[101] The rabbis associate the offense with the misfortune.

In the Aggadah, Absalom glories in his hair. His punishment is to be hung by the hair from a terebinth. When Absalom seeks to cut himself down, the netherworld opens up to swallow him. He is left suspended from the tree.[102] The rabbis add the threat of incorporation. The threat of incorporation makes Absalom prefer the lesser pain of hanging. He desists from cutting his hair. This can be seen as a symbolic preference for castration rather than incorporation, in which the cutting of the hair is symbolically equivalent to castration.

Finally, Absalom is included among those who will have no share in the world to come.[103] According to rabbinic tradition, the ultimate punishment awaiting the unrepentant sinner is denial of a share in the world to come. This is worse than the death penalty. A sinner sentenced to death might ultimately be saved. *Perek Helek* of Tractate Sanhedrin (the chapter on the "share") is the Talmudic chapter which contains one of the most important rabbinic discussions concerning the actions and the fate of unrepentant sinners. The discussions revolve very largely around the issue of who is to be denied the world to come and the reasons for their exclusion. The rabbis believed that the righteous would be resurrected to life eternal in the world to come but that the unrepentant sinner would be eternally condemned. The wording of the Mishnah in describing the fate of Korah and his band makes it clear that the final punishment is utter annihilation: "The company of Korah shall not rise again, for it is written, 'And the earth closed upon them,' in this world, 'And they perished from among the assembly,' in the world to come."[104]

As we have seen, Freud was convinced that fear of death was frequently derivative.[105] Fenichel had a similar opinion concerning the fear of incorporation. There can be little doubt that a *morbid* fear of death covers unconscious anxieties other than annihilation. Annihilation and incorporation can mean many things on many levels. Nevertheless, if one understands coitus in terms of thalassic regressive tendencies as did Ferenczi—the desire to return, at least symbolically, to the oceanic bliss of the womb—castration anxiety would ultimately reflect a later developmental aspect of the child's ambivalent feelings toward its earliest maternal environment.

Those existentialists who have explored the phenomenology of anxiety hold that castration anxiety is derivative. They regard *Urangst*, existential anxiety, man's primordial, ineradicable, and unmediated reaction to the nonbeing that forever threatens to envelop him, as primary. They maintain that it is cognitive without being conceptual.[106] However, following Kierkegaard, who referred to anxiety as a "sympathetic antipathy," they too recognize the ambivalent character of the phenomenon.[107] One yearns for the very nothingness against which anxiety is the primordial defense.

The existentialists' perspective is phenomenological; that of psychoanalysis is dynamic and developmental. The difference is rooted in differences of perspective. In phenomenological description, there is a very strong reluctance to go beyond the given and the apparent. The dynamic approach of psychoanalysis is not without merit. Clinical experience frequently reveals that a regression to earlier modes of behavior, a flight from the phallic to the oral, for example, is motivated by a flight from later conflicts.[108] Strong castration anxieties could express themselves as if they were earlier oral anxieties. Our evidence cannot rule out the possibility that the incorporation anxieties evident in the Aggadah may contain disguised phallic elements. Nevertheless, the phallic elements do not exclude the earlier oral conflicts that are so evident in rabbinic legends.

There is probably less distance between the existentialist and the Freudian views than is sometimes supposed, at least with regard to the primary object of anxiety. Freud posited a universal yearning of all life to return to the inorganic security which preceded the ecstasy of existence.[109] "The goal of life is death" in Freud's formulation. The last anxiety, the anxiety lest one be utterly annihilated, expresses both the earliest anxiety and the oldest yearning. In the final analysis, we yearn most deeply for that which we fear most insistently. Death is as much return to the source as goal and final end. Fear of and yearning for annihilation and incorporation are related to the organism's oldest strivings, the infant's yearning to return to the womb and its concurrent fear that it will be consumed by the cannibal mother.[110]

There is a basis for equating incorporation, the predominating punishment in the rabbinic legends, with annihilation, the punishment meted out to the most unrepentant sinners according to the rabbis. Both annihilation and incorporation involve the terminal riddance of reality. Death is a reincorporation of the organism by the earth. It was thus understood by many preliterate groups whose unconscious perceptions were often more accurate and closer to the surface than modern man's. Burial in the fetal position is not uncommon.[111] Death dissolves the ego and ends its capacity to resist the environment. This is evident in the coldness of the corpse and in its biological vulnerability.

The rabbis had no illusions about what happened to the body in death. They had no doubt about its return to the earth.[112] They faced the reality of death with an almost total lack of illusion. Nevertheless, they did not regard death as necessarily equivalent to *final* annihilation. Only denial of a share in the world to come was absolutely final. Death, even for the unrepentant sinner, could be the entrance into the world to come. The rabbis believed that God would ultimately resurrect the dead and so alter nature which He Himself had created that there would be no further dying.[113] Only those whom God had utterly rejected were to be totally incorporated into the earth whence they came. One might say that in the rabbinic perspective, the worst punishment of the unrepentant sinner was to be abandoned by the Father and, in consequence, to be finally and completely consumed by the Mother. Here annihilation and denial of the world to come are equivalent to final incorporation.[114]

Among the biblical sinners whom rabbinic tradition assigns no place in the world to come were Jeroboam, Ahab, Manasseh, Balaam, Doeg, Ahitophel, Gehazi, the generation of the Flood, the generation of the Dispersion (the tower of Babel), the Sodomites, the spies, the generation of the Wilderness, and Korah and his band. These were the sinners par excellence in rabbinic tradition. They served as negative models in the Aggadah. In other traditions, Balaam, the generation of the Flood, the generation of the Dispersion, and the Korahites also suffer punitive incorporation and burning.

Most punishments were partial and subject to revision. Even death could serve as an atonement.[115] There is a pedagogic element in the application of many of the lesser punishments suggested in the Aggadah. The rabbis continually stressed that God did not desire the death of the sinner, but his repentance.[116] It was always hoped that limited punishment would serve as a deterrent against further sin. The conception of punishments as of the *y'surim shel ahavah*, the chastisements of love, contained this idea.[117]

Most punishments serve as a double deterrent. Anxiety lest one be smitten prompts the ego to defend the organism against the pain by avoiding offense. Memory of the actual punishment is a deterrent against further misbehavior. Denial of a share in the world to come is different. It is only meted out to those for whom all possibility of return is excluded. The rabbis distinguished very carefully between sins for which reparation and repentance are possible and sins for which reparation is no longer possible.[118] They directed their special condemnation against those who had led others astray. The gravity of this type of sin stemmed from the fact that, even were the sinner to make reparation, he could only restore himself but could do nothing for those whom he had led astray.[119]

Denial of a share in the world to come could only deter *before* the fact. The matter is in reality extremely complicated. The primordial yearning evident in the Aggadah for the quiescence of the grave is ultimately identical with the most terrible threat envisaged by rabbinic Judaism. For some, the threat of annihilation may actually be an enticement. For the moment, let us recognize that it is the final and ultimate punishment in both the Halakah and the Aggadah. Whatever differences of perspective are to be discerned between the domains of law and legend in Judaism recede at this point. There is unanimity on the question of ultimate punishment. That punishment was not castration. It was annihilation.

The legends cited are but a sample of very many which could be offered to indicate the persistence of prephallic incorporative anxieties in the Aggadah. There can be no doubt that phallic and castrative elements are present. They have been noted.

Whether by accident or intent, Freud's comment that his discovery of the importance of the pre-Oedipal mother came to him with as much of a surprise as the discovery of Minoan-Mycenaean civilization, was pregnant with meaning.[120] He recognized that his own discovery of the decisive character of the archaic elements in the development of the psyche was analogous to the discovery of the significance of the hitherto unrecognized Minoan matriarchal culture for the development of Western civilization.

The fact that incorporation anxieties predominate over castration anxieties in the Aggadah suggests that the dichotomy between matriarchal and patriarchal religions is untenable. Matriarchal religions may not reflect the dilemmas of phallic religion. The archaic strivings they reflect precede and anticipate phallic development. The phallic stage does not cancel out earlier archaic stages in the development of the individual; neither does that stage entirely cancel earlier stages in religious life. No matter how violently patriarchal religions attempt to uproot traces of matriarchal religions, the results are at best only partially successful. The incorporation legends indicate how deeply rooted the older anxieties remained in supposedly phallic rabbinic Judaism. In all likelihood, they had a greater capacity to deter behavioral deviance than the traditions which reflected castration anxiety. Historically and psychologically, there was a far more direct involvement of the people in the tales of the Flood, the demise of the Egyptians, and Korah's rebellion, than in the less significant stories of Ham's violence or the frogs' castration of the Egyptian nobles. The latter were isolated stories; the former were widely told and repeated. The drowning of the Egyptians is rehearsed daily in Jewish liturgy.[121]

Parenthetically, it is interesting to observe that the laws of eating remain to this day the predominating disciplines of traditional Judaism. Among religious Jews, there is a vast concern with what one may and may not eat. This preoccupation is simply without parallel in any other Western religion. Jewish concentration on dietary matters begs for psychoanalytic study in its own right. We must rest content with noting the existence of the phenomenon. The dietary regulations of Judaism constantly remind the Jew with dramatic forcefulness of the importance of what one takes in with the mouth. Oral activities are emotionally overdetermined in Judaism. The dietary laws tend to confirm the hypothesis that, no matter how preoccupied the rabbis were with phallic and Oedipal matters, they were far more insistently and continuously concerned with oral strivings and anxieties.

A psychoanalytic interpretation of Judaism which ignores the centrality of its oral preoccupations must be woefully incomplete. Any attempt to interpret the severe eating disciplines of Judaism only as unconscious attempts on the part of the community to defend its members against the temptation to repeat the primal crime, that is to commit cannibalistic acts against the fathers, will also be incomplete. An examination of the rabbinic tales of the ways in which sinners were punished strongly suggests that there was far greater fear of the mother than of the father in rabbinic Judaism. I must again suggest that the primal crime simply isn't primal enough.

This conclusion seems to be borne out by the evidence of the history of religion. Too frequently, the image of a mother-goddess conjured up by those who contrast the "restrictive" Jewish Father-God with the "permissive" mothers of ancient paganism is that of the compassionate Mother of Sorrows of Roman Catholicism. Mary, however, represents an Oedipal rather than a pre-Oedipal mother. A far better perspective is attained when we contrast the God of the Aggadah at His angriest and most punitive with such goddesses as Cybele and Kalima. The mother-goddess had two sides. She was the loving giver and sustainer of life. She was also an incomparably hideous and terrifying ogress. She inspires infinitely greater terror than the God of Judaism at His worst. The unmeasured terror inspired by the great cannibal Earth-Mother reflects the child's first confrontation with its environment unaided by previous learning. The child's project is not merely to eat but so to consume its environment that the hideous pains of hunger which thrust it into reality will be appeased and sated. Its greatest unspoken fear, unrefined by experience or concept, is that this nourishing environment will do unto it as it has done. The cannibal child is in terror of a cannibal world, the world of the Mother. It is that world which we see objectified in the religions of the Great Mother. Something of that world never disappears in later life in any of us. It is helpful to compare the punishments in the Aggadah with the misfortunes inflicted by the Great Mother on the fruit of her womb. The predominant fears of incorporation in the Aggadah correspond to the decisive fears of matriarchal religion. This is most vividly evident in the tales of death by earth-incorporation or drowning. This corresponds to the negative side of the Great Mother. It is she as earth, womb, and tomb who consumes her own children. Erich Neumann has described this aspect of the Great Mother with especial forcefulness:

> Just as world, life, nature and soul have been experienced as a
> generative and nourishing, protective and warming Femininity, so

their opposites are also perceived in the image of the Feminine; death and destruction, danger and distress, hunger and nakedness, appear as helplessness in the presence of the Dark and Terrible Mother.

Thus the womb of the earth becomes the deadly devouring maw of the underworld, and beside the fecundating womb and the protective cave of earth and mountain goes the abyss of hell, the dark hole of the depths, the devouring womb of the grave and of death, of darkness without light, of nothingness. For this woman who generates life and all living things is the same who takes them back into herself. . . . This Terrible Mother is the hungry earth which devours its own children and fattens on their corpses; it is . . . the flesh-eating sarcophagus voraciously licking up the blood seed of men and beasts, and, once fecundated and sated, casting it out again in new birth, hurling it to death, and over and over again to death.[122]

I would not dispute that the God of rabbinic Judaism was essentially a Father-God and was so regarded by the rabbis. Nevertheless, the evidence of the legends suggests that earlier archaic feelings toward the mothers were never lost and actually remained a very significant component in the new piety. In reality, the God of the rabbis was considerably less terrifying than His female Syrian neighbor, Cybele. She in turn was prototypical of the best and the worst in the Great Mother.

The God of biblical and rabbinic Judaism demanded circumcision as His token of loyalty from male worshippers. By contrast, the *galloi* expressed their priestly worship of *dea Syria*, the Mother-Goddess of Syria, by castrating themselves and offering their dismembered genitals, rather than just their foreskins, to their celestial mother.[123] The mother-goddesses permitted a greater range of license to their faithful, a fact often emphasized. Nevertheless, this tells us little about the anxiety content of these activities for those who participated in them. They may indeed have been fraught with inner fright and terror that Judaeo-Christian sexual discipline was actually a relief and a defense against anxiety. It is by no means certain that sexual discipline produces greater anxiety than sexual license. The ego often uses repression as a mechanism to defend itself against anxiety induced by unacceptable sexual promptings. Similarly, the religious disciplines of Judaism were defenses against the permissiveness of the Mother and the terrible price she exacted for her freedom. The disciplines of rabbinic Judaism cannot be interpreted as reflecting the prohibitions of the Father-God alone. The prohibitions of the Father-God were a relief in contrast to the unmeasured and uncontained fear of the Great Mother. The mother is the first object of love. She is the object of the later conflicts of father and son. However, the other side of the picture must not be ignored. The mother is the first object of anxiety by any reading of psychoanalytic literature, religious history, or mythology.

Patriarchal religions may very well reflect defenses of the ego, both individually and collectively, against the barely suppressed but infinitely greater fear of the mother-goddesses and the actual maternal figures they presuppose. The defenses of the ego are not necessarily pleasant. Repression is one of the most important of such defenses. Defenses are elected because the ego finds no other way to avoid greater pain or greater conflict. If this interpretation of patriarchal religion has merit, it would seem that many of the characteristic features of rabbinic Judaism are far less projections of the superego, though this element cannot be denied, than defenses of the ego. By extending our conception of the psychogenetic factors operative in Judaism *backward* to include the oral stage, we also extend them *forward* to include the defensive and the integrative functions of the ego. We thus arrive at a psychological interpretation of rabbinic Judaism that is more compatible with the broader aspects of contemporary psychoanalytic ego psychology than the earlier view which stressed the phallic aspects of Judaism almost exclusively.

The *lex talionis*, or measure-for-measure principle, must also be seen in perspective. It is the irrational application of the measure-for-measure principle, rather than the principle itself, which is archaic and harsh. In some respects, the principle must be seen as a principle of mercy and limitation. Punishment is frequently a psychic need of the sinner himself. Equitable punishment was calculable. It allowed for continued effort thereafter. Perhaps, calculable punishment was welcomed by some because it cleared the slate. Much criticism has been needlessly placed on the "barbaric" character of the measure-for-measure principle and on Judaism as an "eye for an eye, a tooth for a tooth" religion. In actuality, the talion principle was by no means the most archaic or barbaric retaliatory norm. The limitation of punishment to no more than a punitive equivalent must have represented a great advance over the old Semitic custom of avenging the crime of an individual many times on his entire clan.[124] In place of Lamech's cry "If Cain shall be avenged sevenfold, surely Lamech seventy and seven-fold,"[125] the talion principle introduced limitation and measure. In the light of archaic Semitic practice, the principle represented a positive advance in both justice and mercy. It is by no means accidental that the principle is associated in the history of religion and psychoanalysis with the Father-God rather than the mother-goddesses. Here again the father even at his most punitive is an agent of limitation and measure in contrast to the unmeasured terrors of the pre-Oedipal mother. The evidence suggests that the turning from the mother to the father in religion was the work of the ego defending itself against infinitely greater archaic fears.

P. J. van der Leeuw has offered a suggestion concerning castration anxiety which accords with my findings in rabbinic legend. He has suggested that castration anxiety is at least partly a defense against earlier and infinitely greater pre-Oedipal anxieties. Follow-ing his suggestion, the fantasy-love of the mother in the Oedipal stage may be a way of resolving an intolerable ambivalence.[126] That ambivalence was so great in the religions of the Father-God as to impel His worshippers to attempt to obliterate all traces of the older mother-goddesses. The history of Judaism and Protestantism at-tests to the violence with which that project was carried out. The evidence of the Aggadah indicates how incessantly she who was repressed returned, not only in the worst fears of the rabbis but also in their deepest yearnings.

I have frequently suggested that the Aggadah preserves or restores archaic insights of the greatest antiquity. The greater importance of incorporation anxiety in these legends may point to one of the most ancient and continuously relevant conceptions of the significance of the Father-God in the history of religion. The Father-God is the *artifex omnium natura*. One of the oldest and most important sources of rabbinic legend, *Bereshith Rabbah*, begins with a discussion of God's role as architect and fashioner of creation.[127] He creates a cosmos out of the primordial wasteland of chaos. He is the author of order, reason, form, and law in both the moral and the physical realms. His creative activity prevents the all too facile return of cosmos to chaos.

In the oldest mythologies, undifferentiated chaos is the abysmal mother out of which earth, sea, and the world of men arise. In the Sumerian myths of the origin of things, the goddess Nammu is referred to as the "mother, who gave birth to heaven and earth" (An and Ki). S. N. Kramer describes Nammu as written with the ideogram for "sea."[128] An and Ki were regarded as the created products of the primordial mother-sea. There are very clear overtones of the womb-birth metaphor in this mythic representation. Chaos becomes truly cosmos only with the organization of the earth. This is the work of the male god En-lil, "who caused the good day to come forth" and who determined "to bring forth seed from the earth."[129] Few activities of the Father-God are as important as His role in creating order out of disorder.

In rabbinic Judaism, the religious Jew was regarded as the partner of God in bringing about the rule of His kingdom. That kingdom is none other than the rule of order, measure, and equity over the ever-present threat of the return of original chaos. The rabbis were aware of the power and the seductive attraction of chaos. Anxiety is cognitive without being conceptual. With its capacity to shake our innermost foundations, it engenders in us a potent awareness of the dissolving nothingness out of which we have come and to which we must return. At one level, the fundamental intent of rabbinic Judaism can be seen as an attempt to create those forms, limitations, and structures which are indispensable to every human activity of significance. For the rabbis, every meaningful encounter contained some element of choice between chaos and cosmos. Forsaking the Goddess who engendered in them their deepest chaotic anxieties, they turned hopefully to the Lord of creation and His statutes, ordinances, and commandments.

NOTES

[1]Søren Kierkegaard, *The Concept of Dread*, trans. Walter Lowrie (Princeton: Princeton University Press, 1944). (Originally published in Danish, 1844.)

[2]Freud, *The Problem of Anxiety*, p. 75. ". . . We assume castration anxiety as the motive force behind the struggles of the ego."

[3]Rollo May, *The Meaning of Anxiety* (New York: Ronald Press, 1950), p. 123.

[4]Cf. Bettelheim, *Symbolic Wounds*, pp. 128 ff.

[5]Paul Tillich, *The Courage To Be* (New Haven: Yale University Press, 1952), p. 38; cf. John Wild, *The Challenge of Existentialism* (Bloomington: Indiana University Press, 1955), pp. 70–71. For an excellent criticism of Heidegger's conception of man as a being-toward-death, cf. Laszlo Versenyi, *Heidegger, Being, and Truth* (New Haven: Yale University Press, 1965), pp. 177 ff.

[6]Freud, *The Problem of Anxiety*, p. 105; May, *The Meaning of Anxiety*, pp. 121 ff.

[7]Cf. Freud, *The Ego and the Id*, pp. 47 ff.

[8]Cf. *supra*, p. 9. [Here and elsewhere in these notes, *supra* citations refer to pages in Rubenstein's *The Religious Imagination*.]

[9]Cf. *supra, loc cit.*

[10]Freud, *Moses and Monotheism*, p. 116.

[11]M. Sotah 1.7 ff. Cf. J. Peah 21b and Ta'anïth 21a in which the teacher of R. Akiba, Nahum of Gamzu, welcomes his extraordinary misfortunes as God's measure-for-measure retaliation for his sins. Cf. Mek. Beshallah, ed. Lauterbach, Vol. I, 243–245, "For with the very thing with which the Egyptians planned to destroy Israel, He (i.e. God) destroyed them." Cf. T. Sotah 3.13; cf. Mt. 5:31, "If your right eye cause you to sin, pluck it out and throw it away. . . ."

[12]Gen. 39:1.

[13]Ps. 37:28.

[14]The Masoretic (i.e. official rabbinic) text of the Bible does not have the reading of the midrash. The Masoretic text reads "saints" as in the English translation.

[15]Ps. 37:28.

[16]BR 86.3.

[17]Cf. Sotah 13b where Rab says that Potiphar was emasculated by the angel Gabriel; Targum Jerushalmi on Gen. 39:1; cf. Tan. B. II, 85 where God does the castrating; MHG on Gen., Vol. II, p. 656, 1.13–15 and p. 657, 1.4–7 which parallels Sotah 13b and also quotes Rab.

[18]Num. 25: 1–18.

[19]Sanhedrin 82a–b; cf. J. Sanhedrin 28b–29a; Sifre on Numbers, ed. Friedmann, p. 131; Sh'moth R. 33.5; B'midbar R. 20.24; Tan. B. IV, p. 148; Tsn., Balak 20.

[20]B'midbar R. 20.24.

[21]B'Midbar R. 20.25; cf. Buber's comments on Tan. IV, p. 148.

[22]Sanhedrin 82b.

[23]Ps. 1: 28.

[24]Tehillim 105: 452 and 78: 350. The latter source describes the frogs as going up through the marble houses but omits the castration story. Cf. Sh'moth R. 10.3, but cf. Buber's *ad loc.* comments on Tehillim 78: 350 where he suggests that the source in Sh'moth R. is medieval.

[25]Gen. 9: 22.

[26]BR 36.7; Sanhedrin 108b; Tan. Noah 12; BR 31.12; BR 34.7; Tan. B. I, 42–43. Tan. B. I, 49–50.

[27]BR 35.1.

[28]BR 36.4 and MHG on Gen., Vol. I, 189, 1.5–6.

[29]Baba Bathra 74 b.

[30]M. Sotah 1.7 ff.

[31]*Ibid.*

[32]Mek. Beshallah (Ed. L.), Vol. I, 243–245. Cf. T. Sotah 3.13; Mek. (Ed. L.) Amalek, Vol. II, 148, 1.8–11; Mek. (Ed. F.), II, 55a. Cf. Ginzberg, V, 427, n. 172 where Ginzberg discusses the rabbinic passages which assert that the Egyptians were punished measure for measure.

[33]ShR 9.10; Tan. WaYera 14; MHG on Ex. 116, 1.16–17. In another tradition it is maintained that the Nile was turned into blood in retaliation for the drowning of the Israelite children. Cf. MHG on Ex., p. 116, 1.15–16.

[34]ShR 10.4.

[35]Tehillim 136, 520. Cf. *supra*, pp. 58 ff.

[36]Cf. *supra*, pp. 47 ff.

[37]Cf. *supra*, p. 54.

[38]BR 87.7 and 98.20; Sotah 36b; J. Horayoth 2, 46d.

[39]BR 87.7

[40]MHG on Gen., II, 668, 1.6–7 and 1.9–15. Cf. BR 98.20 where he sees his mother.

[41]Gen. 39: 11.

[42]BR 87.7; cf. BR 98.20 where the tale is slightly less explicit.

[43]BR 87.7.

[44]Fenichel, *The Psychoanalytic Theory of Neurosis*, pp. 170 ff.

[45]Gen. 20: 18.

[46]BR 52.13.

[47]BR 52.13; cf. Tan.B., I, 101, where the tradition omits the angel and the drawn sword; cf. MHG on Gen., Vol. I, 328, 1.15–16 where Gabriel is the angel; PRE 26.

[48]Gen. 12:17.

[49]BR 40.2 in the current edition. In Theodor's critical edition the tradition appears in chapter 41. Cf. MHG on Gen., Vol. I, 225, 1.6–10 where R. Tarphon is quoted as saying that Pharaoh was smitten with leprosy on the eve of Passover as a hint of the later fate of the Egyptians. PRE 26.

[50]Cf. Erikson, *Childhood and Society*, pp. 67–73; Fenichel, *The Psychoanalytic Theory of Neurosis*, pp. 62 ff. For a most interesting discussion of the development of psychotoxic reactions in the skin of eight-month-old babies, cf. René A. Spitz, *The First Year of Life* (New York: International Universities Press, 1965), pp. 224 ff.

[51]WR 16.1.

[52]M. Margulies' *ad loc.* comment on WR 16.1 in his critical edition.

[53]Ketuboth 77b; cf. WR 16.1 which contains this tradition and the one cited in n. 54. However, Margulies removes this tradition in his *ad loc.* comments on the text. On *ra'athan* cf. T. Ketuboth 7 *ad fin.* Cf. MHG on Gen., Vol. I, 225, 1.11–15.

[54]BR 41.2.

[55]BR 41.2.

[56]Shabbat 149b.

[57]Cf. *supra.*, pp. 43 ff.

[58]Cf. Ginzberg, Vol. VII, 586–598, for an index of Church Fathers and medieval Christian writers using material from the Aggadah. This is by no means an exhaustive list.

[59]WR 16.1.

[60]Sotah 35 a; Kohelet R. 9.12.

[61]Num. 14: 37. Scripture refers to the "plague" rather than leprosy. The rabbis understood the plague to be leprosy.

[62]Kohelet R. 9.12.

[63]Sotah 35a.

[64]Sotah 35a.

[65]ARN 9, 39.

[66]Judges 11: 31.

[67]Judges 11: 34–40.

[68]WR 37.4; BR 60.3; Tan. B. III, 112–114; Tan. Behukkotai 5; Kohelet R. 10.15; Ta'anit 4a; Midrash Tannaim 100; Sifre D. 148; ER II, 55–57.

[69]Judges 12: 7.

[70]Num. 12.10.

[71]WR 16.1, ARN 9.39, Shabbat 97a.

[72]Cf. Bertram Lewin, *The Psychoanalysis of Elation* (New York: W. W. Norton and Co., 1950), pp. 109–110; Lewin, "Sleep, Mouth and the Dream Sequence" in *The Psychoanalytic Quarterly*, Vol. XV, 1946, 240; Geza Roheim, *The Gates of the Dream* (New York: International Universities Press, 1958), pp. 88 ff; René Spitz, *No and Yes: On the Genesis of Human Communication* (New York: International Universities Press, 1958), pp. 70–85.

[73]Cf. Edith Weigert-Vowinckel, "The Cult and Mythology of the Magna Mater From the Viewpoint of Psychoanalysis" in *Psychiatry*, Vol. I (1938), 348–349; Bettelheim, *Symbolic Wounds*, pp. 154–164.

[74]2 ARN 9, 39.

[75]For the flood traditions, cf. Sanhedrin 57a, 108b; WR 7: 6, BR 26.4, 5 and 32.7, AZ 23b; Hulin 23a; cf. Ginzberg, V, pp. 182–183.

[76]WR 7.6.

[77]WR 7.6 and 20.2. Korah is depicted as boiling like "flesh in a pot" in Baba Bathra 74a; cf. Sanhedrin 110a–110b; Tan. B., IV, 94.

[78]Lev. 10: 1, 2.

[79]Sanhedrin 52a.

[80]*Ibid.*; cf. Tan. B. I, 50.

[81]Rashi on Sanhedrin 110a.

[82]Sanhedrin 106b.

[83]Sandor Ferenczi, *Thalassa: A Theory of Genitality*, trans. H. A. Bunker (New York: The Psychoanalytic Quarterly, 1938).

[84]Num. 16: 32, 33.

[85]Num. 16: 33.

[86]B'midbar R. 18: 13; Tan. B. IV, 96–97.

[87]*Ibid.*

[88]J. Sanhedrin 10, 28a which reads 'flew up.'

[89]Baba Bathra 74a; Sanhedrin 110a-T n. B. IV, 94.

[90]Gittin 56b–57a; cf. AZ 11a and A. E. Silverstone, *Aquila and Onkelos* (Manchester: Manchester University Press, 1931), pp. 1–22 and 148–160.

[91]Gittin 56b–57a.

[92]Ex. 14: 26; Mek. Beshallah (ed. L.), Vol. I, 243, 1.3–p. 244. 1.7, Mek. RS (ed. E.), p. 66, 1.20–44. The story of the Egyptian drowning is rehearsed throughout Jewish liturgy. It thus received the widest currency of any of the punishment traditions.

[93]Ex. 4: 24–27.

[94]Cf. Salo Baron, *A Social and Religious History of the Jews* (New York: Columbia University Press, 1952), Vol. II, 107 and 374; Justin Martyr, *Dialogue with Trypho*, tr. A. Lukyn Williams (London: S.P.C.K., 1930), p. 107; M. S. Enslin, "Justin Martyr: An Appreciation," JQR (new series), XXXIV, 179–205; cf. Nedarim 31b–32a and Bacher II a, 22.

[95]Mek. Amalek (Ed. L.), Vol. II, 168, 1.93–p. 169 1.105; Mek. Jethro (Ed. F.), I, 57b–58a.

[96]Ex. 4:25, 26. The rabbinic source is Nedarim 32a.

[97]Ran on Nedarim 32a printed in the standard edition of Ayn Ya'acob (reprinted, New York: 1953).

[98]Mahrsh'a on Nedarim 32a printed in the standard edition of Ayn Ya'acob.

[99]MHG on Ex., 78, 1.2–4; ShR 5.8.

[100]But cf. Fenichel, *op. cit.*, pp. 63 ff and 83 ff. Fenichel tends to reduce incorporation anxiety to castration. Nevertheless, his description of archaic object relations does not necessarily call for that reduction. The intersection of anxiety over castration and incorpora-

tion is described by Freud in the case of "little Hans." Cf. Freud, "Analysis of a Phobia in a Five-Year-Old Boy" in CP, Vol. III, 149–179.

[101]II Sam. 15: 1 ff and II Sam 18: 15.

[102]M. Sotah 1.8.

[103]M. Sanhedrin.

[104]M. Sanhedrin 10.3.

[105]Freud, *The Problem of Anxiety*, p. 105.

[106]John Wild, *op. cit.*, pp. 70–71.

[107]Søren Kierkegaard, *The Concept of Dread*, pp. 38, 55.

[108]Fenichel, *op. cit.*, pp. 206 ff.

[109]Freud, *Beyond the Pleasure Principle*, pp. 67 ff.

[110]From the point of view of psychoanalysis, one of the earliest anxieties is the archaic anxiety of incorporation. This is stated succinctly by Fenichel: "The content of the primitive ego's idea of anxiety is determined in part directly by its biological nature and in part by its animistic ways of thinking, which make the ego believe that its environment has the same instinctual aims as it has itself (combined with more power). In these animistic misunderstandings the punitive talion principle is at work, according to which any deed may be undone (or must be punished) by a similar deed inflicted on the original doer." Fenichel, *op. cit.*, pp. 43–44. Since one of the fundamental aims of the archaic oral stage is the striving to unite, by means of the mouth, with the predominantly maternal environment, it follows that the anxiety lest one be incorporated is decisive at this stage. Cf. Erikson, *op. cit.*, pp. 67–73.

[111]Ferenczi, *op. cit.*, pp. 81–95.

[112]Cf. Aboth 3.1 and 4.1.

[113]M. Sanhedrin 10.1. There are extremely complicated problems connected with the question of the rabbinic view of the time of the Messiah and the World to Come. R. Johanan held that, though the prophets spoke of the days of the Messiah, nevertheless concerning the World to Come "no eye has seen what God has prepared for those who wait for him." Berachoth 34b. In the present context, what is important is that the rabbis never doubted God's power to make alive and to annihilate. For some views on the problem, cf. Joseph Klausner, *op. cit.*, and Montefiore and Loewe, *A Rabbinic Anthology*, pp. 580–608.

[114]The rabbis were mindful of the analogy between the womb and the tomb: R. Tabi further said in the name of R. Josiah: "What is meant by the text, 'There are three things which are never satisfied. . . . the grave and the barren womb'? (Prov. 30: 15, 16) How come the grave next to the womb? It is to teach you that just as the womb takes in and gives forth again, so the grave takes in and will give again. . . . Here is a refutation of those who deny that resurrection is taught in the Torah. . . ." Berachoth 15b.

[115]For the conception of the sinner's death as atonement, cf. M. Sanhedrin 6.2 and T. Sanhedrin 9.5: "Those who are put to death by the (rabbinical) court have a share in the world to come, because they confess all their sins."

[116]For a succinct summary of rabbinic attitudes toward repentance, cf. Maimonides, *Mishneh Torah*, Hilkoth T'shuvah (reprinted New York: Otzer Harambam, Inc., 1960).

[117]Cf. Berachoth, 5a–5b.

[118]Cf. Maimonides, *op. cit.*, Hilkoth T'shuvah, 4.2 ff.

[119]Maimonides, *loc. cit.*

[120]Freud, "Female Sexuality" in CP, Vol. V, 254.

[121]Cf. Hertz, *The Authorized Daily Prayer Book*, pp. 101 and 129.

[122]Erich Neumann, *The Great Mother*, trans. Ralph Mannheim (New York: Pantheon Books, 1955), pp. 149 ff. Cf. Heinrich Zimmer's description of the bloody worship of Kali-ma quoted by Neumann (p. 152). Cf. Heinrich Zimmer, "Die Indische Weltmutter" in *Ernanos-Jahrbuch* (Zurich: 1938), pp. 179 ff. The entire issue of the *Ernanos-Jahrbuch* for 1938 is devoted to the problem of the Great Mother.

[123]Weigert-Vowinckel, *loc. cit.*

[124]Cf. W. Robertson Smith, *Kinship and Marriage in Early Arabia* (Cambridge: 1885), pp. 22 f.

[125]Gen. 4: 24.

[126]P. J. van der Leeuw, "The Preoedipal Stage of the Male" in *The Psychoanalytic Study of the Child*, Vol. XIII, 352–374. Cf. Edmund Bergler, *The Basic Neurosis: Oral Regression and Psychic Masochism* (New York: Grune and Stratton, 1949), p. 16.

[127]BR 1.1.

[128]Samuel N. Kramer, *Sumerian Mythology* (New York: Harper Torchbooks, 1961), p. 39.

[129]Kramer, *op. cit.*, p. 42.

Freud and Jewish Marginality

Moses and the Evolution of Freud's Jewish Identity

Martin S. Bergmann

EDITOR'S COMMENT

This essay is reprinted from the *Israel Annals of Psychiatry and Related Disciplines*, Volume 14, Number 1, pages 3–26, March 1976.

Analysts have learned from daily clinical experience that the history of a person's career can be seen to express the vicissitudes of the process of his resolution of fundamental conflicts. This thesis becomes especially interesting when the person has made significant contributions to culture or science. We can observe then that his readiness to solve important and difficult problems in the outside world is influenced by his struggle to solve his inner problems. On the basis of this principle, the discipline that has been called psycho-history was established.

Psycho-history is both a promising and a treacherous discipline. Though it tells us nothing about the validity of contributions to science, or the esthetic value of contributions to art, or the intellectual value of contributions to culture, it can tell us something of the motivation and the struggle of the contributor. Properly done, it requires complete respect for facts and sufficient self-discipline to avoid seeing what is not there. Without the corrective and directive influence of the constant flow of material from the patient on the couch, the psycho-historian can easily find whatever he wishes to find.

Perhaps psycho-history can be said to have started with Freud. To illustrate the principles of dream interpretation, he described and analyzed his own dreams, and so introduced us to the history and outcome of his own conflicts. Taking this material together with other autobiographical writings and a large number of letters, one can attempt a psycho-history of Freud himself. In fact many essays have been written on that subject.

In this paper, Martin Bergmann, a man of wide and deep learning, equally at home in psychoanalytic theory and Jewish culture, has attempted to reconstruct Freud's struggle to come to terms with his Jewishness, from the various biographical sources available to us and from Freud's writings. He does not concern himself here primarily with the social influences upon this conflict, the marginal situation of post-emancipation Jews in Vienna, but rather with Freud's attempts to deal with his marginality.

Bergmann's paper is followed by a discussion I offered when the paper was read before the New York Psychoanalytic Society in 1975. While some of my suggestions were incorporated into Bergmann's essay, I believe that some other points may be of interest to the reader.

I have added, too, an informal discussion of the paper, comments included in a letter to Dr. Bergmann by Dr. Robert Jay Lifton, Professor of Psychiatry at the School of Medicine of Yale University. In this letter Dr. Lifton responds to some ideas in the paper and felt free to speculate about a number of related matters.

*Sigmund Freud's family came from the Galician "Stadtle" Buczacz, incidentally the home town of the Hebrew writer and Nobel Prize winner, S. J. Agnon (Simon, 1957). Freud's father, Jacob, belonged to a group of wandering Jewish merchants that travelled between Galicia and Freiburg, Moravia, the current Czechoslovakia. Freud's birthday was recorded in the family Bible under the Hebrew name, Schlomo, according to the Hebrew calendar, "Rosh Hodesh Iyar 5616." (The first of the Hebrew month of Iyar.) (Aron 1956/1957; Ellenberger 1970).

A photograph of Jacob and Sigmund Freud appears on the title page of Volume 20 of the *Standard Edition* and in Jones' Biography of Freud (1953). There is nothing to suggest religious observances in the father's appearance. According to Jones, "Jacob Freud was undoubtedly a liberal-minded man of progressive views, but it is not likely that he kept up orthodox Jewish customs after migrating to Vienna." Jacob and Sigmund Freud grew up in different eras, but both were rationalists in their outlook. In 1896, when Jacob Freud died, his life span covered the entire period of Jewish emancipation from the highly structured orthodox community life in Eastern Europe to the voluntary Jewish ghetto Leopoldstadt in Vienna.

Jones relates that on Freud's 35th brithday, his father, then 75, returned to him a childhood Bible with the following dedication in Hebrew, that is, in a language the recipient could neither read nor understand:

"My dear Son,
It was in the seventh year of your age that the spirit of God began to move you to learning. I would say the spirit of God speaketh to you: 'Read in My book; there will be opened to thee sources of knowledge and of the intellect.' It is the Book of Books; it is the well

*A modified version of this paper was read at the Jewish Museum in connection with the Exhibit *Berggasse 19, The Office and Antiquities of Sigmund Freud*, on November 24, 1974 and on January 12, 1975. The paper was presented to the New York Psychoanalytic Society on September 30, 1975. I wish to express my gratitude to the discussants of the paper Drs. Kurt Eissler and Mortimer Ostow for their valuable contributions and criticism.

115

that wise men have digged and from which lawgivers have drawn the waters of their knowledge.

"Thou hast seen in this Book the vision of the Almighty, thou hast heard willingly, thou has done and hast tried to fly high upon the wings of the Holy Spirit. Since then I have preserved the same Bible. Now, on your thirty-fifth birthday, I have brought it out from its retirement and I send it to you as a token of love from your old father." (Jones, 1953, Vol. 1, p. 19).

The dedication confirms Freud's statement (Freud, 1929 S.E. vol. 20, p. 8), that he was engrossed in Bible stories almost as soon as he could read. However, if the dedication is analyzed as a Hebrew document it becomes apparent that Jacob Freud was neither a religious nor a nationalist Jew, but a member of the Haskala, a movement that saw Judaism as epitomizing the religion of enlightenment. No orthodox Jew would speak lightly about the Spirit of God speaking to a seven-year-old. Nor would any religious Jew see the Bible as belonging to mankind as a whole. Biblical flowery language (Melizot in Hebrew), also marks Jacob Freud as a member of the Haskala. It was this aspect of the Jewish tradition that Freud learned from his father, and he could, therefore, equate the freedom to use the intellect with his Jewish heritage.[1]

Freud's wife, Martha Bernays, was the daughter of a well-known rabbi in Hamburg. She was an observant Jewess in her youth. During her betrothal to Freud, she wrote to him daily, except on the Sabbath. Eventually, however, the prohibition against writing on the day of rest yielded to love and she started to write on the Sabbath too, but only in secret and only with a pencil (Jones, Vol. 1, p. 116). During the years of the betrothal, Freud waged a sustained campaign to emancipate his bride from the domination of her mother. The writing on the Sabbath was one of the many tokens of love he demanded from her (Jones, Vol. 1, Chapter 7).

Among Freud's letters to his fiancée, the following lines are of interest in the current context:

February 2, 1886

"Do you know what Breuer said to me one evening? That he had discovered what an infinitely bold and fearless person I concealed behind my mask of shyness. I have always believed that of myself, but never dared to say it to anyone. I have often felt as if I had inherited all the passion of our ancestors when they defended their Temple, as if I could joyfully cast away my life in a great cause. And with all that I was always so powerless and could not express the flowing passion even by a word or a poem. So I have always suppressed myself, and I believe people must notice that in me."

(Jones, Vol. 1, p. 197)

This letter is of psychological significance because in 1886 the cause that Freud wished to defend as the zealots defended the Temple against the Roman Legions was not yet discovered, but the predisposition to fight for a cause is already present. This wish Freud experiences as his Jewish heritage.

These strong feelings are in sharp contrast to Freud's knowledge of matters pertaining to Jewish life. When he visited the Catacombs in Rome, he wrote to his wife that the Jewish graves can be distinguished from the Christian by the relief of the candelabrum, but he was not sure if the candelabrum was called Menorah. Jones, (Vol. 2, p. 36) who records the incident, interprets it to mean that Freud was not familiar with the synagogue. But this issue cannot be dismissed so easily for the Menorah ranks with the Star of David as the Jewish symbol par excellence.

In the famous letter No. 69 to Fliess, when he announced to his friend that his seduction theory of the origin of neurosis proved erroneous, Freud relates that he has no feeling of shame, but adds, "Of course, I would not tell it to Dan and talk about it in Askelon." This is a reference to David's lamentations over the death of Saul and Jonathan, the Biblical quotation: "Tell it not to Gath, publish it not in the streets of Askelon, lest the daughters of the Philistines rejoice, lest the daughters of the uncircumcised triumph." (II Samuel, I: 20) Dan, however, unlike Gath, is not one of the five cities of the Philistines, but the Northern Israeli tribe. The slip confuses friend and foe. (Vol. I, p. 260)

There was one area of Jewish life that Freud knew and loved, that was the Jewish joke. The book, *Jokes and their Relation to the Unconscious* (Freud, 1905 S.E. vol. 8) abounds with examples of Jewish humor. It is a book of a man at home with the Jewish attitude toward life, an attitude which has found its expression in the great Jewish writers, Shalom Aleichem and Mendel, Mocher Sefarim. The Jewish joke, a unique creation of the Jews, requires no adherence to Judaism in any organized sense, and can, therefore, become a vehicle for the expression of feelings of solidarity for those who have retained a sense of belonging, without religious or national affiliation. In Freud's case, one must also add that Jewish superstitions, particularly with regard to lucky and unlucky numbers, continued to exert an influence. (Schur, 1972, p. 25)

I would like first to examine the evolution of Freud's conscious attitude toward being a Jew. Freud was once exhorted by an American physician to accept the Bible as God's word, and Christ as his personal Saviour. Freud replied:

> "God has not done so much for me. He had never allowed me to hear an inner voice; and if, in view of my age, he did not make haste, it would not be my fault if I remained to the end of my life what I now was[2]—an infidel Jew'."

> (Freud 1928, S.E. vol. 21 p. 170)

The paradoxical term 'infidel Jew' coined by Freud expresses his position well. "Incidentally," Freud asked Pastor Pfister, "why have the religiously devout not discovered psychoanalysis, why did one have to wait for a totally Godless Jew?" (Letter October 9, 1928). Freud looked upon religion in general as a collective neurosis and looked forward to the time when mankind would outgrow it. Toward Zionism he was a shade more positive. In a letter to Professor Thierberger, dated April 25, 1926 Freud said, "Toward Zionism I have only sympathy, but I make no judgment on its chances of success and the possible dangers facing it." (Simon 1957)

In a letter to the B'nai B'rith, Freud commented on his attitude towards Judaism:

> ". . . before long there followed the realization that it was only to my Jewish nature that I owed the two qualities that have become indispensable to me throughout my difficult life. Because I was a Jew I found myself free of many prejudices which restrict others in the use of the intellect; as a Jew I was prepared to be in the opposition and to renounce agreement with the 'compact majority'."

> (Freud 1926, S.E. vol. 20 p. 274)

A year earlier, Freud expressed a similar sentiment:

> "Finally with all reserve, the question may be raised whether the personality of the present writer as a Jew who has never sought to disguise the fact that he is a Jew may not have had a share in provoking the antipathy of his environment to psychoanalysis. An argument of this kind is not often uttered aloud. But we have unfortunately grown so suspicious that we cannot avoid thinking that this factor may not have been quite without its effect. Nor is it perhaps entirely a matter of chance that the first advocate of psychoanalysis was a Jew. To profess belief in this new theory called for a certain degree of readiness to accept a situation of solitary opposition—a situation with which no one is more familiar than a Jew."
>
> (1925a, S.E. vol. 19 p. 222)

In the preface to the Hebrew Translation of *Totem and Taboo*, written in 1930, Freud said:

> "No reader of (the Hebrew version of) this book will find it easy to put himself in the emotional position of an author who is ignorant of the language of holy writ, who is completely estranged from the religion of his fathers—as well as from every other religion—and who cannot take a share in nationalist ideals, but who has yet never repudiated his people, who feels that he is in his essential nature a Jew and who has no desire to alter that nature. If the question were put to him: 'Since you have abandoned all these common characteristics of your countrymen, what is there left to you that is Jewish?' he would reply: 'A great deal, and probably its very essence.' He could not now express that essence clearly in words; but some day, no doubt, it will become accessible to the scientific mind."
>
> (Freud 1912/1913, S.E. 13 p. XV)

Freud is clearly referring here to an unconscious sense of belonging, perhaps based on identifications which themselves have become repressed. His is an original answer and it fits the man who was both a rationalist and the discoverer of the unconscious. We should note, however, that these affirmative statements of belonging to the Jewish group all date from a late period in Freud's life, when the major battles had been won, and he was already a man of world renown. The positive attitude discernable in these utterances was achieved by incorporating in the "personal myth" in the sense in which Kris (1956) used this term, the ability to stand alone and the use of the intellect as two peculiarly Jewish trends.

During the formative years of psychoanalysis Freud seems to have been primarily concerned lest his being a Jew become an obstacle to the spread of psychoanalysis. In a letter written on May 3, 1908, he urged Abraham to adopt a more tolerant attitude toward Jung, since, thanks to him, "psychoanalysis escaped the danger of becoming a Jewish National Affair." (Abraham and Freud, 1965, p. 34) In another letter, dated July 23, of the same year Freud wrote: "We as Jews, if we wish to join in, must develop a bit of masochism, be ready to suffer some wrong, otherwise there is no hitting it off. Rest assured that if my name were Oberhuber, in spite of everything my innovations would have met with far less resistance." (p. 46) In a different vein, on December 26 of that year, Freud shared with Abraham his observation that the analysis of patients in whom the therapist takes an "excessive personal interest" frequently fails. He then added: "Do not lose heart, our ancient Jewish toughness will prove itself in the end." Only a Jew was likely to discover psychoanalysis, but the spread of psychoanalysis was handicapped by the Jewishness of its founder. Lowenberg (1971) cites this passage as an example of Freud's ambivalence towards being a Jew. And Ellenberger (1970, p. 427), believes that Freud was prone to feel rejected because of his Jewishness. He often misjudged the situation, for example, when he felt that the travelling grant to Paris would be given to a non-Jew (Letters, 1960, p. 147). Merely to point out that Freud was ambivalent towards being a Jew, given the social and psychological environment in which he grew up, is of little interest. What matters is the creative use to which this ambivalence was put. While this ambivalence was never entirely overcome, Freud's attitude, as already indicated, grew increasingly positive. In this evolution the figure of Moses played a significant role. We can probe into Freud's unconscious attitude towards being a Jew by examining some of the dreams recorded in *The Interpretation of Dreams*.

In a recent article the historian, Carl E. Schorske (1973, p. 330), aptly described the dream book (Freud 1900) as follows:

"Its surface organization is governed by its function as scientific treatise, with each chapter and section systematically expounding an aspect of dreams and their interpretation. To this scientific structure Freud explicitly subordinated the personal content of the book, designating the dreams and memories that constitute it only as 'material by which I illustrated the rules of dream interpretation.' Yet, a closer look reveals a second, deep structure of the work which, running from one isolated dream of the author to the next, constitutes an incomplete but autonomous subplot of personal history. Imagine Saint Augustine weaving his *Confessions* into *The City of God*, or Rousseau integrating his *Confessions* as a subliminal plot into *The Origins of Inequality;* such is the procedure of Freud in *The Interpretation of Dreams.* In the visible structure of the scientific treatise he leads his readers upward, chapter by systematic chapter, to the more sophisticated reaches of psychological analysis. In the invisible personal narrative he takes us downward, dream by major dream, into the underground recesses of his own buried self."

One of the persistent day residues of Freud's dreams was his concern with academic advancement, that is, becoming a Professor. It is well known that under the Hapsburg Monarchy, academic advancement was made easier for Jews through conversion. The problem was particularly difficult for the "marginal Jews," that is, those without strong religious or national convictions. Jones describes how very much Freud hated the Jewish marriage ceremony and on one occasion briefly considered changing his "confession," but Breuer dissuaded him when he murmured: "Too complicated." (Jones, Vol. 1, p. 167)

A number of writers, particularly Velikovsky (1941), have attributed to Freud a persistent and overwhelming wish to become a convert. These writers evoked in Jones a rather vehement denial. (Vol. II, p. 17)

Velikovsky, for example, interpreted all Freud's dreams to contain the wish to convert. He could demonstrate this thesis by usurping the dreamer's right to free association. To take only one example in the "Dream of the Botanical Monograph" (Freud 1900, p. 1169) Velikovsky finds that 'herbarium' conceals the word 'Hebrew,' the genus crucifers refers to crucifix, and to turn over colored plates alludes to conversion (p. 492). It is obvious that a technique in which the interpreter rather than the dreamer dismantles words, is characteristic of dream interpreters in antiquity, a technique not open to psychoanalysis. On the other hand, Jones' statement, "that worldly success meant little to him (Freud) and it would never have occurred to him to sacrifice any principle for such a reason," oversimplifies a complex problem, when we deal not only with conscious but also with unconscious ideas that emerge in dreams and free associations in spite of much resistance. There is no evidence that Freud consciously ever entertained the idea of conversion for the sake of academic advancement, but it does appear in his dreams. After Freud learned that "denominational considerations" stood in the way of his promotion, he had the dream "My uncle with the yellow beard" (Freud 1900, S.E. vol. 4, p. 137). Association to the dream led to a childhood memory. Freud recalled political events that took place in Austria in 1867, when he was eleven years old.

> "Those were the days of the 'Bürger' Ministry. . . . There had even been some Jews among them. So henceforth every industrious Jewish schoolboy carried a Cabinet Minister's portfolio in his satchel. The events of that period no doubt had some bearing on the fact that up to a time shortly before I entered the University it had been my intention to study Law; it was only at the last moment that I changed my mind. A ministerial career is definitely barred to a medical man."

The cheerful hopes of 1867 are contrasted with the dreary present. Freud turned tables on the anti-Semitic ministers, identifying with the aggressor, mishandles eminent colleagues because they were Jews, and denying in the dream his worry that anti-Semitism would stand in the way of his promotion (Freud 1900, S.E. vol. 4, p. 193).

After this disclosure, Freud breaks off the narrative and in a new paragraph tells the reader that he had "a series of dreams which are based upon longing to visit Rome" (p. 193). If following a standard technique of dream interpretation, we disregard the fact that Freud started a new paragraph and allow the trends of thought to continue, we will be able to establish a connection between anti-

Semitism and the dreams that follow. In these dreams Rome is ever elusive. Freud sees Rome but it is shrouded in mist and yet Freud is surprised that the view of the city is so clear, or the train moves on before he can "so much as set foot in the city" (p. 194). Freud had developed an inhibition, called by Schorske (1973) a "Roman neurosis." Between 1895 and 1898, Freud travelled to Italy five times without reaching Rome. At times Freud came as close to Rome as Orvieto or Assisi without venturing into the Eternal City. Obliquely, Freud reports how he overcame the inhibition to visit the "mother of cities."

On one of the visits to Italy Freud was going to by-pass Rome when the following sentence came unbidden to his mind, "Which of the two it may be debated, walked up and down his study with the greater impatience after he had formed his plan of going to Rome—Winckelmann, the vice principal, or Hannibal, the commander in chief?" (Freud 1900, S.E. vol. 4 p. 196). Strachey notes that the original of the sentence has not been traced but the origin seems less significant than the possible dynamic meaning. Was Freud only contrasting a military man with a scholar and lover of Rome? I believe that Schorske (1973) came closer to deciphering the meaning of this enigmatic sentence.[3] Hannibal wanted to conquer Rome, Winckelmann, the noted art historian converted to Catholicism in order to make Rome his home. Winckelmann, according to Butler (1935), was the first of a series of Germans to have been struck with passion for Rome.[4] Unconsciously, Freud may well have been struggling with two attitudes toward Catholicism represented by Rome, to "conquer it," as he ultimately did in exposing religion as a collective neurosis, or to convert, with the chances of academic advancement that conversion offered in Austria. We can take it for granted that the prohibition to enter Rome symbolized the oedipal taboo. Of interest in the current context is how the Jewish theme is interwoven with the oedipal. The analysis of the Hannibal-Winckelmann conflict led Freud to a crucial childhood memory:

> "At that point I was brought up against the event in my youth whose power was still being shown in all these emotions and dreams.

I may have been ten or twelve years old, when my father began to take me with him on his walks and reveal to me in his talk his views about things in the world we live in. Thus it was, on one such occasion, that he told me a story to show me how much better things were now than they had been in his days. 'When I was a young man,' he said, 'I went for a walk one Saturday in the streets of your birthplace; I was well dressed, and had a new fur cap on my head. A Christian came up to me and with a single blow knocked off my cap into the mud and shouted: 'Jew! Get off the pavement!' 'And what did you do?' I asked. 'I went into the roadway and picked up my cap,' was his quiet reply. This struck me as unheroic conduct on the part of the big, strong man who was holding the little boy by the hand. I contrasted this situation with another which fitted my feelings better: the scene in which Hannibal's father, Hamilcar Barca, made his boy swear before the household altar to take vengeance on the Romans. Ever since that time Hannibal had had a place in my fantasies."[5]

(Freud 1900, S.E. vol. 4, p. 197)

Simon (1957) has observed that the 'fur cap' was probably the "streimal," the special hat worn by some groups of hasidim.

The memory is a critical one for it marks the point at which Freud became disillusioned with his father, Jacob. It should be recognized that within the framework of organized Jewish life the behavior of Freud's father was anything but undignified. A Jew was expected to be able to control his anger, not to be provoked; his feelings of inner dignity were sustained by a belief in his own spiritual superiority which a ruffian and "Goy" can in no way touch. But during Freud's childhood, Jewish community cohesion had already dissolved so that the twelve-year-old Freud came to see his father's behavior not as exemplary, but as cowardly.

The identification with Hannibal is of interest, it seems to have lasted until Freud heard Goethe's essay *On Nature*, and abandoned the wish to become a Minister in favor of a medical vocation. Today, we would be inclined to see a boy's admiration for a historical figure as a precursor to the establishment of an ego ideal. In Freud's case, the "Hannibal-Minister" ideal on the one hand represented the fulfillment of Jacob Freud's ideals. On the other, it was built upon a disappointment in his father. It is possible that this contradictory origin of the precursor to an ego ideal was a predisposing factor in Freud's future idealizations and subsequent disappointments that took place at regular intervals in his relationships with Breuer, Fliess and Jung. We note that Freud was the same age at the time of the episode of the Bürger ministry and when he was told of the fur cap incident.

Another Rome dream that deals with Freud's ambivalent attitude toward being a Jew is the dream "My Son the Myops" (Freud 1900 S.E. vol. 5 p. 441; see also Lowenberg 1971). Freud dreamt: "On account of certain events which had occurred in the City of Rome, it had become necessary to remove the children to safety." The day residue to the dream was Theodor Herzl's play, "The New Ghetto," which as Freud says, deals with the "Jewish problem, concern about the future of one's children, to whom one cannot give a country of their own, concern about educating them in such a way that they can move freely across frontiers." (S.E. vol. 5 p. 442) Simon (1957) and Lowenberg (1971) attach significance to the fact that Freud omitted Herzl's name as the author of the play. Further associations lead to King Herod and the *Massacre of the Innocents*, in Bethlehem. But his dream revises St. Matthew, so that the anxiety is averted, the massacre does not take place and the children are removed to safety. The lines, "By the waters of Babylon we sat down and wept," occur to Freud, his associations go to Siena and Rome—cities of many fountains. However, the line is taken from Psalm 137, which in the King James' translation reads:

> "By the rivers of Babylon there we sat down, yea, we wept, when we remembered Zion."

The Psalm is one of the strongest psalms of mourning over the destruction of the Temple, but Freud's associations stop short of Zion, and go to Rome.

The dream is of further interest because a Hebrew word "Auf gezeres," and "Auf ungezeres," replaces the German "Auf Wiedersehn" (S.E. 4:442). Freud writes that he consulted a philologist to learn that the word means, "imposed suffering or doom." This is not entirely accurate, the Hebrew word "gezerot" is specifically used to denote anti-Jewish laws. That Freud unconsciously knew the correct meaning of "gezerot" can be deduced from the manifest content of the dream. The removal of the children from Rome alludes to such a law only it refers to the New and not the Old Testament. The neologism "Auf Ungezeres" then could mean that Freud would be exempt from the anti-Jewish laws. What Freud called slang, was the Jewish Viennese dialect in which the word 'gezeres' was used to connote fuss. For example, do not make 'gezeres' out of it, meaning do not exaggerate or make a fuss. In this sense, the word was recalled by Freud (p. 443). The associations lead on to leavened and unleavened bread. Freud here makes a slip when he calls Passover Easter. The fact that a Hebrew word intrudes into a dream about Rome I would interpret as additional evidence that the dreamwork was not entirely successful in bringing about a displacement from the original Promised Land (Israel), to the adopted Promised Land (Rome).

In the *Edition* of 1900, Freud is still rationalizing his inability to visit Rome because of climatic considerations. In 1909, he adds:

> "I discovered long since that it only needs a little courage to fulfill wishes which till then have been regarded as unattainable;

Finally in 1925, the triumphant sentence is added: ". . . and thereafter became a constant pilgrim to Rome." (p. 194)

Schur (1972, pp. 103 and 466) observed, that the metaphor of the Promised Land is one of Freud's favorites. It appears frequently in the correspondence with Fliess. What the Promised Land is, changes from time to time. At times, it is the solution of the riddle of the dream. At other times, it is the key to the cause of the neurosis. Finally, at the end of his life Freud experienced the publication of *Moses and Monotheism*, as the Promised Land. To my knowledge, the first conscious identification with Moses appears in a letter to Jung, dated February 8, 1908. There Freud compares Jung to Joshua, who is destined to enter the Promised Land, while he, like Moses, will only view it from afar.

Up to the encounter with Michelangelo's statue of Moses (Freud, 1914), the identification with Moses can only be inferred from the symptoms of Freud's "Rome neurosis" and from the prominence of the metaphor of the promised but forbidden land.

Freud visited the Moses statue upon his first visit to Rome in 1901, that is after he successfully analyzed his "Rome neurosis." He wrote to his wife: "I have come to understand the meaning of the statue by contemplating Michelangelo's intention." (Jones, Vol. II, p. 96)

Although Freud in the study of Moses reviewed the views of some of his predecessors, recent work by art historians has changed our perspective on the Moses statue, and therefore requires some further comments. Vasari, Michelangelo's contemporary described the statue as "unequalled by any modern or ancient work. . . . God has permitted his body to be prepared for the resurrection before the others by the hand of Michelangelo. The Jews still go every Saturday in groups to visit and admire it as divine." (Hind's translation, Everyman's Library, Vol. 4, p. 121) Condivi, who was also Michelangelo's contemporary described the statue as follows:

> ". . . the marvelous statue of Moses, leader and captain of the Jews. He is seated in the attitude of one wise and thoughtful, holding under his right arm the tables of the law, and supporting his chin with his left hand, like a man tired and full of cares. . . . His face is full of vitality and spirit apt to arouse both love and terror."
>
> (Quoted in Pope-Hennesy, 1970 p. 322)

DeTolnay (1970, p. 103) reviewing the various interpretations given to the Moses statue concluded:

> "The question of whether Michelangelo's intention was to give a timeless character image of the lawgiver, or whether he wanted to represent his hero in a significant historical moment in his life was the chief problem of interpretation concerning the statue."

Panofsky (1939) believes that in the Moses, Michelangelo translated into stone the vision of the Florentine Neoplatonists, who believed that Moses and St. Paul were both struck by the splendor of divine light and saw God with an inner eye. Thus, in Panofsky's interpretation, Moses showed neither anger nor surprise but supernatural excitement (p. 193). Janson (1968), has amassed historical evidence in support of the interpretation that the gesture of grasping of the beard should be interpreted along similar lines as, "awe in the presence of the divine." To him, the Moses statue connotes "action in repose." By contrast to these contemporary art historians, the 19th Century observers, probably under the influence of Lessing's Essay on the Laocoon, assumed that Michelangelo portrayed Moses in a moment before he will rise and break the Tablets. Freud (1914), also felt that Michelangelo had a specific moment in mind, but interpreted it following the lead of W. W. Lloyd (1863). Freud said:

> ". . . the Moses we have reconstructed will neither leap up nor cast the Tablets from him. What we see before us is not the inception of a violent action but the remains of a movement that has already taken place. In his first transport of fury, Moses desired to act, to spring up and take vengeance and forget the Tables; but he has overcome the temptation, and he will remain seated and still, in his frozen wrath and in his pain mingled with contempt. Nor will he throw away the Tables so that they will break on the stones, for it is on their special account that he has controlled his anger; it was to preserve them that he kept his passion in check. . . . He remembered his mission and for its sake renounced an indulgence of his feelings." (Freud 1914, S.E. vol. 13, 229–230)

Freud was well aware that his interpretation did not fit the Biblical text where Moses in fact broke the Tablets. His defense is most interesting:

> "Michelangelo has placed a different Moses on the tomb of the Pope, one superior to the historical or traditional Moses. He has modified the theme of the broken Tables; he does not let Moses break them in his wrath, but makes him be influenced by the danger that they will be broken and makes him calm that wrath, or at any rate prevent it from becoming an act. In this way he has added something new and more than human to the figure of Moses; so that the giant frame with its tremendous physical power becomes only a concrete expression of the highest mental achievement that is possible in man, that of struggling successfully against an inward passion for the sake of a cause to which he has devoted himself." (Freud 1914, S.E. vol. 13, p. 233)

Since there is no reason to assume that Michelangelo intended such a far-reaching revision of the Biblical text, I must assume that it was Freud who wished both to elevate Moses and to obliterate his outstanding human characteristics, namely the wrath of Moses.[6]

Professor Meyer Schapiro has kindly drawn my attention to the influence of Goethe's Laocoon on Freud's Moses essay. In the Laocoon, Goethe postulates that great works of plastic art fulfill a civilising function in that they tame and moderate the human passions for the onlooker. The great artists select a moment in which one emotion is superseding another and both are still in evidence. Freud's identification with Goethe is well known. Eissler has pointed out that both Goethe and Freud identified themselves with Joseph, each was the first born male child to a young mother and an aging father and both found themselves in the unusual position of being closer in age to the mother than their respective father (Eissler, 1963).

Even though Freud's interpretation of the Moses statue reads like an example of Goethe's Laocoon, I do not believe that this borrowing was conscious to Freud. Rather I assume that they emerged from repression due to the special circumstances in Freud's life at the time, to which I will return. Freud quoted Sauerland as calling the statue "Moses with the Head of Pan" (Freud, 1914, S.E. vol. 13, p. 213) but otherwise ignored the horns of the statue. In the Biblical text (Exodus 32:19) Moses is not yet "horned" when he breaks the tablets; "Moses' anger waxed hot, and he cast the tablets out of his hands, and broke them beneath the mount." Moses became "horned" only after the second descent from Sinai, the so-called renewal of the Law (Exodus 34:30): "Aaron and all the children of Israel saw Moses; behold, the skin of his face shone; and they were afraid to come nigh him." Unfortunately for Freud's interpretation, this mark of distinction was bestowed on Moses only after the breaking of the tablets.

The horns of Moses have their origin in the Hebrew word "Karan" derived from the Hebrew Keren, meaning either horn or ray. It is possible the two words are related since the rays of the sun could have been seen as the horns of the sun. It is interesting to note that the famous Hebrew medieval intepreter of the Bible, Rashi, interpreted the passage to mean "the light radiates and stands out like a horn."

When St. Jerome translated the Bible into Latin in the Fourth Century, he chose to translate Karan as cornuta (horned) although the Septuagint translated Karan as glorified (Mellinkoff 1970, p. 77). Early translators of the Anglo-Saxon Bible followed St. Jerome and translated Karan as "gehyrned." The horned Moses became the Moses whose face shone in the English Bible only after 1560.

Of great interest in this context is Mellinkoff's observation that the Egyptian Gods, Isis and Ra, as well as the Mesopotamian Shamash, are represented with horns as well as with a solar disc. Rosenfeld (1951), offered a psychoanalytic interpretation for this change from the horned (totem) Moses to the Moses with the shining face. The shining Moses is in her interpretation "the internalized father image, the fantasy creation of a guilty people, the image of their superego." (p. 87)

Freud's interpretation of Michelangelo's statue left a mark on art historians. DeTolnay (1970, pp. 39–40) described the statue as follows:

> "The Moses is the figure of a seated colossus trembling with indignation: a cataclysm made man. The overriding force of passion unleashes here elemental powers. The swell of the enormous beard, the strength of the rugged knee which breaks through the flowing cloak as through boiling lava, are only emanations of an internal agitation set up by anger and indignation. He rears his head sharply, and looks towards his left, but his body instinctively moves to the other side while his hands touch the waves of the beard. The outburst of anger has been subdued. . . . Thus Michelangelo simultaneously incarnates in this figure the birth of passion, its climax, and its ebbing away."

The interpretation that "the anger has been subdued," or that the statue shows not only, "the birth of passion, the climax," but also "its ebbing away," reflects Freud's influence.

Freud's hesitation in publishing the essay and its anonymous publication may attest to the fact that he was dimly aware that in this case he may have projected his own ideas on Michelangelo. One is left with the question of why he wrote the essay at all. Hanns Sachs, (1941) suggested that by shifting the identification from Hannibal to Moses, and one might add, to a Moses figure that

Freud himself created, Freud symbolically overcame the temptation to fight his backsliding disciple and to waste his energies in a futile battle. For 1914 was the year when Jung, Freud's beloved heir and "Crown Prince," finally broke with psychoanalysis and founded his own "heretical" school. This disappointment was severe and at this crucial moment, Freud may have created the wrath-conquering Moses as a new ego ideal to help him overcome the pain and to maintain sublimation.

Dr. Ostow in the discussion of this paper before the New York psychoanalytic society offered a deeper interpretation. The Moses statue appeared angry to Freud because he had broken the "Rome Taboo." If Ostow is right, we may go a step further and say that the wrath-conquering Moses connotes an intrasystemic change within Freud's own superego, a less destructive father figure is created of Freud. The new Moses who is not violent is a shade closer to Jacob Freud who also conquered his wrath in the fur cap incident. When this paper was translated into Italian, Freud wrote to Eduardo Weiss, "My feeling for this piece of work is like that towards a loved child." (Jones, Vol. II, p. 367) If this interpretation is correct, then the love for the essay itself would suggest that it did in fact accomplish the intrapsychic purpose for which it was written.

The year Freud visited the Moses statue daily, while he was in Rome, also saw the publication of *Totem and Taboo* (1912/1913). Freud assumed there that civilization began with the killing and eating of the primeval father which was followed by the establishment of the incest taboo and the totem feast. The first gods, therefore, were totem animals, but increasingly they attained human form. The Egyptian gods were still theriomorphic, but the Olympians anthropomorphic. What they were in totemistic times, had been relegated to an animal holy to them, or their steady companion. The last is also typical of Indian mythology. Horns and wings are the last animal organs to disappear. Among Mesopotamian gods, Marduk is the only God still portrayed with horns. (Farnell, 1911, p. 52)

The gods of Greek mythology, like the sons of the primeval father, have only limited power. They must respect the prerogative of their fellow gods. This "balance of power," in the Olympus is reflected in the Iliad and the Odyssey. Mythology celebrates the original slaying of the primeval father in the many myths in which the hero slays the monster. It also celebrates the Oedipal victory in the portrayal of youthful gods, like Attis and Adonis, who commit incest with their mother, usually seen as Mother Earth, and are in turn torn asunder by a wild animal before the year is over. This wild animal represents the primeval father. To this general and repetitive myth, Christianity offered a new variation. Christ, too, is a Son God, but he neither kills the father, nor commits incest. He sacrifices his own life to redeem the brothers from "original sin." To Freud, original sin meant the killing of the primeval father. There is no reference to Moses or to the religion he founded in *Totem and Taboo.*

In 1919, Theodore Reik published his book on *Ritual.* It appeared with a preface by Freud, and won Reik the prize for Applied Psychoanalysis. Particularly relevant for our purposes is the last chapter of his study of the Shofar (Ram's Horn) entitled, "The Moses of Michelangelo and the Events on Sinai." Since Freud had not at the publication of that essay acknowledged his authorship of the essay on Michelangelo's Moses, he is referred to in Reik's work as, "the gifted author of the study of the Moses by Michelangelo." (p. 354)

The horns of the Moses statue which play no role in Freud's essay on the Michelangelo Moses, are the point of departure for Reik. Quoting the same sources that Freud does, Reik stresses the fact that the statue evokes a mixture of horror and admiration, that it both attracts as well as repels. Reik cites many observers that have been impressed by the bovine nature of Moses' head. Reik does not believe that the horns of Moses are a mere error in the vulgate translation, but rather that the translators grasped intuitively the totemistic nature of these events.

Although disguised, the events on Mount Sinai recapitulate the kernel of the Mediterranean myth of the struggle of the hero against the monster. The Israelites originally worshipped a bull or a ram. Moses destroyed the totem animal, burned it, and gave the remains to the Israelites to drink, a reenactment of the totem feast.

In Reik's interpretation, Moses ascends Sinai not to receive the Ten Commandments, but to fight Jahweh, the Bull God; he returns horned, and victorious. This Bull God was worshipped through a stone holy to him. The destruction of the Tablets alludes to the destruction of the holy stone. When Moses forbade the worship of graven images, it was a parricidal act. In a secondary revision of these historical events victory returned to the father. To commemorate the revision of these facts, the bull was changed into a calf. The calf like the Christian appellation, Lamb of God, connotes a son. The name, Moses, derived from the Egyptian, means child. The rebellion of the son, Moses, failed, and Moses was transformed into the mediator between God and his people who now had to be satisfied with being the Almighty God's chosen children. But the sense of guilt over the unsuccessful rebellion remained, only to be resumed once more in the struggle between God and Christ; but unlike Judaism, Christianity became a successful Son religion.

Historically speaking, Reik's study forms a bridge linking *Totem and Taboo* with *Moses and Monotheism*. I will not here attempt to recapitulate the content of this book, but wish to draw attention to its unique methodology. *Moses and Monotheism* consists of a small number of interwoven historical and psychological hypotheses. The historical hypotheses are that Moses was an Egyptian and a follower of the monotheistic Pharaoh Ikhnaton. It was the latter's monotheism that Moses bequeathed to the Hebrews. This hypothesis was not as bold as one has generally assumed since Breasted (1934) had reported a few years earlier that the morality that we associate with the Old Testament has come down to us through the Hebrews, but was not created by them. According to Breasted, conscience originated three thousand years earlier in Egypt. One can well imagine that the idea that traced the origin of human conscience back to 4,000 B.C., appealed to Freud, for here was a parallel on a grand scale to his own discovery of the significance of the distant past.

The second hypothesis, Freud derived from the work of Sellin (1922), who thought he discovered in the Old Testament traces that the Hebrews killed Moses. The third historical hypothesis original to Freud, postulated the existence of two Moseses: one, a follower of the monotheistic Ikhnaton; the other a priest of the volcano god, Jahweh, who was described as: "a coarse, narrow-minded local God, violent and bloodthirsty." A compromise between the monotheism of the Egyptian Moses and the Henotheism of Jahweh was achieved before the conquest of Canaan. All that is noble, ethical and universal was assigned by Freud to the Egyptian Moses; all that was trivial, narrow, and violent to Jahweh.

The psychological hypotheses stated that the murder was repressed, but nevertheless left an abiding sense of guilt. Freud conjectured that it was the remorse for the murder of Moses that provided the stimulus for the wishful fantasy of the Messiah. (p. 89) Furthermore, this sense of guilt was passed on from one generation to the other, and ultimately erupted in the theology of St. Paul. Upon these guilt feelings, St. Paul founded the religion of the Son who died for the atonement of the sins of mankind. In Christian theology the murdered one is also the savior, whereas Judaism separated the dean of the prophets from the expected Messiah. Christianity imposed a more severe instinctual renunciation on the pagan world. The Jews who refused the happy tidings of salvation became the scapegoats. Hence, the paradoxical position of Christianity toward Jews. The Death of Christ was a necessary atonement for the sins of all mankind. But the Jews are nevertheless responsible for this death. Christianity, as a consistent theology cannot blame the Jews, but the gospels and generations of Christians did. Theological anti-semitism is a logical absurdity, but psychologically well founded.

Finally, the boldest of all Freud's hypotheses states that the murder of Moses represents a unique event in world history: the return of the repressed. For behind the killing of Moses looms the much earlier killing of the primeval father. Unlike Reik, Freud did not assume that the events on Sinai refer back to primeval times, but represent a return of the repressed in a highly civilized group. Sellin, with whom this hypothesis originated only thought that Moses died in a religious war between the followers of Jahweh and the followers of the Baal of Peor, another local divinity, an event of no consequence in world history. Freud deprived the Hebrews of their discovery of monotheism but restored them psychologically to a central position: for among them alone the repressed returned with fateful results for the spiritual history of mankind. The first hypothesis that Moses was an Egyptian had no historical consequence, beyond the wounding of the narcissism of some Jews. However, the murder of Moses, according to Freud, gave Jewish history a dynamic quality that determined its fate. What to Reik was only an example of the ideas expressed in *Totem and Taboo*, now received a dynamic elaboration. The primeval trauma does not belong to the past, it is still exerting its influence on contemporary events.

In the years preceding the publication of *Moses and Monotheism*, Biblical scholars were engaged in demonstrating that Hebraic monotheism emerged during the Babylonian exile (see bibliography to Kaufmann, 1970). The religion of the earlier Hebrews is characterized by them as Henotheism or Monolatry. In this more primitive religious view the tribe has one God, but the God's jurisdiction is limited to the territory of the tribe. Deutero-Isaiah is generally given credit for the transformation of Henotheism into Monotheism (see Meek, 1936, and for an excellent summary of the role of Deutero-Isaiah see Kaufmann, 1970). Freud was aware of the distinction between Henotheism and Monotheism (see p. 128) but instead of the usual evolutionary point of view, he emphasized the original trauma and a latency period in Jewish history for the eight hundred years that separate Moses from Deutero-Isaiah.

In a recent publication, Shengold (1972) has drawn attention to what he believes to be a parapraxis of Freud—the omission to mention Abraham's 1912 study of *Amenhotep IV*, a study that first aroused Freud's interest in Egyptian monotheism. He traced the parapraxis back to the rivalry between Abraham and Jung, and further back to Fliess. However, Freud omitted not only Abraham's contribution, but also Reik's. And what is psychologically more interesting, he omitted any reference to his own essay on the Michelangelo statue. It is possible that Freud did not wish to be reminded that he had dealt with Moses a quarter of a century earlier, and yet both works on Moses have in common the attempt to idealize and purify the dean of the Hebrew prophets. In 1914, he attributed this idealization to Michelangelo. In 1939, he achieved the same aim by creating a dichotomy between two Moses. It would be fascinating to know what role Freud played in the development of Reik's ideas. We know from another publication of Reik's (1940) that Freud allowed him, in one case, to publish a contribution of Freud's under his own name. We also know that the two were in close personal contract. It is possible that in this case too, Freud allowed Reik to publish some of his budding ideas under Reik's own name. At any rate, it is unthinkable that Reik would have published an interpretation at odds with Freud's own. We may assume therefore that before the twenties Freud too saw Moses as a son figure. In *Moses and Monotheism* he is clearly a father figure and denying him access to the Promised Land ceased to have a dynamic meaning. Freud now interpreted the same legend as a denial that Moses was killed in the desert.

Blum (1956) has drawn attention to an essay by Friedrich Schiller entitled *The Mission of Moses* written in 1789. In that essay Schiller postulated that Moses as the foster child of an Egyptian princess had access to the mystery religions of Egypt, in which the initiated were introduced to monotheistic beliefs. Moses transformed the religion of the Egyptian mysteries into the national religion of the Hebrews. To conceal this alien element he presented the new religion as if it were that of their patriarchs, and added the doctrine of the chosen people as a further inducement. The dilution of a universal monotheism by tribal concessions was the price Moses had to pay to make monotheism acceptable. Schiller's hypothesis bears more than an accidental similarity to Freud's ideas. Blum pointed out that it is unlikely that Freud did not know of this essay during his adolescence; therefore the germ of the ideas contained in Freud's last book may have had their origin much earlier than Freud remembered.

Freud did not consider the possible impact of *Moses and Monotheism* on subsequent Jewish history, beyond the wounding of Jewish pride, by making Moses an Egyptian. However, since he believed that the Jews were held together by a trauma that took place at the very beginning of their history, it seems to me at least possible that Freud felt that making that trauma conscious would loosen the cohesive power that held this group together. At the end of the book, Freud says:

> "A special enquiry would be called for to discover why it has been impossible for the Jews to join in this forward step which was implied, in spite of all its distortions, by the admission of having murdered God."

(S.E. Vol. 12, p. 136)

To call Christianity a forward step over Judaism, introduces a value judgment, not supported by historical or clinical evidence. Freud assumes that to acknowledge guilt, however indirectly, is superior to the repression of the parricidal act. Even in an individual analysis this need not be true. Ostow, in the discussion of this paper, has pointed out that to admit guilt is consistent with the psychodynamics of depression and not with greater health. I am led, therefore, to believe that the old wish to convert that I assumed operated in some of the dreams dreamt forty years before the publication of the book, broke through, to be sure in a much larger historical context, once more at the end of Freud's life. My surmise is at variance with Eissler's (1965) view who believes that *Moses and Monotheism* by making conscious a trauma that was repressed for twenty-five hundred years may have enabled the Jews to master it. The book may thus have been instrumental in bringing about the creation of the State of Israel. Thus, Eissler believes the Jews may be the first to have achieved mastery of their own destiny through insight. (p. 231)

For a generation the basic thesis of *Moses and Monotheism* was rejected by Biblical Jewish scholars. However, there are signs that the book may receive a new evaluation. The evolutionary point of view is becoming less fashionable and a new search for a paradigm for psycho-history may account for a beginning change in the evaluation of the book. (See Lifton and Olson, 1974) Two psychoanalytic studies, one by Eissler, 1965, and the other by Waelder, 1971, demonstrate the productive impetus of *Moses and Monotheism*. Eissler has pointed out how the trauma inflicted on Japan by the humiliation suffered from Commodore Perry, influenced recent Japanese history. Waelder explained recent

American history as a result of the success of the American revolution:

> "Just as childhood experiences have a great impact on the organism and make a disproportionate contribution to character, psychopathology, and destiny, so do experiences in the childhood of a nation, its formative period, lastingly and indelibly influence national character and outlook. . . . The cause of this preeminent influence can be easily surmised; because it is the period in which the group is formed and stabilized it is also a time of success in terms of the group values. The behavior and the methods of the time have thus 'worked' and become deeply ingrained in the people's memory as the methods of choice, the obvious thing to do." (pp. 24–35)

If Eissler and Waelder are both right, trauma as well as success in a nation's history may be influential in creating a "repetition compulsion" in a nation's history.

It is not the aim of this presentation to pass judgment on the validity of Freud's historical construction. What interests us here are the inner motives that led a man of eighty, gravely ill, on the threshold of death, to harness his energy to write a book which breaks the continuity of Freud's last books, books that led to psychoanalytic ego psychology, to an earlier era when the repressed alone was the focus of interest.

Earlier in this essay I have quoted Schorske's observation that the surface organization of the *Interpretation of Dreams* is that of a scientific treatise, while below the surface runs a sub-plot of personal history. If my reconstruction is correct then the same sub-plot can be traced also in the Moses of Michelangelo through to *Moses and Monotheism*. It is awe-inspiring to see Freud at the end of his life once more struggling with the same inner forces while he is creating a new model for the study of history. What I have said so far can also be confirmed in other writings of Freud in the same period.

In 1925 Freud published *An Autobiographical Study*, an essay in which he recapitulates in a more concise way the development of the basic concepts of psychoanalysis. The term, "Autobiography" in the title, as Strachey has pointed out, is misleading. Freud's task was to present the development of psychoanalysis, not his own personal history. The following is not congruent with the rest of the "biography". "My parents were Jews, and I have remained a Jew myself." (p. 7) The German reads: "Auch ich bin Jude geblieben," which, more precisely, would be translated, "I, too, remained a Jew." Freud has taught us to pay attention to nuances and the word "remained" in this context may connote resignation, (in German even more than in English) and I believe confirms the unconscious conflicts of which I have spoken. In addition two further sentences also seemingly unrelated to the purposes for which the Autobiography was written, were inserted in 1935, possibly under the pressure of ideas that Freud was working through in the Moses. Stated here in the two sentences below, we find the ideas that I believe were interwoven in *The Interpretation of Dreams*; Freud's political ambition and the ambivalent identification with Moses:

> "My deep engrossment in the Bible story (almost as soon as I had learnt the art of reading) had, as I recognized much later, an enduring effect upon the direction of my interest. Under the powerful influence of a school friendship with a boy rather my senior who grew up to be a well known politician, I developed a wish to study law like him and to engage in social activities."
>
> (Freud 1925, S.E. vol. 20, p. 8)

At the end of his life, perhaps also under the pressure of National Socialism and the rising anti-semitism Freud once more returned to his great discovery, the Oedipus Complex, and its role in World History. At the same time he returned to the Bible, the first book he read that impressed him so much, to deal with the imposing figure of Moses. At last, Freud could bring to bear the full power of his speculative genius which brought together psychoanalysis, his love of archeology and ancient history, and for the first time, Jewish history.

The Midrash, somewhere contains a story in which the Angel of Death has come to take the soul of Moses. But Moses commands the Angel of Death to wait outside the tent, until he is finished writing the Pentateuch. One can imagine Freud too holding the Angel of Death at bay, until he completed *Moses and Monotheism*.

REFERENCES

Aron, W.: (1956/1957) Notes on Sigmund Freud's Ancestry and Jewish Contacts. Yivo, *Annual of Jewish Social Studies*, 2: 286-295.

Abraham, H. C. and Freud, E. L.: (1965) A Psychoanalytic Dialogue. The letters of S. Freud and K. Abraham. Basic Books, N.Y.

Abraham, K.: (1912) Amenhotep IV, Psychoanalytic Contribution Toward Understanding of His Personality and the Monotheistic Cult of Aton. In: *Clinical Papers and Essays on Psychoanalysis*, Hogarth Press, London 1955 pp. 262-290.

Bakan, D.: (1958) Sigmund Freud and the Jewish Mystical Tradition. Van Nostrand Company, Princeton, New Jersey.

Blum, E.: (1956) Uber Sigmund Freuds: Der Mann Moses und die Monotheistische Religion. Psyche, 10: 367-390 Klett Verlag, Stuttgart.

Breasted, J. H.: (1934) The Dawn of Conscience. London.

Butler, E. M.: (1935) The Tyranny of Greece over Germany. Cambridge University Press.

De Tolnay, C.: (1970) Michelangelo, Volume 4, The Tomb of Julius II, Princeton University Press.

Ellenberger, H. F.: (1970) The Discovery of the Unconscious, Allen Lane. The Penguin Press, London.

Eissler, K. R.: (1965) Goethe, a Psychoanalytic Study 2 Vol., Wayne State University Press, Detroit.

Eissler, K. R.: (1965) Medical Orthodoxy and the Future of Psychoanalysis.

Farnell, L. R.: (1911) Greece and Babylon, T & T Clark, Edinburgh.

Freud, E. L. (1960) editor, Letters of Sigmund Freud. Basic Books, N.Y.

Freud, S.: S. E. Vol. 1, 4, 5, 8, 13, 19, 20, 21, 23 publ. Hogarth Press and the Institute of Psychoanalysis London.

Freud, S.: (1954) The Origins of Psycho-Analysis, London: Imago Publishing Company New York: Basic Books, Inc.

Freud, S. and Pfister, O.: (1963) Briefe 1909-1939. S. Fischer, Publ.

Freud, S. and Jung, C. G.: (1974) The Freud/Jung Letters. Bollingen Series No. 94, Princeton University Press.

Goethe, J. W.: Über Laokoon, Jubileums Ausgabe, Vol. 33, P. 124-137.

Janson, H. W.: (1968) The Right Arm of Michelangelo's "Moses", In: Festschrift Ulrich Middeldorf. Walter de Gruyter, Berlin.

Jones, E.: (1953/55/57) Sigmund Freud: Life and Work, Volume I-III. New York: Basic Books, Inc.

Kaufmann, Y.: (1970) The Babylonian Captivity and Deutero-Isaiah. Union of American Hebrew Congregations, New York.

Kris, E.: (1956) The Personal Myth. *J. A.M. Psychoanal. Ass.* 4: 653–681.

Lifton, R. J. and Olson E. eds: (1974) *Explorations in Psychiatry*. Simon & Schuster, New York.

Lowenberg, P.: (1971) A Hidden Zionist Theme in Freud's "My Son, the Myops . . . Dream." *J. History of Ideas*, 31: 129–131 Sigmund Freud As a Jew: A Study in Ambivalence and Courage. *J. History Behav. Sci.*, 7: 363–369.

Lloyd, W. W.: (1863) The Moses of Michelangelo. London.

Mellinkoff, R.: (1970) The Horned Moses in Medieval Art and Thought. University of California Press.

Meek, T. J.: (1963) Hebrew Origins. Harper, New York.

Panofsky, E.: (1939) Neoplatonic Movement and Michelangelo, In: Studies in Iconology Harper Torch Books, New York 1962.

Pope-Hennessy: (1970) Italian High Renaissance and Baroque Sculpture. Phaidon Press Ltd., London.

Reik, T.: (1919) The Shophar (Ram's Horn), In: Ritual Psychoanalytic Studies Preface by Sigmund Freud, English Translation Farrar Straus, New York 1946.

Reik, T.: (1940) An Unknown Lecture of Freud's. *American Imago*, vol. 1, pp. 4–23.

Rosenfeld, E. M.: (1951) The Pan Headed Moses—A parallel. *Int. J. Psychoanal.* 32: 83–93.

Sachs, H.: (1942) The Man Moses and the Man Freud, In: The Creative Unconscious, Sci-Art Publishing Boston, Massachusetts pp. 132–134.

Schiller, F.: (1789) Die Sendung Moses. Ausgewahlte Werke Bd. 5 W. Kohlhammer Verlag Stuttgart 1955.

Schorske, C. E.: (1973) Politics and Parricide in Freud's Interpretation of Dreams. *Amer. Historical Rev.* 78: 328–347

Schur, M.: (1972) Freud, Living and Dying. International Universities Press, New York.

Sellin, E.: (1922) Mose und seine Bedeutung fur die israelitisch-judische Religionsgeschichte. Leipzig.

Shengold, L.: (1972) A Parapraxis of Freud's in Relation to Karl Abraham. *Amer. Imago*, 29: 123–159.

Simon, E.: (1957) Sigmund Freud, The Jew. *The Leo Baeck Institute Year Book*, No. 2, London.

Szondi, L.: (1973) Moses Antwort auf Kain. Bern: Huber.

Velikovsky, E.: (1941) The Dreams Freud Dreamt. *Psychoanal. Rev.* 30: 487–511.

Waelder, R.: (1971) Psychoanalysis and History: Application of Psychoanalysis to Historiography, In: The Psychoanalytic Interpretation of History Editor: B. B. Wolman, Basic Books, Inc.

NOTES

[1]My conclusions are diametrically opposed to those of Bakan (1958) who attempted to derive psychoanalysis from the Jewish mystical tradition.

[2]The word "was" is a mistranslation of the German "sei." The passage should read "what I now am."

[3]There is no proof that Freud knew that Winckelmann was a convert to Catholicism but Schorske (1973 p. 338) points out that Carl Justis' biography "Winckelmann und Seine Zeitgenossen" appeared when Fraud was still in the Gymnasium. A second edition appeared in 1898. Goethe had also written an essay on Winckelmann in which the conversion was mentioned.

[4]Winckelmann, the first to describe Greek art as "noble simplicity and serene greatness," avoided the Acropolis, in a way reminiscent of Freud's "Rome neurosis," but unlike Freud he never mastered or analyzed this anxiety. (Butler, 1935).

[5]In 1883, on a train trip to Leipzig, Freud himself was called "a dirty Jew," by other passengers, but unlike his father he challenged them to a fist fight. (*Letters of Sigmund Freud*, p. 78).

[6]In a recent work, Szondi (1973) derived the fate of Moses the law giver from his overwhelming guilt for having killed the Egyptian overseer in his wrath.

DISCUSSION OF MARTIN S. BERGMANN'S PAPER
by Mortimer Ostow

Dr. Bergmann reviews some of the indications of Freud's ambivalence to Judaism. On the positive side there is a defiant openness about being Jewish, including activity in the local B'nai Brith, and there is a late sympathy with Zionism.

On the negative side we find the following. There is a studied hostility rather than indifference to any practice of the Jewish religion. In a letter to Martha Bernays in July 1882—Letter #7 (Freud, E. L., editor, *Letters of Sigmund Freud* [Basic Books, New York, 1916])—Freud attempts to deal with this ambivalence as follows. "And as for us, this is what I believe: even if the form wherein the old Jews were happy no longer offers us any shelter, something of the core, of the essence of this meaningful and life-affirming Judaism will not be absent from our home." Nevertheless, judging from Jones and from Martin Freud's description of his father, there is no indication that this promise was fulfilled. Second, there was a preference, in early life at least, for non-Jewish heroes over Jewish ones, e.g., Hannibal and Alexander. Third, there was a preference for non-Jewish classical writings over Jewish ones. Fourth, there was the resentment that his being Jewish encouraged hostility to psychoanalysis. Fifth, we know that he briefly considered the possibility of conversion to Christianity but was discouraged by Breuer. Sixth, pressing Martha to give up religious practices must be considered at least mischievous; but considering conversion to escape the Jewish religious wedding must be considered frankly hostile. Seventh, he was preoccupied with Rome and Athens, symbolic enemies of the Jews, political in the first instance and philosophical in the second, rather than with localities associated positively with Jewish tradition. Eighth, calling Christianity a "forward step" betrays a discontent with being Jewish. In fact, it suggests an identification with the enemy.

Herman Nunberg has told me that Freud was intensely hostile to religion in his early years, but that in later years he mellowed considerably.

Dr. Bergmann brings us some information dealing with Freud's difficulty in controlling his anger.

He quotes a letter to Martha in which Freud makes the statement that Breuer had discovered, "What an infinitely bold and fearless person I concealed behind my mask of shyness." Then he says, "I have often felt as if I had inherited all the passion of our ancestors when they defended their Temple, as if I could joyfully cast away my life in the great cause."

Freud was disappointed some time around his eleventh or twelfth year to hear of his father's unheroic behavior when provoked by an anti-Semitic Gentile. He attributes his selecting Hannibal as his ideal to Hannibal's heroic hostility to Rome—and to the fact that Hannibal had a militant father.

In 1883, Freud challenged an anti-Semitic Gentile to combat, when provoked on a train.

This issue of control of anger becomes the leading theme of Freud's paper on Michelangelo's Moses whose greatness lies in his self-control, as distinguished from the temperamental leader of the Bible story. "The highest mental achievement that is possible in a man is struggling successfully against an inward passion for the sake of a cause to which he has devoted himself."

Martin Freud (*Sigmund Freud: Man and Father* [New York: Vanguard, 1958], pp. 205 f.) records an incident which reminds one of Freud's description of Michelangelo's Moses. It was 12 March 1938, and German troops were known to have crossed the Austrian frontier. Freud was concerned, and when he heard the cries of the newspaper sellers that Saturday afternoon, he sent for the paper. "After gently taking the paper from Paula's hands, he read through the headlines and then, crumpling it in his fist, he threw it into a corner of the room. Such a scene might not be unusual in any happy land not enduring political convulsion; but father's perfect self-control seldom, or never, permitted him to show emotion; and thus all of us remained silent in the living room, well aware that a turn of events which would allow him to fling a paper from him in disgust and disappointment must have alarming implications."

(Comment added in 1980: Dr. Bergmann quotes the message with which Jakob Freud returned to his son, on the occasion of the latter's thirty-fifth birthday, the Bible that he had studied, and discarded, in his youth. The version quoted is that given by Jones. But it is an incomplete version. The full version, in an archaic translation from the original Hebrew is given by Roback (A. A. Roback, *Freudiana* [Cambridge, Mass.: Sci-Art, 1957]). The latter version contains the following phrase: "For long since the Book has been lying about like the broken tables, in a closet of mine . . ." There is a well-known legend to the effect that the fragments of the original tables of the law were preserved in a separate container (L. Ginzberg, *The Legends of the Jews* [Philadelphia: Jewish Publication Society, 1911], Vol. III, p. 158). This sentence obviously refers to the legend and so implicitly compares the worn Bible to the fragments of the tables that Moses had broken.

Freud received and read this message in 1891. It was ten years later that he first saw the Michelangelo statue, though he did not write "The Moses of Michelangelo" until 1913. His interpretation of the meaning of Michelangelo's version, if he associated the breaking of the tablets with his rejection of his Bible, suggests that he now saw the virtue of self-control; he should not discard his paternal heritage.)

Dr. Bergmann speculates that the Michelangelo's Moses paper may have been written at a time when Freud was trying to deal with his own anger with unfaithful disciples. We do not know what other frustrating situations he may have been encountering in his personal life, that might have required control of anger. Dr. Bergmann explains Freud's father's passive response to anti-Semitic attack as derived from a confidence in his own spiritual superiority, whereas Sigmund Freud himself, at age twelve, was no longer in touch with this Jewish tradition.

This is a matter of some interest and it deserves a few minutes' discussion. Freud's attitude at age twelve is the same as that which accuses the Jews who perished in the Holocaust of having been accomplices in their own destruction because they had been too passive in the face of attack. It is also the same attitude as that of the Jews who support Israel because Israelis have demonstrated that Jews can fight. In fact, before the destruction of the second Temple in 70 c.e., history records that the Jews were great fighters who more than held their own in the ancient world, and held off the might of the Roman legions for years. The Bible recounts tales of military prowess, and Chanukah is actually a holiday which celebrates not only the rededication of the Temple, but also a military victory, the only şuch holiday that is retained in the Jewish calendar.

The destruction of the Temple—for many reasons—was a trauma from which the Jews have never recovered. It changed the modus vivendi of the Jews, their view of how to survive in the world, and the nature of their religion. The legend is that Rabbi Johanan ben Zakkai escaped the Zealots defending Jerusalem, appeared before Vespasian, hailed him as a future emperor, and requested permission to set up an academy in Yavne. Thereafter, Judaism lost its umbilical attachment to Temple and city, and became predominantly a religion of study. Most rabbis then opposed military activism. More than a millennium before Michelangelo, to whom Freud attributes it, the Mishnah celebrates the virtue of self-control. "Who is mighty? He who subdues his impulses." The Mishnah here had adopted the stoic, hellenistic principle (see *Avoth* 4: 1).

Since this episode in Jewish history, Jews have made their way on this planet by accommodating themselves as best they could—to the social and political climate in which they lived. On some occasions, for example during the Crusades, when all appeared lost, they stood and fought, usually to their death. Similar heroic stands took place during the Chmielnicki massacres of 1648, and again recently, in many of the ghettos of Eastern Europe, of which the Warsaw ghetto is the best known. But by and large they have survived by accommodating, sometimes even to the point of conversion, for example by some Sephardim who became Marranos, and by unknown numbers of Ashkenazim as well. Even the ideologic architects of Zionism saw the Jewish state established with the consent and encouragement of the surrounding states and great powers. Military defense began only when the Jewish settlement came under attack. Before the emancipation, the wisdom of the strategy of accommodation was evident to all Jews, including Jewish youths. However after emancipation, Jews became more aggressive, realizing that social organization was no longer as fixed as it had been previously, and that there was room for Jewish advancement. Sigmund Freud therefore had little sympathy for his father's pre-emancipation mentality.

In 1908, Freud, in apparent resignation, wrote to Abraham that "We Jews, if we want to cooperate with other people, have to develop a little masochism and be prepared to endure a certain amount of injustice. There is no other way of working together." Yet he hoped as long as possible to remain in Vienna, and to defy the Nazis. But when he finally left, he saw himself as a modern-day Johanan ben Zakkai, escaping the burning city to found an academy elsewhere. On March 13, 1938 (the day following the incident which Martin Freud described), Jones says that at a meeting of the Board of the Vienna Society, "It was decided that everyone should flee the country if possible, and that the seat of the Society should be wherever Freud was settled." Freud commented: "After the destruction of the Temple in Jerusalem by Titus*, Rabbi Johanan ben Zakkai asked for permission to open a school at Jabneh for the study of the Torah. We are, after all, used to persecution by our history, tradition and some of us by personal experience." Freud finally understood at eighty-two what he had failed to understand at twelve, that is, that his father's behavior had been discreet rather than cowardly, and that when you are in a physically weak position, as the Jews in the Diaspora are, physical defiance is a poor strategy. With the reestablishment of the State of Israel, Jews have reverted to militance as a tactic for survival. The armies of Israel have done wonders for the self-esteem of Jews around the world. And we earnestly hope that they will continue to protect the State.

With respect to Freud's concern with Moses, I find reasonable Jones' suggestion that Moses may at times represent Freud's father, and at other times himself. Jones suggests that the statue may have represented Freud's father because "he used to flinch from its angry gaze as if he were one of the disobedient mob" (see E. Jones, *The Life and Work of Sigmund Freud*, Vol. II [New York: Basic Books, 1955],

---

*In most traditional accounts, Johanan ben Zakkai approached Vespasian, not Titus; during the siege of Jerusalem, not after the destruction. M.O.

p. 365). If that is so, then he may have been attributing to the Moses he saw before him, anger at his breaking of the "Rome taboo." Similarly, the fantasy that the Jews had murdered Moses and stubbornly refused to admit guilt for doing so, could express his own feelings of guilt toward his father. At the time that he wrote it, he was suffering from his painful and final illness, and at the time *Moses and Monotheism* was released for publication, he was already in exile. He did not respond to these two afflictions of his old age with anything resembling clinical depression, so far as I know. However, to consider it a "forward step" for the Jews to admit guilt for murdering the father would be consistent with the psychodynamics of depression, and might represent an attempt to contend with a depressive tendency by working, that is, writing, and by confession.

Dr. Bergmann reminds us of Freud's flirtation (I choose the word carefully) with the city of Rome—"the mother of cities." Rome signified for Freud two things, the Oedipal wish and Christianity. Freud wrote in 1900, "To my youthful mind, Hannibal and Rome symbolized the conflict between the tenacity of Jewry and the organization of the Catholic Church" (S.E., Vol. IV, p. 196). In each case there was a wish and an inhibition. In the first case, the Oedipal wish, the inhibition resulted in the "Rome neurosis" which delayed his entering the city. In the second case, the wish was probably the wish to embrace Christianity, as Dr. Bergmann suggests, and the inhibition, his reactive insistence on his pride in "remaining a Jew." For a Jew to relate Psalm 137, "By the rivers of Babylon, there we sat and wept," to Rome rather than Jerusalem, as Dr. Bergmann observes, is remarkable, and calls into question the single-mindedness of his identity as a Jew. The Hannibal-Winckelmann antithesis, to which Dr. Bergmann calls attention, expresses just this conflict.

What this combination of conflicts suggests to me is that the Jewish conflict about converting follows the Oedipus complex as a paradigm. That is, conversion means murdering one's father and making love to the forbidden woman. From what I read, I infer that Jewish tradition was conveyed to Freud by his father, but disdained by his mother. The two areas of conflict come together in "marrying out." Here the non-Jewish woman represents the literally forbidden woman, and the Jewish father is openly defied. The unattainable "Promised Land," is no longer Canaan, but Rome. I realize that this contention differs from that of Abraham's "Neurotic Exogamy" (K. Abraham, *Clinical Papers and Essays in Psychoanalysis*, edited by H. Abraham [New York: Basic Books, 1955], pp. 48–50), which has become the classic psychoanalytic position. That is, one marries out to defend against incestuous wishes. But I propose that marrying out, for the Jew especially, permits a return of the repressed. He selects a vehicle to defend against incest that accomplishes a similar result, defying father and marrying the forbidden woman. While Freud did not marry out, he pressed his fiancée strongly to give up Jewish practices, and considered conversion to avoid even a Jewish marriage ceremony.

The distinguished historian of Judaism, Yehezkel Kaufmann, in his book *Gola ve-Nekar* (see reference in Chapter 1), proposes that the eternal conflict confronting the Jew in the Diaspora is that between his wish to become assimilated to the surrounding culture and society, and his refusal deliberately and openly to convert. This conflict becomes sharper the greater the opportunity to assimilate, and the greater the practical advantages of doing so.

Freud adopted a position which satisfied both tendencies, a position which appeals to many and is especially popular in the United States today, that is, the conflicted Jew embraces a movement which is universalist in its goals and strives for the classical, humanitarian, prophetic ideals. The movement is nonsectarian. He does not openly deny Jewishness, he makes no attempt to pass, but takes little interest in the Jewish community or its activities, and raises his children with little or no education in Judaism, which is considered too particularist, but with a strong dose of universalistic idealism.

Freud seems to have adopted this position in terms of actual social and professional conduct despite his occasional assertions of loyalty to the Jewish community. He saw psychoanalysis as a discipline and movement which could truly claim to be universalist in its melioristic goals, and ethical by strictest Biblical standards. To be sure, in the Vienna of his day he remained far more Jewish than many of his contemporaries in the academic and medical world. He did retain his membership in B'nai B'rith, he seems gradually to have extended his learning about Jewish matters, and he finally adopted a low-key but positive Zionist orientation.

Many of his Jewish disciples in the psychoanalytic movement have been even more universalist than he, and less assertive about their Jewishness. For example, Fenichel, in the index to his monumental *Psychoanalytic Theory of Neurosis* (New York: Norton, 1945), does not list the word "Jew," but has three entries under "Christian Science." The word "religion" is listed with sub-rubrics: "obsession," "schizophrenia," and "psychotherapy," and the word "religious" is associated with sub-rubrics: "ecstasy," "obsessions," "submissiveness," and "delusions." This soft-pedaling of particularistic Jewishness and dedication to a melioristic, universalistic humanitarianism has become the unspoken convention among Jewish analysts. Only in the last few years have a small number of Jewish analysts permitted themselves some overt sympathy for Israel as a relatively noncontroversial assertion of Jewish identity.

Finally, Dr. Bergmann has, in this paper, made a very strong case for the importance, in the analysis of any Jew, of careful study of the nature of his feelings about his Jewishness and his conflicts about it. Freud, in his discussion of his dreams, occasionally brings up Jewishness and its problems. In the case of the Hannibal fantasy, he relates it to the formation of a childhood ideal; and in other places, he does not hesitate to deal with Jewishness as a significant determinant of his own behavior. Dr. Bergmann has reviewed for us the evidence that Freud's conflicts about his Jewishness made an important contribution to shaping his interests and his career.

When I was a student at the New York Psychoanalytic Institute, there was an unspoken gentleman's agreement that in psychoanalysis one does not discuss Jewishness, except to demonstrate to an occasional religious patient that his piety is a sign of neurosis.

It has been my experience that analysis of a patient's conflicts about Jewishness is vitally important for a full understanding of his attitude toward his parents, his children, towards society and toward himself. Omission of this area leaves large lacunae in the analysis. Reconstruction of Jewish identity is vital to the completion of the analysis. Dr. Bergmann demonstrates in this paper that our understanding of Freud is far from complete unless we understand his attitude toward his Jewishness.

DISCUSSION OF MARTIN S. BERGMANN'S PAPER
by Robert Jay Lifton

I believe that Freud's lifelong preoccupation with Moses can be illuminated a bit by immortality themes I have tried to conceptualize in my work. My assumption is that everyone requires a sense of historical connectedness with what has gone on before and what will continue after his limited life-span, but that with great men like Freud the imagery of symbolic immortality tends to be closer to consciousness, and tends to be a powerful organizing principle. While Freud considered all imagery of immortality as denial of death, he was himself, especially when close to death, profoundly preoccupied with the fate of his ideas and of the psychoanalytic movement. (This is clear in Jones, Schur, as well as in a little, somewhat erratic but interesting book on Freud by Maryse Choisy.) And his unconscious attraction to the idea of converting to Catholicism, which I think you rightly emphasize, could be understood within his immortalizing quest.

I think he was ambivalent about whether Christianity was an advance or regression—it was an advance for him, as Bergmann says, in that Christians admit to their "parricidal guilt" while Jews do not, but he thought it a regression in its promise of immortality as opposed to the more stern and admirable Moses-Jewish insistence upon renunciation of such illusion. But Christianity and Catholicism had the powerful attraction of universalization—we can postulate that an early model for that appealing universalization developed from the influence of his Catholic nursemaid, who represented both a mothering influence and the dominant society, and that as Freud began to focus on psychoanalysis as his life project and path to symbolic immortality (via works), the question of its universality came to matter enormously for him.

Freud was clearly concerned about the extent to which psychoanalysis could be viewed by others as a "Jewish science"— and Jung's importance to him was as a vehicle of universalization. As his only really brilliant Christian disciple (I do not think he ever thought of Jones as more than an extremely intelligent, able, and loyal number-two man), Jung came to symbolize the breakout of psychoanalysis from its Viennese-Jewish environment to the larger world, much as many have viewed the Christian sequence of Judaism as a similar breakout from the remnants of monotheistic tribalism. It is even possible that Freud needed the kind of evidence Jung could give him to believe in the universal applicability of his insights, especially of the Oedipus complex.

But the trouble with that Christianizing sequence toward universalization, apart even from gargantuan conflict between the two men (or perhaps significantly contributing to that conflict) was Freud's simultaneous awareness that his creative power derived importantly from his Jewishness—from that Jewish capacity to hold (one might add, imagine in the first place) unpopular ideas and stand in opposition to the majority. Indeed I think that part of Freud's fascination for us—certainly for me—is the model he provided of the authentic modern secular Jew, a proud and loyal (whatever his unconscious conflicts) member of a people whose religious practices he not only rejected but directly confronted and attacked.

His way of evoking and identifying with Moses was his brilliant resolution to his immortality struggles. In the *Moses of Michelangelo* paper, he already attributes to Moses, at least by implication, a fundamental human advance around the control of violent passion—a theme he reiterates in *Moses and Monotheism* around his concept of "the great man" and his capacity to elevate his followers to that degree of renunciation of instinct. My sense is that Freud does things with Moses that we have not yet quite entirely figured out. Sachs may be right about the shift in identification from Hannibal to Moses at that time, and Ostow also right in associating Freud's reading of controlled anger because of his own violation— and conquest—of the "Rome taboo." But in breaking that taboo Freud was, in effect, subsuming Rome to Jewish purposes— acknowledging (with his own growth as well as the loss of Jung) his own autonomy and its Jewish source. That is, he moves toward accepting a secular-Jewish base for his psychoanalytically-centered symbolic immortality.

What he does with Moses later on (in *Moses and Monotheism*) is more confusing. I would suggest that he simultaneously idealizes Moses further and cuts him a bit to size (by divesting him of his Jewishness and seeing him as eventually rejected and killed by the Jews). Now this could reflect Freud's ambivalence about his Jewishness—all the more so in the light of Bergmann's further evidence about his temptations toward conversion—but I think that the more important process was Freud's reassertion of his immortalizing claim. That is, by reinterpreting the Moses story in terms of his *Totem and Taboo* theory, he connects the central source of Jewish identity ("the one man, the man Moses, who created the Jews") with his own (Freud's) nuclear principle, that of the Oedipus complex. The sequence from *Totem and Taboo* to *Moses and Monotheism* (and I see more similarity than difference in the two) is the rendering of history an apologia for the Oedipus complex. It is that principle which takes precedence over Moses (to the point of being responsible for his death)—and therefore psychoanalysis itself (rather than Freud the individual) to which Moses is subsumed. Yet Moses at the same time becomes a central model for Freud's ultimate statement about the historical process, and as Bergmann says, for subsequent psychohistory. Here I would stress the innovator's need to connect his universalizing doctrine with his own person—which I have always thought to be the basic issue in Freud's self-analysis, even more so than the discovery of the Oedipus complex as such. So here we can say that by extending the Oedipus complex (Freud's original and lasting connecting principle between self and doctrine) to serve as an explanation for the historical process, Freud both reasserts and transcends his Jewish-Mosaic identification in the service of conquering the death he anticipated and furthering his "psychoanalytic immortality."

As to the future of *Moses and Monotheism*, I strongly agree with you about its continuing importance. But I think we have to raise more fundamental questions about the extent to which the Oedipus complex—and the individual psyche writ large—can be organizing principles for the broader historical process. It is of course easy—though correct—to reject Eissler's literalization of the model of "history as patient now cured"; but it may be just as important to look critically at the other Eissler use of the *Totem and Taboo* model (concerning modern Japan) and the Waelder use of it that Bergmann quotes as well. I agree that these last two are more evocative—there is clearly something to them—but they still may be misleading precisely in their maintaining the model of the individual psyche for a particular country's history. The idea is interesting as metaphor, but what is needed is a more precise set of distinctions, which must include a kind of psychohistorical interface where individual experience connects with prevailing historical currents and ideologies (which I struggle with in my work around the idea of "shared psychohistorical themes"). Without doing that, one runs the risk of eliminating history in the name of studying it, and of "explaining away" certain forms of collective ethical passion (as, for instance, the expressions of rebellion among the young in this country in the late '60s in response to the Vietnam War and other social issues) as nothing but reactivated Oedipus complex. Also involved importantly are conceptual principles around cultural and historical transmission of ideas and attitudes.

Clinical Psychoanalytic Studies

The Psychologic Determinants of Jewish Identity

Mortimer Ostow

EDITOR'S COMMENT

This essay grew out of, and reflected the approach of, the study group on the Jewish response to crisis, the findings of which are summarized in "The Jewish Response to Crisis". This essay, and the next two, are based primarily on clinical experience, but my observations here are coordinated with some of the principles and generalizations elucidated by that study.

In another place in this volume (p. 13) I call attention to the fact that the term "identity" as a psychoanalytic concept was first used by Freud with reference to his Jewish identity, while Erikson, who elaborated the concept, acknowledges that his interest in the subject was stimulated partly by what he called "the Jewish part of my background as an identity issue." Identity becomes an issue of significance for those who are born into a minor community that is obviously demarcated from a surrounding major community.

The chief contribution of this essay is the suggestion that identity is composed of an unconscious core, established in childhood, and a manifest identity determined by the influence of environmental circumstance and current psychic mental disposition. Therefore manifest identity may change from time to time, even though core identity remains fixed. Manifest identity is profoundly influenced by the personality consolidation of adolescence, and also by current cultural and political pressures. The early home environment shapes the core identity of the child, while subsequent education merely contributes content to his manifest identity.

This essay was published primarily in the *Israel Annals of Psychiatry and Related Disciplines*, Volume 15, Number 4, pages 313–335, December 1977. It was reprinted in *Perspectives on Jews and Judaism; Essays in Honor of Wolfe Kelman*, edited by Arthur Chiel (New York: Rabbinical Assembly, 1976).

We use the term "Jewish identity" to signify one's identity with special reference to one's Jewishness. The term "identity" itself deserves a little interest. Literally it means sameness. Applied to one's personality, it denotes those features that are characteristic and distinctive, and that are relatively enduring. It would not be incorrect, therefore, to speak of one's identity in terms of those features of one's personality visible to *others*. However, in common use, it is taken to signify one's image of one's *self*, using the term *image* broadly, to include physical, intellectual, moral, psychologic and social characteristics. The term "Jewish identity" therefore loosely denotes the Jewish components of one's self-image. When we are concerned about a person's "Jewish identity", we are concerned with how prominent a place Jewishness occupies in his view of himself.

A man of German-Jewish descent, who had been taught by his parents, and encouraged by his liberal and radical associates to disdain religion and all other kinds of Jewishness, when he became depressed, found comfort in associating with a moderately observant family and participating in their observance. He developed an interest in Jewishness. When he recovered from his depression, this interest subsided but remained consistently well above the level which had prevailed before his illness.

A man whose parents had turned away from the Jewish religion which had been practiced by their parents, and brought up their children with little or no concern for their Jewishness, associated with almost no Jews and gave little thought to his Jewish roots and ties. When his wife died in 1939, he became depressed. He left home and office, went to France, and there, using his own resources and his friendships and connections, he occupied himself with bringing Jews out of the gathering Holocaust and to the United States. After the better part of a year in which he had rescued over 50 Jews, he returned to his home, resumed his profession and his indifference to the Jewish community.

A man who was contemptuous of the profession of his father, an Episcopalian clergyman, and contemptuous of religion, became depressed. As his illness became more intense he described visions of the face of his dead mother, and alongside it the face of the baby Jesus. It was surprising to hear this expression of religious sentiment by a man so antipathetic to religion, but it is not uncommon to encounter a reversion (the proper technical term would be "regression") to childhood attitudes in the course of mental illness. What was more surprising was his desperate exclamation a few days later, as his decline continued (drug therapy of depression in many cases requires at least four weeks of treatment before improvement begins), "I feel like an old Jew at the Wailing Wall." His mother had been Jewish. When he recovered, any thought of his considering himself Jewish was inconceivable.

Similar cases are encountered not infrequently. They demonstrate that under the influence of mental illness, one's view of oneself changes. Usually there is a reversion to components of one's self-image that were *conscious* in childhood but which seemingly were discarded subsequently. We see here that they were not discarded, but repressed, that is, excluded from consciousness. As illness evolves, it facilitates the escape of these earlier aspects of the self-image from repression.

In general, close study of identity—and this is as true of its Jewish components as it is of others—reveals that over the course of the life cycle, manifest identity changes. There are two types of change: There is the change that occurs gradually, as an aspect of the process of passing through the life cycle, from birth to death. One sees oneself differently as one matures, acquires experience, and alters the nature and objects of one's affection. There is the change that occurs more abruptly from time to time as one's mental state responds to stress or its removal, especially when the response involves lapse into illness.

I believe we are justified in making the following generalization: Identity, as we ordinarily use the term, refers to the self-image of which one is conscious. However this manifest self-image changes in response to maturation and aging—and in response to changes induced by stress. What is probably fairly fixed after childhood, is an unconscious core self-image, individual components of which become conscious as one's position in life and in the community demand. Let us consider first the determinants of this unconscious core and then the determinants of the manifest expression of the individual components of this core.

One of the earliest tasks of the infant is to differentiate his image of himself from his image of his mother. While we can never know with certainty the contents and processes of the infant's mind, we can make some reasonable guesses based upon our observations. We infer that as the first conscious sensations and impressions appear in the infant's mind, he does not at first "know" of any distinction between his own body and his mother's. During his first and second years, he learns to make that distinction and at the same time to attempt to make himself more independent of his mother. He wants to see himself as separate—and to act as if he were separate and independent.

Yet, despite this tendency to differentiate, the opposite tendency, to remain close to mother—and conceptually part of mother—becomes stronger, even as the need to separate grows. Separation, and, as time goes on, ultimately emancipation and independence are driven by a biologic maturational thrust. However complying with this thrust implies facing the danger of the unfamiliar and forgoing the comfort of the familiar. For the small child, his need to cling to mother—and later to father too— influences both his behavior and his view of himself. Psychologically, the regressive tendency to cling to parents finds expression in seeing oneself as similar to them. The child tends to maintain an identity, or at least a similarity between his image of himself and his image of his parents. We say that he "identifies" with them. The identification becomes more and more subtle as the child becomes aware of the finer, more abstract and more subtle features of his parents' identity. While in the earliest years he does not identify with their Jewishness as distinguished from other aspects of their personality, nor does he distinguish between their Jewishness and the non-Jewishness of other parents, nevertheless his identification does incorporate indiscriminately the Jewish components together with all others. It is only after the age of 5, when he begins to associate with peers, that he begins to recognize both distinctions and similarities between *his* parents and *other* parents, and therefore between his image of *himself* and his image of his *friends*. These distinctions may include many of the ways in which a person is Jewish. In a sense, the child becomes Jewish before he knows that Jewishness exists. The earliest identifications arise out of the child's need to retain the gratification and protection of the earliest love relations, even as these relations must be permitted to weaken in order to make way for new love relations and for independence. However it is also true that parents enjoy seeing their children identify with them, and encourage identification. Therefore by identifying with the parent, the child earns the bonus of the parent's continuing love.

Identification is one method by which the young child copes with the need to separate from mother; continuity is another. At some point in his early years, the child becomes aware that some people are separated from their families, for a shorter or longer time, and some separations are permanent. He can use identification to prepare for such a loss, and to defend himself against its impact when it does occur. He can also create the illusion of changelessness by making himself sensitive to the quality of continuity: continuity of the life of the individual, and continuity of life across the generations. He becomes interested then in the concept of ancestors and forebears, and sees his grandparents as living demonstration of generational continuity. Generational continuity is expressed in family and community tradition. Among Jews, Jewish tradition carries the feeling of continuity, and therefore it appeals to the child who is trying to protect himself against the feared separations and discontinuities of life. Grandparents are not only themselves the living representatives of the past, and therefore a guarantee of an unending future, but they also teach tradition. They are therefore as influential in making the child Jewish as the parents, and sometimes more so. The child seeks continuity not only through the generational chain, but by relating to a wider circle of family members, the family then coming to replace the mother, as the exclusive relation with her is gradually relinquished. At each point in time, the child draws a circumferential line between the extending family which he finds *familiar;* and strangers. No matter how large a group is encompassed within the area of familiarity, the child always feels more comfortable with them than with the strangers, towards whom he is always more or less defensive. To help him in drawing this line, he strives to discern those qualities that distinguish the familiar from the strange; and to establish that he is a member of the familiar, he assumes these qualities as fully as he can. In a society in which the Jewish child comes into contact with non-Jewish children, to the extent that he learns from his parents that the distinction between Jewish and non-Jewish is significant, he becomes sensitive to the difference and includes it among the criteria that distinguish between the familiar and the strange.

Cohesive groups tend to reinforce their cohesion by elaborating on their common origin. These accounts, usually partly history, and partly fiction, are, in the process of group repetition and transmission, given a form which serves the current needs of the group. As the needs of the group alter, the specific content of the myth changes accordingly. (I shall use the term "myth" here to designate stories, including history or fiction or both in any proportion, that achieve currency within a group and purport to be accounts of significant events in the life of the group.) Subscription to this myth establishes the individual's membership in the group. To be useful, the myth must serve the needs of both the group and the individual. It can do so because, in most instances, the history of the individual and the history of the group are congruent, or can be made to seem so.

Among the most powerful of such myths are myths of origin and myths of crisis. In the former, the origin of the group is portrayed as a remarkable event which came to pass despite the hostility of the environment. In the latter, the existence of the group is threatened by an enemy or a natural event. An *actual* threat to a group impels its members to reinforce their commitment to each other for purposes of defense of the group; a *recollected threat* exerts a similar influence. The elaboration and propagation of the crisis myth is a group function which elicits maximal commitment from its members. Individuals subscribe to these myths for two reasons. They perceive and enjoy the cohesive influence of these myths; and the account of surviving attack and triumphing over enemies, reminds the individual that he too had overcome danger, and it confers upon him a sense of potency and optimism. Both of these reasons appeal to children as much as, or perhaps even more than to adults. Children too enjoy hearing these myths and committing themselves to the group process which they engender.

The Jewish myths which contribute to the core identity of the Jewish child, are offered to him in folk form by his parents, especially on the occasion of Jewish holidays, and by instruction in the earliest grades of Jewish schools. He identifies with the Jews and their legendary victories and defeats, and retains the identification and the values conveyed by the myths, at least unconsciously, even when, as a result of maturation and higher education, the myths are displaced by more realistic historical accounts. It is because the childhood experience of the major events of the Jewish calendar have made such a strong impression on the child, that they continue to exert a major attraction to the adult as well.

What we learn of the earliest memories of awareness of Jewishness, teaches us that it is conveyed by specific vehicles, usually conventions and rituals. One of the most potent cohesive influences in any group is the use of a specific language, distinctive for the group. The use of the language, realistically but not always accurately distinguishes members of the group from non-members. In encountering strangers, it helps to ascertain whether the stranger is a member of the group. (The unthinking application of this test has at times led Jews into traps set by their enemies who have employed renegade Jews or even non-Jews speaking the prevailing Jewish language.) However the language, because it binds the members of the group together, seems to possess a magical power, calling for, and usually eliciting a sympathetic response from the hearer. The accents, intonations and sounds of the language convey a message apart from its content. Mother's lullaby, when heard in later years, powerfully re-evokes the feelings of love, closeness and identity which it originally elicited. Even the language in which it is sung, acquires some of the lullaby's magic. The children of Jewish immigrants to the United States have, for the most part, abandoned Yiddish, but they will still use it, or individual words or expressions, when an assertion of their Jewishness is appropriate. *Their* children were exposed in childhood to only these fragments and so they can scarcely utilize Yiddish for asserting Jewish identity. They will still respond to it, but they will not be able to convey it to their children. Encouraged by the revival of Hebrew in Israel, many self-conscious young Jews are becoming familiar with it, and are using it as the language of Jewish identity. It is not likely however to become nearly as widespread in the United States as Yiddish was in the past.

A second "magical" identifying device is the *name*. In an alien environment, language is often given up, but names, signifying actual continuity with one's literal parents are abandoned less readily. Yet the tension between old and new, between the requirement for continuity and the desire for change, manifests itself in manipulation of names. The first change to be made is to abandon clearly Jewish given names. That is, babies are given names characteristic of the surrounding culture. These names reflect the desire of the parents to be accepted without minority and inferior status. Either or both of two concessions are generally made to continuity. A second name, in Hebrew or Yiddish, is given along with the first. The second name is a parallel name (not a middle name), to be used on religious occasions, but not to be employed in school, at work or in social relations. The second name is usually that of a deceased relative whom the parents wish to honor, often a deceased grandparent, memorialized out of respect for a surviving parent. Frequently the initial letter of the ("English" as distinct from "Jewish") given name or names corresponds to the initial letter of the name of the ancestor who is being memorialized. A third possibility, utilized by Jews who do not wish to be assimilating, and yet who feel that a specifically Jewish name might be a handicap in daily affairs, is the use of a name from the Jewish Bible, since the latter is used as a source of names by Christians as well. This practice often has significant consequences, for the child will not infrequently identify with his historical namesake and choose his career and shape his destiny accordingly.

Abandoning a characteristically Jewish family name of one's parents is a more difficult step. Often the name is shortened and made to appear less distinctively Jewish. Since the name is one of the principal components of core Jewish identity, the gradual abandonment of characteristic names does diminish the content of this core. In general, a child is likely to interpret his name as an assignment. If it is a characteristically Jewish name, the assignment is to take one's Jewishness seriously. If it is the name of one who is spoken of frequently by the parents and who perished in the Holocaust, the assignment is to become a living memorial to the victim. How he reacts to this assignment will depend upon how he reacts to his core identity.

Dress is commonly used to intensify group cohesiveness. On occasion when group cohesiveness is critically important, for example in war time, uniforms are used. Uniforms also help to distinguish members of a group from non-members. The uniform itself comes to signify the group, just as the flag does. Adolescents will assert their membership in their peer group by dressing alike, but differently from their parents.

Jews do not dress in any particularly Jewish way—at least not deliberately. Hassidim dress to assert their adherence to Hassidic tradition. Orthodox Jews in the street in a hatless environment will be recognized by the fact that they are wearing hats while others are not. Orthodox Jewish women will generally dress more modestly than non-Orthodox or non-Jewish women. One element of dress which does label the male Jew is the skullcap. When a man wearing a skullcap is seen on television or in photographs in the newspaper, the entire Jewish community becomes alert to whether he will make a good or bad impression and thus reflect credit or discredit on the entire Jewish community. The tallith is the uniform of the synagogue; t'fillin to a much lesser degree, since they are used when the congregation is smaller and therefore are seen so much less frequently. The young child's view of the synagogue includes these distinctive elements of dress, skullcap and tallith, and they become incorporated into his core view of Jewishness, so that his donning them, in his view, makes him a Jew.

Ritual is a device employed when individuals fear a tendency to fail to perform a necessary act, or a tendency to perform a destructive act.

An obsessive-compulsive man who was torn between a desire to repudiate a demanding father, and a feeling of guilt toward him, made a daily practice of kissing the tallith bag which his father had given to him. To him the act had religious significance. In terms of the religion it had none. He did not use the tallith or its container for any other purpose and neglected almost all other religious obligations. In caricaturing religious practice, he was degrading his father and his father's religious practices. Since the form of "worship" that he selected was kissing, we may infer that his conflict dealt with his affection for his father. The ritual therefore signified both rebellion and submission simultaneously.

To take an example from normal daily life, in the operating room, or in the cockpit of an airliner, when it is necessary to prevent individual error, many maneuvers are reduced to ritual form. To the child, ritual signifies the continuity which he craves. Children love to hear the same story, read exactly the same way, any number of times. They must prepare for bed in exactly the same way every evening. Rituals are developed by children especially in the face of separation, for example at bed time, or when going to school. The child's ritual promises continuity in two ways. First, in form it represents sameness. Second, in content, it symbolically wards off or cancels separation and change. Children find religious ritual agreeable, and when introduced to it in childhood, will incorporate it into core Jewish identity, so that whether or not it is subsequently abandoned, it will always elicit an affective response.

One cannot speak of Jewish identity without considering circumcision, for millennia an integral part of the Jewishness of the male. While it is not at all distinctive in the Middle East or in the United States, in Europe, during the Holocaust, it was used to identify Jews for persecution. Circumcision does not easily fall into the category of core Jewishness, at least to the extent that the latter is created in childhood. Few Jewish children, before 8 or 9, are aware of circumcision. Being circumcised is never something relegated to the unconscious. After one has become aware of it, one always knows whether one is or isn't. When we think of those aspects of our behavior or personality which demonstrate our Jewishness, we seldom think of circumcision. I suppose it should be considered "core" because of its centrality and great symbolic value. It is usually the last thing even the assimilating Jew gives up.

The act of circumcising is authorized by the parent. The father whose child is being circumcised feels that *he* is making the commitment to Judaism, accepting his own father's imperative. Circumcising one's child then should be considered an act of assertion of Jewish identity, though the circumcision itself probably does not play a central role in the young child's view of his being Jewish.

It occasionally happens during the course of life, that we are confronted by mystical images that come to the surface, or to which we find ourselves responding. While most sophisticated American Jews will disavow belief in an anthropomorphic god, the image that comes to mind during earnest prayer or during the intensity of the Kol Nidre or the Ne'ilah service of Yom Kippur, will often tend to assume anthropomorphic characteristics. A painting, a song, a play will sometimes elicit an affective response, often powerful, often without specific content. Under psychoanalytic scrutiny, such moving experiences can usually be traced back to childhood memories. Among Jews the significant events of life, such as weddings and funerals, are usually experienced within a religious context. They too usually elicit powerful feelings, some concerning the principals of the event, some concerning the subject himself. Inevitably they tend to elicit memories of childhood, especially the earliest experiences of separation, and of reunion. These experiences will usually reflect early childhood impressions of oneself, of the people one loves, and of the nature of the love. To the extent that one's early childhood is colored by Jewishness in the ways that we have discussed, the mystical images of adult life will tap one's Jewish identity.

It is difficult to select any small sample of Jewish myths without including instances of misfortune and sacrifice: flood, *Akedah*, Egyptian slavery, desert hardships, wars of conquest, exile, destruction of Temple and City, Maccabean wars, Roman persecution, Moslem and Christian persecution, Holocaust, defense of Israel. Although one would expect that such dismal events might discourage youngsters from identifying with a group which had encountered so many misfortunes, in fact, they do not. On the contrary, they seem to elicit sentiments of loyalty, as though the sacrifice of others were an obligation which demanded one's own loyalty.

I should like to suggest that the theme, not merely of danger, but of actual sacrifice exerts a powerful mobilizing influence. The principal theme of Christianity is that Christians were saved by the sacrifice of Jesus, and that they are thereby obligated to accept him as their Savior, and commit themselves to his community. The role of obligating martyr, which Jesus plays in Christianity, is played in Judaism by the long list of Jewish victims, including recent victims of anti-Semitic persecution. The Christian theologic doctrine that the victim is also the Savior, reflects what I take to be the psychic reality that individual salvation (read: reunion with lost parents) can be obtained by sacrifice, even by the sacrifice of another member of the group. In the Rosh Hashana service, Jews invoke the merits of their forefathers (Z'chuth avoth) and especially the merit of Isaac who permitted himself to be bound for sacrifice, as a justification for their prayer for redemption. (In current, as distinguished from historical practice, the repetition of the Akedah story and the accompanying invocation of merit, form part of the daily morning service.) One can see circumcising one's child as an act of sacrifice to God and to community which creates the feeling of having acquired merit for both oneself and the child.

One of the most painful acknowledgments which the young child is forced to make is that he must share his parents with brothers and sisters, and each parent with the other. Each child likes to see himself as special in some way so that he may make special claims upon each of his parents. The Jewish conception of election, though it offers the child no advantage with respect to his literal siblings, does offer the comfort of special divine protection. It reinforces the child's self-esteem and helps him to resist indications of impaired self-esteem among discontent parents or other members of the community. This concept of specialness may become significant subsequently whenever issues of self-esteem, especially communal self-esteem are raised.

Many adolescents and adults who acknowledge commitment to

the Jewish community but feel that they must dissent from one or more aspects of Judaism like to distinguish among the various kinds of Judaism: religious, secular, Zionist, philanthropic, cultural, and ethnic. These distinctions are not made by children in their earliest experiences of initiation into the Jewish community and they therefore probably do not exist in the core concepts of Jewish identification. In making these distinctions, the individual is actually distinguishing which of these features with which he has already identified in childhood, he will consciously and deliberately accept, and which he will reject, as an adolescent or adult.

The influence of the experiences which we have discussed persist as a core identity, though not all of this core is readily accessible to consciousness during adolescence and adult life. Some components of this identity are consciously accepted; others are consciously rejected; some are ignored; some are not even retrievable by conscious thought. However the whole of this core identity persists as a reservoir from which elements can be extracted and to which they can be returned as external circumstances and current psychic need require.

The process of adolescence is a complex and profound one which could certainly not be encompassed properly even by the whole of an essay of this size. It is the process by which the young person becomes transformed from a child who sees himself primarily under the protection of his parents, to an independent person oriented toward playing a role in society, and undertaking the care of spouse and children of his own. The process is driven by the somatic and psychologic changes characteristic of this period. In a sense, these changes "demand" of the individual the revision of his attitudes toward himself and others. The dimensions of the adolescent transformation include sexual identity and behavior, attitude toward parents, attitude toward society, readiness to undertake responsibility for self and others, and the crystallization of a personality and character in which changes in all of these dimensions are integrated. These processes are never really completed even by the close of adolescence, and continue throughout life, as social expectations and physiologic state change.

Obviously some of these changes must affect the individual's view of himself as a Jew. For example, in his struggle to emancipate himself from the influence of his parents, he may reject aspects of his earlier identification with them. If the peer group among whom he finds himself is self-consciously Jewish, he may use his Jewishness as a means of identifying with them, this latter identification succeeding and building upon the basic identification with the parents, and reinforcing it. If the peer group is non-Jewish, his eagerness to identify with them, may involve consciously rejecting his core Jewishness. Note that such rejection does not imply that the Jewish identification is eradicated; merely that it is inactivated for the time being, while retaining the potential to be reactivated when and if the occasion should arise in the future.

In a sense the process of adolescence resembles the process whereby the young child separates from his parents in his second and third year. In early adolescence as in this childhood period, the separation, though driven by a maturational thrust, is nevertheless frightening. In early adolescence therefore, as in childhood, many young people will take defensive measures. One may be a reinforcement of childhood identification with the parents. In the case of Jewishness, the young person may reinforce his Jewish identity, less as a matter of commitment to Jewishness as such, but more for the purpose of pleasing his parents and securing their continuing affection. Another may be the effort to assert continuity within the family and across generations.

This need for the assertion of continuity, within the generation and across generations, may also be satisfied by seeing oneself as a member of the Jewish community. It is elicited primarily by confrontation with separation. The young adolescent does not often in the course of the ordinary vicissitudes of life face serious threats of separation. Being sent off to boarding school and to a lesser degree, summer camp are generally the most upsetting of such experiences. Of course the separation and divorce of the parents, or the death of a parent are far more serious but less frequent examples. However, separations recur throughout life, and they are usually met, at all ages, by reassertions of continuity. It is for this reason that people turn to their religious heritage on the occasions of life's milestones, marriage, illness, death and the birth of children. For many Jews, the invoking of religious tradition on such occasions, is their only association with the Jewish community.

One of the major issues for the adolescent is that of commitment to society. There is the inner need on the part of the adolescent himself to make such a commitment. It is an aspect of his maturation. Biologically it is the expression of his readiness to sacrifice himself for the defense and well being of his family and community. It includes such things as the readiness of the young man to risk his life in battle, and the readiness of the young woman to accept the discomfort, pain and risk of pregnancy and parturition. Complementing this inner need is the expectation of society that it possesses the adolescent's loyalty and can call upon him and depend upon him for service and sacrifice. It is this readiness for commitment that finds expression in the sacrifice and martyr myths which we have discussed above.

The adolescent's readiness to make sacrifices for the group depends upon his courage, that is upon the advancement of his maturation. Some adolescents are eager for the opportunity to commit themselves; others are timid but will respond to clear and present danger; still others will avoid commitment under all circumstances. Since the Jewish community in many times and places requires the defensive efforts of its young people, and since being a committed Jew has often meant the incurring of hostility and danger, timid adolescents are often fearful of making commitment to the Jewish community.

It has scarcely been possible to get even this far into the discussion of the determinants of the expression of Jewish identity without referring to the nature of the environment in which the Jew lives. In *galuth* the Jew is always a small distance away from non-Jewish and potentially hostile neighbors. In Israel, the individual Jewish family does not feel threatened by living in the midst of a non-Jewish community, but the knowledge of the hostility of closely neighboring nations is always immediate. Clearly the surrounding community and the relation of the Jewish community with it, play a signal role in influencing the individual's Jewishness. The very visible relative advantages of being a non-Jew in a non-Jewish environment, with respect to physical safety, to opportunities for economic advancement, to achievement of prestige, has resulted in the past in the loss of large numbers of Jews by assimilation. A deliberate decision by a young person to "pass" as a non-Jew signifies merely a rejection of the childhood core identity. That the latter can be activated once more under adequate stress, was illustrated by the cases cited at the beginning of this essay.

Low self-esteem is one of the frequent findings in mental illness, presenting among the most prominent symptoms in melancholic depression, schizophrenia and the common personality disorders. We do not understand its origin too well, but many of the manifestations of mental illness are devices designed to protect the individual against his self-condemnation. I should like to note parenthetically that I am not considering in this essay the influence of mental illness on Jewish identity, except when it can throw light on the normal. Problems of self-esteem occur widely among individuals who are not mentally ill, and often play a significant role in determining what we ordinarily consider normal behavior.

The relevance to the subject of our concern is that the individual with problems of self-esteem may occasionally attribute the felt inferiority to his Jewishness. Some of the reasons are fairly obvious. Since the Jewish minority community is often viewed with condescension if not contempt by the host community, it requires a vigorous self-respect to resist this external influence. A second reason lies in the rabbinic renunciation of military resistance following the destruction of the Temple, and the subsequent policy of the Jews to purchase security by submission and self-effacement.

The Jewish community attempts to resist these influences. The emphasis on the doctrine of election, the frequent reference to the nobility of our ancestors, the pride in our way of life, all serve this resistance. I am reminded here of Goldin's protest in his introduction to the English version of Agnon's *Yamim Noraim* (Days of Awe) that the latter omitted the saying attributed to Rabbi Solomon of Karlin, "Der grester yezer horeh is az mi far-gest az mi is ein ben melekh." ("The worst of the impulses to evil is to forget one's royal descent.")

Given then, an individual with problems of self-esteem arising from his own imperfect development, or his inability to meet current challenge, he tends to blame his felt inferiority on his Jewishness, and the real challenges to the Jew's self-respect lend verisimilitude to his fantasy.

> A man descended from a distinguished Jewish family failed at everything to which he turned his hand, although he was given many special advantages out of respect for his family and their position in the Jewish community. As the only failure in a brilliantly successful family, he entertained a low opinion of himself. But he blamed his failures on anti-Semitic prejudice.

Among the issues determining the adolescent's position with respect to his Jewish identity, we have discussed issues of identification with parents, influence of peers, threats to continuity, demands of the Jewish community for commitment and sacrifice, advantages of "passing" out of the Jewish community, and problems of self-esteem. These are probably the central determinants, but not the only ones. His attitude toward religion is often influenced by the adolescent's need, on the one hand, to control importunate sexual impulses; and on the other, by a temptation to retreat from social obligations to a self-indulgent sensuality. The attitude toward idealism and morality are influenced by a need to overcome persistent childhood selfishness. The attitude toward religious tradition and authority is influenced by the need to overcome—or at least to appear to overcome—dependence upon parents and a childlike need to submit to authority.

However mental evolution does not cease with the passage from adolescence into adult life. Subsequent changes influence most aspects of the individual's personality, including those which determine his Jewishness. Freud called attention to the phenomenon which he named *deferred obedience*. The adolescent, out of his need to assert his independence from his father, rejects the latter's values, and pursues a very different modus vivendi. However, as he grows older, and the need to rebel and assert independence subsides, he may attempt to recapture his feeling of unity with his father by adopting his values and life style. Such a delayed resumption of identity is especially apt to be precipitated by the death of the father and by the individual's becoming a parent. It is this principle which accounts for the familiar observation that young people who as adolescents had ignored the Jewish community, return to it when they become parents. One need not credit fully their claim that they are doing it only "for the children."

Often during the late teens and early twenties, there is a surge of courage which impels the young person to seek adventure and to favor militancy in defense of some group under attack. When the Jewish community is in need of defense, he may become militantly Jewish. When the Jewish community is at ease and others are apparently oppressed or in danger, he may turn militantly toward the latter and away from, or even against the Jewish community. In either case, after twenty-five, this aggressiveness subsides and the associated attitude toward the Jewish community relents.

As parents die, and as the individual himself begins to observe his powers and faculties waning, his search for continuity becomes more active. He may pursue it by strengthening his interest in religion. At all ages, individuals tend to respond to danger to the Jewish community by renewing their commitment to it; and they tend to respond to situations of relaxation of danger by relative indifference.

The foregoing considerations apply to Jews living in the Jewish community of the Diaspora in general. Let us consider some of the details of our current situation in the United States, as they affect the Jewish identity of American Jews.

The early childhood of the children of the American Jewish community is, by and large, not nearly as saturated with Jewish experiences or folk ways as that of children growing up in the more homogeneously Jewish communities of say, the shtetl. In the United States the saturation of this early exposure does vary from community to community, and from family to family. Obviously, the children less intensively exposed will be left with a weaker identity core than those more intensively exposed. Fortunately in his first few years, the child is impressed easily by experiences which are significant for his problems of closeness and distance, continuity and separation, similarities and differences. Such impressions, occurring infrequently or even once, appealing to his current anxieties or defenses, may remain within conscious memory throughout his life. In the instances of surprising recurrence of conscious Jewish identity, exhibited in the illustrative reports at the beginning of this essay, the identity was, in each case, based upon brief exposure to grandparents and their ritual practices, or, in one case, merely to mention of them. To the extent that American Jewish families today are more dispersed than in the past, and that young children are less exposed to their grandparents, the Jewish identity core will be less vigorous. The decrement in outcome however will be considerably less than proportional to the decrement in exposure.

One of the reasons for our current concern with Jewish identity is the disturbing evidence of Jewish young people who seem to be turning their backs on the Jewish community. They include: the political radicals who oppose Israel's struggle for survival, those who marry out, and those who commit themselves to the many non-Jewish religions and quasi-religious sects. It is important to distinguish between the most shocking examples of this anti-Jewishness, usually adolescents whose struggle to resolve the conflicts of adolescence take a deviant form; and similar but usually more temperate instances among young people whom one could not consider deviant. True, it would be difficult to find instances of actual betrayal of one's own group which one would not consider pathologic. Similarly, adherence to sects which, from the point of view of one's origin in the middle class American Jewish community, must be considered bizarre, cannot easily be labeled normal. The deviant young people, that is, those whose turn away from the Jewish community results primarily from inner struggle, need not necessarily be considered a great loss. If their illness had taken a different form, say depression or just helpless resignation, they would make no greater contribution to the Jewish community. They may be a source of real difficulty in two eventualities. If they have children, their children will probably be lost to the Jewish community. In times of social unrest, they may set unwholesome example to contemporaries who are troubled and confused but not disabled by illness. Our interest in these young people, from the point of view of Jewish identity, is that the environmental influences and the dynamic mechanisms which determine the pathologic outcome in their case, are often the same as those which are active in the normal as well, though the outcome is less extreme.

Perhaps the most troublesome issue with regard to Jewish identity today, is the problem of intermarriage. I shall not discuss either *marrying down*, that is, marrying someone clearly inferior socially, economically or educationally; or *marrying up* which is marrying someone above one in these respects. The first is a common neurotic attempt to deal with the problem of low self-esteem by choosing a partner whose evident low status makes one feel higher. The second, often encouraged by a non-Jewish environment which rewards assimilation, also attempts to deal with low self-esteem, in this instance by attaching oneself to a partner of higher station, and acquiring his or her prestige by association. The troublesome issue today is *marrying across*, that is, marrying a partner, appropriate in every respect except in being non-Jewish. It is more common in the United States today than in recent years and seems to pose a threat to the strength of the Jewish community. It is interesting that in most instances, there is no effort to deny one's Jewishness, no change in name, no rejection of friends or family, and often an effort even to introduce a Jewish component into the marriage ceremony. In many instances, the partner is asked to convert to Judaism. Usually the children are expected to consider themselves Jewish.

It would be misleading to try to account for this phenomenon without considering many relevant influences which we have discussed above. One necessary but obviously not sufficient condition favoring intermarriage is that Jewish young people are now more easily accepted by their non-Jewish peers than previously. One might think that these young people are wandering away because they are not close to their parents. The fact is that many of them are close, and though they may understand that they are hurting their parents, they do not wish to be rejected. I believe that a fear of commitment is usually involved here. One formula which seems applicable to many cases is the following: The adolescent retains too strong an attachment to his parents. To demonstrate his independence, he attempts to dissociate himself from them in symbolic ways, including his choice of peer group to which he attaches himself. Fearfulness and timidity accompany excessively strong parental attachment, and in turn make the individual hesitant about making a commitment to a person or group. The Jewish community, with its intense cohesiveness, with its demands and expectations, seems overwhelming to the timid young person. He feels less threatened by a non-Jewish community which is more easy going, less threatening and less demanding. However, as is the case with the resolution of all neurotic conflict, small differences in the relative strength of the contending forces may induce large differences in outcome. For example, the individual may be *too timid* even to make gestures of independence. He may look upon the Jewish community as an extension of his family, and as a refuge, and assert his Jewishness in order to obtain the protection of the community. On the other hand, the adolescent who is *courageous* may welcome the opportunity to undertake a serious commitment to defend the Jewish community. He will find in this commitment, fulfillment of his maturational and social responsibilities. If we do not examine carefully what Jewish identity means to each of these two adolescents, we shall miss the significant difference. It matters not only *whether* one sees oneself as Jewish, but also *how* one sees oneself as Jewish. I suspect that in many instances of intermarriage, the timid young Jew attempts to deny his fear of anti-Semitism by assuring himself via marriage, that he is really loved by the gentiles.

It follows from our discussion than when and if significant threat to the Jewish community materializes, many of those who resisted making a full commitment to it previously, will be motivated to respond with vigor and new found courage, since the willingness to sacrifice, to a certain extent, is a function of the awareness of clear and present danger. The man in the second case history which I cited, was responding not merely to his depression, but to the impending Holocaust. Such instances illustrate that, given an unconscious core of Jewish identity, the social and political climate which prevails during one's adolescence and adulthood, will influence the degree of one's conscious Jewishness.

Our discussion also throws some light on the influence of Jewish education upon Jewish identity. It is evident from everyday observation, as well as from the argument which we have been considering, that Jewish education, though very helpful in the individual's cultivation of his Jewish identity, is neither sufficient nor even necessary for its inception and development. Core identity is established early in childhood by home influence, though the early years of education can contribute to it. The evolution of conscious identity is influenced by inner psychic disposition and by external demands and expectations. Jewish education can play a significant environmental role in encouraging Jewish identification. Jewish education provides content to associate with Jewishness and to replace the content of childhood Jewish mythology. The realistic content can now carry the values and emotional commitment of the mythology. For example, the history of the Holocaust and of the creation of the State of Israel lend meaning to the ancient history of Egyptian slavery and redemption. Education in Jewish schools, camps and social groups provides a peer community with which the young person can identify as he tries to emancipate himself from his parents. Jewish education provides instruction in How to be a Jew. If Jewish education is limited to a few years of elementary material, the young person is left with a child's eye view of Jewishness which favors his disparaging it, and seeing it as detracting from his self-esteem. Higher Jewish education permits one to see Jewishness as admirable. But a respectful view toward Jewishness is probably necessary before the adolescent will accept higher Jewish education. While it will reinforce Jewishness as a source of self-respect, it cannot be counted on by itself to serve as an instrument for strengthening Jewish identity in the uncommitted.

It is obvious that the Holocaust has strongly influenced the Jewish identity of American Jews. But the nature of the influence is complex and composed of several factors. When one thinks of the Holocaust or reads about it, the first reaction is guilt. American Jews, influenced by the current mode of social activism, believe that they could have made more aggressive efforts to protect their brothers. It is a kind of "survivor guilt." The term "survivor guilt" implies that the survivor feels guilty toward the victim, as though he had contributed to the victim's death. I believe the explanation for guilt, when it occurs, may be slightly more complicated. It may be that the guilt applies not simply to surviving, but to having failed to offer oneself on the field of combat in defense of the common cause. It is not that the individual has personally victimized the one who perished; it is that he has not offered to make an equivalent sacrifice for the group. What I am suggesting is that the guilt that does recur at certain times among some survivors, often called "survivor guilt," is a manifestation of the individual's tie to the group, rather than an interpersonal transaction.

A second reaction of Jews to the Holocaust, is the feeling that utopian and universalist hopes which Jews had held in the first quarter of this century, were disappointed. Therefore Jews are not only justified in closing ranks against the outside, but are obligated to do so. We have already discussed the tendency of young Jews in the United States to intermarry, as an effort to escape the intensity of Jewish family ties, into the apparently more relaxed casualness of the surrounding non-Jewish world. A second reason for the tendency to intermarry is a hopeful restatement of a belief that anti-Jewish hostility has indeed ended, and the era of universalism has finally come. This continued resurgence of hope for acceptance by non-Jews arises from the need to escape the emotional intensity, the possessiveness, the expectations and demands of the Jewish community; the impairment of self-esteem implicit in being a second class minority group within a first class majority culture and community; and the need to deny both the historically demonstrated recurrent dangers to the Jewish community, and the obligation which Jewish destiny imposes on the individual. Therefore those young people whose personal disposition welcomes obligation and challenge will respond to the Holocaust with militancy, while those whose disposition does not easily tolerate obligation and challenge will be impatient with recollection of the Holocaust, will try to minimize it and attempt to act as though anti-Semitism were eliminated forever. A test of the orientation of the young person with respect to this dimension, is his attitude toward the "sh'foch chamathcha . . ." during the Passover Seder service. Identification with it indicates militant, self-assertive Jewishness, while a rejection of it betrays the universalist orientation designed to resist the hazards and obligations of Jewishness.

One sees these reactions more intensely displayed among the

children of actual concentration camp survivors. These survivors, by virtue of their own experience, generally exhibit an aggressiveness in pursuit of self-interest, the interest of their children, of the community of survivors and the interest of the Jewish community as a whole. This aggressiveness and the possessive protectiveness toward their children are not easy for the children to accept. While some of the latter accept and identify with their parents' militance, many others attempt to escape and deny by embracing universalist attitudes and orienting themselves away from the Jewish community.

Since we are considering here the secondary encouraging and discouraging influences upon manifest Jewish identity, rather than its unconscious core, it follows that the attitudes we have been discussing may change as circumstances change and as the individual matures. A new round of dangerous anti-Semitism may compel the loyalty of the universalists. Or, as the individual leaves the early decades of life, he often becomes less militant and more accommodating and compromising. We should not overlook the fact that although most Holocaust survivors feel committed to aggressive defense of the Jewish community, a few others have responded by an assimilationist strategy, hoping thereby to protect their descendants from similar persecution in the future. Such assimilationist survivors often refuse to circumcise their children. Note that although the manifestation of this type of assimilationism resembles those of the universalist young, its psychologic basis is quite different, and so is its fate. In the face of renewed persecution, those who are attempting to escape Jewish destiny will be spurred to intensify their dissociation from the Jewish community, while those who are trying to escape only the psychic demands of the Jewish family and community, are likely to assert their Jewishness more positively.

A third response to the Holocaust is a feeling that Jews have acquired a certain claim on the rest of the world for respect and protection. In oversimplified form, this claim is a claim for financial reparation. In practice it may take the form of expecting the rest of the world to acknowledge a moral obligation to protect the State of Israel. I believe that underlying both of these ideas is the conviction of having acquired merit and a feeling of being deserving by identifying with the victims of the Holocaust. A readiness to make a sacrifice for the community confers a sense of distinction, or merit, and a feeling of deserving special consideration and indulgence. It is interesting that the non-Jewish world understands this response of the Jews. Germany has acknowledged obligations and paid financial reparations. Other countries and many non-Jewish individuals acknowledge a moral obligation toward Jewry and the State of Israel. Still others whose self-interests seem to them to run counter to such sentiments, deny that the Holocaust of Jews ever took place. They seem to acknowledge in this way that if it did, the obligation to Jews and to Israel would be valid. Therefore they attempt to disavow the obligation by denying the event.

It is obvious that the self-esteem of American Jews has been elevated by the heroism of Israel and Israelis. The hitherto passive, accommodating, acquiescent role of the Jew which has been traditional since the Roman destruction of the Temple, has been replaced with military and aggressive self-defense that has been universally admired. In addition, American Jews see themselves and are seen by their neighbors as meritorious not merely by identification with the victims of the Holocaust, but also by identification with the Israelis who defend themselves and their country so courageously and effectively. American Jews attempt to give substance to this identification by making financial sacrifice and by visiting Israel. Also, the State of Israel, its Biblically named cities and regions, its embattled positions among many ferocious enemies, all recall Jewish myths and mythologized fragments of history, which have been recorded in the core of Jewish identity. It is as though this current reality lends verisimilitude and affective cogency to the positive experiences which formed the basis for the childhood unconscious nucleus of Jewish identity.

We have spoken of Holocaust and Israel individually. However there is a sense in which they belong together. Apocalypse is a fantasy which has long attracted adherents in the Western world. The classical fantasy is that there will be a final catastrophe in which very large numbers of people will be destroyed by forces of Evil, but the latter will be conquered by forces of Good. Out of the desolation, the world will be reborn and in the reborn world, Good will prevail. That in the course of human history there have been catastrophes, and that many of them have been followed by reconstruction, seems to validate the apocalyptic idea of the succession of death by rebirth. The apocalyptic expectation that Good will triumph over Evil is often in the mind of those who initiate apocalyptic wars, though succeeding generations wonder how their predecessors could have been so naive. The construction of the State of Israel immediately upon the termination of the Holocaust conforms to the scheme of apocalypse, and seems to confer supernatural sanction to both the State and to surviving Jews. It seems to confirm the core concept of election.

Since its inception, the State of Israel seems to have been endowed with divine sanction, and yet to be threatened by mortal political, military and economic forces. The concept of messianism is for many people a component of core Jewish identity. It has been widely observed that Zionism has functioned as a real political movement which has carried with it a messianic flavor. It is the latter and its appeal to unconscious Jewish identity which has served to make a movement which was politically so improbable, actually such a success. The messianic role of Zionism confers, in the mind of the Jew, an additional quantum of supernatural sanction and vitality to the State of Israel.

SUMMARY

Jewish identity is based upon two components. One, the core, is established in the early years of childhood and much of it may become and remain unconscious. The second, the manifest identity, may vary from time to time in response to external circumstances and the individual's current psychic state.

The unconscious core of Jewish identity is established by identification of the young child with the parent; his need for generational continuity; his sensitivity to the distinction between family and non-family; his acceptance of group myths; and his use of sensitivity to language, names, dress and ritual as a means of establishing identification with family and community.

Manifest Jewish identity is determined by the operation of several influences upon core identity. These include: the vicissitudes of adolescent development; adolescent need for continuity; adolescent need for and fear of commitment; the pluralistic American social environment; the problems of regulation of self-esteem; as well as changes of outlook and social expectation after the first two decades of life.

On the current American scene, the core identity offered to Jewish children is attenuated in several respects but not critically so. While one is distressed by obvious problems in Jewish identity exhibited by many deviant young people, their problems should not be confused with the situation prevailing among more wholesome adolescents. One result of troubled Jewish identity is the increase in intermarriage. Jewish education, as we know it, may reinforce Jewish identity, but it is neither sufficient nor necessary for its establishment or manifestation. The Holocaust, and the State of Israel, individually and together, influence manifestations of Jewish identity in a number of different ways which lead to a flavoring of the recognition of the problems of Jews in the real world with a feeling of supernatural election and protection.

A Psychoanalytic Study of a Religious Initiation Rite: Bar Mitzvah

JACOB A. ARLOW

EDITOR'S COMMENT

The religious ceremony in which the attainment of the status of Bar Mitzvah is observed is widely recognized nowadays as the equivalent of a puberty ordeal. Arlow provides clinical evidence, in this essay, of the fusion of the induction of the young man into the Jewish community with his transition to sexual maturity. His cases illustrate problems in adolescent resolution of the Oedipus complex, sibling rivalry, and timidity in facing ordeals. He notes that even though the ceremony symbolically sanctions sexual activity, in practice the sexuality and the aggressive impulses associated with it are diverted into substitute channels of religious study, ritual observance, and community loyalty.

In one of his footnotes, the author comments that his clinical material provided evidence also that the Bar Mitzvah ceremony encouraged the boy's separation from his mother, and from women and sexuality in general. This theme should be developed further with respect especially to the problem of the boy's fear of his initial sexual encounters with girls, and problems of potency which for so many centuries might have been threatened by the implicit training of the young Jew in exile to suppress aggression.

More recent developments in the synagogue have resulted in diminishing the differences between the roles of males and females in the service. In many congregations of the Conservative movement, women are now counted along with men to constitute the required quorum of ten, they are invited to accept the honor of being called to ascend to the reading table to read or have the Torah read on their behalf, they are encouraged to participate in a Bat Mitzvah ceremony, and, in the Reform movement, some are being ordained as rabbis and leading the service as cantors. It will be interesting to see what the Bat Mitzvah ceremony will mean to the girls who participate in it, and what it will mean to boys who are losing this traditionally male prerogative, who must compete now with girls as well as with boys, and whose cohort of ordeal participants now includes both sexes. Clinical case material should provide us with some answers to these questions and to others that arise from these changes in synagogue practice.

Arlow emphasizes the role of the Bar Mitzvah tutor as a new ideal and model. These models become especially effective if they are themselves impressive individuals worth emulating, and if they are only a few years older than the Bar Mitzvah. Too often the person who serves as tutor is one who knows the required material and who needs the income supplement that Bar Mitzvah tutoring brings. I should like to take this opportunity again to suggest that Bar Mitzvah tutors be carefully selected and carefully trained for this particular function, for they have an opportunity to exert an especially strong influence in the determination of the adolescent's Jewish identity, his loyalty to the Jewish community, and his religious and ethical standards.

We shall have to wait to see whether problems will arise out of the appointment of female Bar Mitzvah tutors for boys and male tutors for girls.

This essay is reprinted from Volume 6 of the *Psychoanalytic Study of the Child*, pages 353–374 (New York: International Universities Press, 1951).

INTRODUCTION

In certain religious ceremonies one can observe how society tends to institutionalize the major universal affect-arousing situations and, by linking them to suitable occasions, utilizes them for purposes of real social values (5, 8, 10). To the extent that these affect-arousing situations constitute a common and significant experience for members of a social group, a community of participants is formed. For such a group, mass participation in the observance of a ceremonial may serve both as a means of arousing and discharging those affects which are peculiarly linked to the particular event. All the members of the wedding, for example, experience to a greater or lesser degree their own emotional relationship to the momentous event of taking a mate for oneself. This is as true for those as yet unmarried as it is for those already married. Clinical psychoanalytic experience makes manifest the various forms of affect aroused in patients who attend such rites.[1]

PSYCHOANALYTIC STUDIES OF INITIATION RITES

Among the affect-arousing situations, few are more dramatic than the transition to biological and sexual maturity. This event, as we know, has been widely celebrated among primitive peoples in awesome and colorful ceremonies which have been the subject of a considerable body of psychoanalytic literature.[2] The essence of these studies may be summarized as follows: The approach of sexual maturity accentuates the affects connected with the conflicted relations between the father and son and their respective generations. In order to integrate the youth with the social patterns of the community and with the traditions and values of his forebears, it is necessary that he master the feelings referred to above, especially those which arise out of oedipal rivalry. The initiation rites of primitive peoples which usually involve circumcision, serve to discharge the fear and hostility which the older generation harbors toward the developing younger generation. By hurting and frightening the initiates the older generation exacts promises of submission and obedience; by interceding in behalf of the youths and protecting them from the hostile spirits, they divert the aggression of the youths toward the spirits and away from themselves, thus allying the new group of adults to the elders in ties of gratitude for helping them into manhood. The twofold way in which the primitive boy experiences the antics of his elders during the initiation ceremonies corresponds to his previous experiences with the men of the older generation. When they make horrendous noises and terrify him almost to death, he re-experiences, as it were, the childish terror of the father and his surrogates. In the benign intercession of the elders, on the other hand, the youth feels once again traces of the protecting intervention of the father and father substitutes who in the past had educated him and had watched over his development. The initiation rites solemnize the granting of such sexual and other privileges which accrue to mature men of the community. Elements symbolizing castration, death and incorporation as well as expulsion, rebirth and phallic endowment have been interpreted in these ceremonials. The members of a "class" of initiates may feel a special type of kinship, sometimes formalized in the term and institution of "blood brothers." The termination of formal initiation is often marked by appropriate festivities during which the initiates sometimes embark, as a group, upon the exercise of their newly won prerogatives. Through these ceremonies a resolution of the hostility between the generations is facilitated and identification with the taboos and values of the group is effected.

In summarizing the literature concerning examinations and examination anxiety, Flugel (6) has shown how certain elements of the motivations described in the initiation rites of primitive peoples survive in the pedagogical and social custom of examinations, particularly in qualifying professional examinations. Apart from this, very little has been written concerning initiation experiences in our culture, in spite of the fact that there has been an increasing interest in the psychology of the latter part of the latency period and of early adolescence.

THE BAR MITZVAH INITIATION

An example of an institutionalized form of initiation at puberty is to be found in the Jewish ceremony of Bar Mitzvah. Jewish boys can undergo two initiations into their faith; circumcision at the age of eight days and Bar Mitzvah at the age of thirteen years. While circumcision is by far the more important rite from the point of view of the religion, the psychological effect of this event cannot be clearly described since we do not know what an eight-day-old infant remembers. The idea of having been circumcised, to be sure, may become very important in retrospective fantasies (15). The state of affairs is quite another, however, regarding Bar Mitzvah, since in this ceremony the central figure is an active, conscious participant who is at the threshold of adolescence.

The essence of the ceremony is as follows: On or about the boy's thirteenth birthday, the father is called to the reader's stand in the synagogue where he pronounces the blessing over the Torah (Law). He then says a short prayer which may be translated as follows: "Blessed (be He) who rid me of this one's punishment." Later in the services the boy is called to pronounce the blessings and to read a section of the Law. Thenceforth the father is no longer considered responsible for his son's moral transgressions and it is understood that the young man assumes the moral and religious obligations of the adults. From that time on the youth may be considered as an eligible adult whenever a group of ten adult males is to be assembled to constitute a quorum for prayer or other religious observances. He is accorded the privileges of being called to the Law and of wearing a prayer shawl (Talith).[3] In addition he thenceforth has the obligation to use phylacteries during the morning prayer.

The purpose of this study of Bar Mitzvah is to examine this institution as an initiation rite, to see how it serves the functions enumerated above in regard to initiation rites in general, and to observe the impact of this affect-arousing experience in its relation to character and symptom development, especially during the pubertal period.[4]

In order to grasp the full emotional impact of the Bar Mitzvah experience, it would be well to describe the details of the celebration in our current cultural context. The essential ceremony may be elaborated according to the social and cultural milieu, the economic status of the parents and their relation to traditional practices.

As the thirteenth birthday approaches, steps are taken to prepare the youth for the part he is to play in the synagogue ceremony; namely, pronouncing the blessings and reading from the Law. If he has not received Hebrew training hitherto, an intensive course of preparation to meet the minimum requirements is undertaken. If he has already received some training, a special tutor or special lessons are arranged for the purpose. In addition to teaching the youngster the essential elements of the ceremony, the tutor instructs him in the application of the phylacteries, the wearing of the prayer shawl and some fundamental religious doctrines. Usually a suitable speech to be delivered at the time of the ceremony is memorized by the initiate. A father rarely prepares his son for the occasion even if he is well qualified to do so.

Frequently, this juncture becomes the occasion for rebellion against the parents. The boy, for various reasons, may refuse to participate in the entire process and may repudiate his parents' authority as represented by the need to go through the Bar Mitzvah initiation.

In any event the need to prepare and to participate in the Bar Mitzvah is usually regarded as an imposition although other secondary motivations, to be described below, may obscure this element. The initiate has to undertake studies from which for the moment his playmates are exempt. He prepares as for a very important examination, with the fear of public humiliation before him should he fail to pronounce the blessings correctly or falter in the delivery of his speech. On the other hand, there is the promise of a celebration and many gifts when the ordeal is over. About this time it is customary to begin to refer to the prospective initiate as "a Bar Mitzvah boy." This appellation means not only that he is in preparation for the ceremony, but also that he has attained a certain level of maturity so that a higher degree of responsibility and performance is expected from him.

The ordeal by recitation finally takes place in the synagogue. Shortly after the father has made the blessings and uttered the short prayer of dissociation, the youth is ceremoniously called to the Law as "the Bar Mitzvah Groom." This striking title is no semantic accident. A bridegroom in orthodox communities was expected to go through the same ceremony the week before his wedding.

Throughout his recitation the initiate is observed intently as a young man on trial undergoing a very difficult examination. A sense of compassionate participation grips the audience, especially the boy's mother. With the successful completion of the recitation, the tension is broken. A great sense of relief is experienced by the friends and relatives as well as by the Bar Mitzvah boy who receives the congratulations of the rabbi, his teacher, and his father. In many communities at this point it is customary to shower the boy with nuts, raisins and sweets, apparently as a token of congratulations and good wishes.

AMBIVALENT FATHER-SON RELATIONS IN THE BAR MITZVAH CEREMONY

The relationship of forces on the synagogue platform is very illuminating. As the initiate awaits his turn to be called to the Law, his father is first honored with similar recognition. It is at this point that he recites the short prayer of five words which is unique in Jewish ceremonialism, namely, "Blessed (be He) who rid me of this one's punishment." The words of the prayer are short, sharp, and impart a definite sense of hostility. Even the name of God is omitted from this prayer and the word *pator*, which means to get rid of, conveys a definite connotation of vexation and distaste. In this prayer no direct reference is made to the son who is disparagingly referred to as "this one." It is considered bad luck for the boy to be called to the Law immediately after his father. During the ceremony, furthermore, the father stands off at a distance and observes his son's performance, while it is the Bar Mitzvah boy's tutor who stands at his side ready to assist him, to correct his mistakes and to supply the words of the prayer which may falter on the lips of the anxiety-ridden initiate. The anxiety felt by Bar Mitzvah boys during the service is traditional and is surprisingly disproportionate to the realities of the situation, for here indeed is one examination in which no one ever fails.

Considerable latitude is permitted the boy to demonstrate his qualifications during the Bar Mitzvah ceremony. He may elect to make this "ordeal by recitation" more rigorous than required. In a cultural milieu which traditionally honors intellectual prowess and learning, the Bar Mitzvah boy, by reading additional sections of the Law or composing an original sermon, may win special recognition and prestige from the congregation. In so doing he has an opportunity to demonstrate his superiority over rivals, inside and outside of the family.[5]

BAR MITZVAH MATURITY—MORAL AND SEXUAL SIGNIFICANCE

What the immediate experience of Bar Mitzvah stands for is made explicit in the speech delivered by the boy.[6] Usually the speech contains three essential points: First, an expression of gratitude by the Bar Mitzvah boy to his parents for having raised and educated him; second, a somewhat bombastic avowal that "Today I am a man"; third, a promise of allegiance to his people and their ideals. With the completion of the service in the synagogue the boy's mood is usually that of having gone through an ordeal successfully.[7]

The meaning of the Bar Mitzvah boy's assertion, "Today I am a man," may seem obscure. In our society certainly, the attainment of the age of thirteen brings with it no truly adult privileges and this probably was the case in the past as well.[8] In spite of these facts, however, this element is so characteristically a part of the Bar Mitzvah celebration that no distortion or rationalization can obliterate it. Even those initiates who deliver no speech are invariably congratulated with the reminder, "Today you are a man." It is only in the biological sense that this statement has any element of validity. It is the transition to sexual maturity as we shall see which furnishes the affective core of the celebration. How this element is appreciated can be observed with utmost clarity in the study of the reactions of women, as one perhaps might have anticipated.

An eight-year-old girl when asked, "How did you like your brother's Bar Mitzvah?," sighed, and with sober gravity gave the following reply: "Years ago when I was a little girl my brother got a watch for a gift. I was terribly jealous and I wanted one too. When his Bar Mitzvah came, I became jealous all over again, but when I saw what they made him go through, with all that studying, I said to myself, 'He can keep it. It's not worth it. I'm glad I'm a girl.' "

An eleven-year-old girl who was intensely jealous and hostile toward her thirteen-year-old brother used to say, "I wish I were a boy. I'd grow up and I'd do all kinds of mean things to girls." At his Bar Mitzvah party she had a temper tantrum, threw herself upon the floor, and insisted upon sitting in the place of honor which had been reserved for her brother.

During her analysis, a woman patient, T., had the following dream: "I saw myself in a blue serge tailored suit." Her associations to this dream were: She had been shopping for a dress to wear at her son's Bar Mitzvah. Her brother, eighteen months her junior, had worn a blue serge suit when he was Bar Mitzvah. She felt jealous and excluded at the time because the celebration drew her brother and her father together. Her mother had been dead for many years. She was curious to find out what the men were doing together in the vestryroom of the synagogue after the service. When the men left she stole into the room and discovered that they had been drinking whisky. Overcome by envy and curiosity, she drank some too. The liquor burned her mouth and throat and she began to cough. She recalled how when she was very young her aunt caught her at a game which she had induced her brother to play. In this game she took his genitals into her mouth. She felt very guilty when caught at this play.

Her reaction to the Bar Mitzvah celebration was, "They are giving him a penis but I do not get any." These unfulfilled yearnings were restimulated by the experience of preparing her own son's Bar Mitzvah. In the dream her frustrated wishes are depicted as already fulfilled. In her associations she demonstrated how she unconsciously hoped to set things right, namely, by an aggressive castrating act of oral incorporation. She unconsciously equated her brother's Bar Mitzvah recitation with phallic exhibitionism.

The transition to sexual maturity, as we know, arouses once again conflicts originally associated with the oedipus complex. Although not as dramatic and as definitive as the menarche in girls, the Bar Mitzvah ceremony serves as a sharp reminder to the boy of his new biological status and forces him to re-examine his attitude toward his masculinity. This attitude is an ambivalent one. Over the triumph at the approach of man's estate falls the shadow of the feared hostility of the older generation. Although secondary motivations, dependent upon the specific life situation, may obscure this element, the feeling that the Bar Mitzvah ceremony is a hostile imposition is almost always present.

One boy, for example, when told that it was time to prepare for his Bar Mitzvah, said, "Why do I have to do it? My sister won't have to go through it. She's always been having things easier than I, just because she's the baby of the family."

Under similar circumstances another boy said, "Just because I am the oldest I have to do everything first. I am always clearing the way for my younger brother."

To a third patient who wet the bed until the age of fifteen and who had never been quite sure of his masculinity, Bar Mitzvah came to represent any humiliating occasion which he could not control. During a session in which he was expressing his feelings of chagrin at having to implore a Credit Bureau to rescind an unfavorable credit rating which they had issued concerning his business, he said, "So I put on my blue Bar Mitzvah suit and hat in hand I set out to see the First Vice-President."

SYMBOLIC CASTRATION

Except for the father's short prayer of riddance the exercise of the ceremony bears no manifest evidence of the hostility of the older generation. This hostility emerges from repression, as it were, in certain customs practiced years ago in other countries. A number of communities decreed that Bar Mitzvah boys were to fast on the day before the ceremony. In others, the boy was required to wear his phylacteries for a full day (17, p. 68). Most striking of all the customs, however, was the practice in vogue among the Jews of North Africa. "When they [the guests] were all assembled a barber was summoned who shaved off the hair of the heads of the Bar Mitzvah boy and his friends. Every adult male who attended contributed a coin to the barber in payment for his services."[9] This example demonstrates almost every aspect of the initiation rite of the primitives, especially the symbolic castration not only of the Bar Mitzvah boy himself, but of his generation of "blood brothers" as well. It is striking, moreover, how these impulses which find discharge in a communal custom may under appropriate circumstances reappear in the spontaneous acts of isolated individuals.

An older brother and cousin who were keenly aware of the competitive strivings of the younger brother taunted him some months before his Bar Mitzvah by saying, "So he's going to be Bar Mitzvah. Look who's going to be a man. Let's pounce on him and see if he has any hair growing around his penis." They promptly proceeded to do so. This act which on previous occasions had constituted a humiliating assault for the younger brother was at this time resisted only half-heartedly, for he knew, with secret pride, that his pubic hair had already begun to grow.[10]

SUCCESSFUL RESOLUTION OF OEDIPAL CONFLICTS AT BAR MITZVAH

The sense of kinship which exists among fellow initiates is expressed in many customs in which the Bar Mitzvah boy and his friends receive special recognition as a group and embark together upon the exercise of certain hitherto forbidden privileges. The North African Jewish boys whose heads were shaven were permitted to go out as a group in the evening and spend without restriction all the gift money which the Bar Mitzvah boy had received. In other communities on this occasion a special party was arranged for the Bar Mitzvah boy and his friends at which they were allowed to stay up all night and drink as much wine as they pleased even to the point of intoxication. The connection between such new prerogatives and their unconscious sexual equivalents may become evident from the following material.

A boy who had just gone through Bar Mitzvah initiated his cousin who was about to do the same into the practice of masturbation. His approach was, "You are old enough. It's about time you had some fun." When they masturbated together they both felt less guilty.

As a member of a Bar Mitzvah class of two, patient U was able to overcome much of the guilt associated with competitive victory and sexual equality with the father. Competition and comparison were two of the predominant themes of his early formative years. He was the first of three children. The trauma of being ousted from the position of the only child when his sister arrived was more than duplicated when his younger brother was born. Several weeks after the arrival of the younger brother, his mother took into her household the family of her recently deceased sister. The competitive antagonism which U felt for his own siblings was sharpened and widened to include these usurping substitute siblings as well. It was with the greatest difficulty that the patient could keep in restraint his merciless antagonism. Fantasies of destroying his rivals and competitors with utmost violence persisted in consciousness throughout his life. On every possible occasion he accented his position as the oldest, the first male, and the most advanced in his studies. He as well as his siblings were outstanding students. This competitiveness was fostered further by the mother who was an active, courageous, assertive and dominating figure. While raising six children from two families, she managed to hold down a job even in the depths of the depression. It was her initiative which kept the family going. While the unemployed father brooded hopelessly, she kept working and managed to find avenues which ultimately led to her husband obtaining employment. The patient was seven years old at the time and was able to appreciate the resigned weakness of his father in comparison to the confident activity of his mother.

In the year before his Bar Mitzvah he became acutely aware of his disappointment in his father. He saw him as an unsuccessful, ineffectual, foreign-born laborer. He realized that his own career held promise of much greater achievement. The knowledge that he would outstrip his parent filled him with contempt for him but at the same time made him feel guilty and depressed. During this period he began to masturbate, a practice which he confided in no one.

In the person of the new rabbi of the congregation he found a superior father substitute. This rabbi had been born in South Africa and educated in England. His bearing was proud and erect, his dress impeccable, and his speech and accent were flawless. To this elevated father figure the patient became most devoted. For the sake of the rabbi he changed from a rebellious street urchin who used to steal from a fruit store to a serious-minded boy who went to work running errands and doing odd jobs in the same store. The patient could not, however, give up the practice of masturbation and continued the practice with a feeling of great guilt.

As it happened the patient and another boy were due to have their Bar Mitzvah at the same time and their parents had both engaged this rabbi to prepare their sons for the ceremony. The rabbi taught them their lessons at his home in a class of two. Frequently the rabbi would assign them a certain amount of work while he left the room for a period of time. During these intervals, the boys became fast friends and spoke to each other about their feelings concerning Bar Mitzvah and growing up. They exchanged confidences and were both relieved to know that the other had also masturbated. They thereupon agreed that after each session they would go up on the roof of the rabbi's house and masturbate together. They followed this practice regularly, their common participation in this new-found sexual activity helping to alleviate their individual guilt. While masturbating they would often exclaim, "Oh, if rabbi X only knew what we were doing behind his back!" Together they were able to overcome their fear of the rabbi, the new ego ideal whose disapproval served to inhibit their individual enjoyment of sexual activities. After the Bar Mitzvah the patient continued to masturbate but by himself and with fewer conscious guilt feelings.

Bar Mitzvah marked for this patient a definite turning point in his relationship to his father and to his own set of values. Following the ceremony, the patient became intensely interested in religious observance and in Jewish culture. Taking the rabbi as his model, he felt morally and intellectually superior to his father who knew much less than he did about Judaism and who was not at all interested in religious observance of any kind. Although before his Bar Mitzvah the patient had had feelings of guilt and depression concerning his changing status toward his father, following Bar Mitzvah he no longer felt this way.

In certain respects, therefore, the Bar Mitzvah ceremony accomplished its "unconscious" purpose. As the result of this initiation, the patient was able to begin the process of detachment from the authority of his father. In this transition to independence and equality the rabbi served in the role of a temporary intermediary, whose acceptance as a superior father substitute constituted for the patient a socially sanctioned repudiation of the father and therefore less fraught with guilt.

The close link between the initiation into religious prerogative and sexual privilege may on occasions become almost conscious.

A boy to whom sexual indulgence represented a great threat because he had only one testicle, was also a particularly poor student. It was necessary, therefore, that he receive very special preparation in order to go through the Bar Mitzvah ceremony. He had a cousin, six years his senior, whom he admired greatly. The parents asked the cousin to prepare the boy for Bar Mitzvah. The boy was impressed with his cousin who appeared to know everything. He was particularly interested in his cousin's college studies. The cousin was majoring in chemistry. During the period of preparation, a warm bond arose between the tutor and the pupil. After some inner struggle, the boy decided to ask his tutor about sex, a problem which was bothering him very much at this time. At the last moment, however, his courage failed him and he asked his cousin instead to demonstrate and to explain to him the flame which is produced when alcohol is set on fire.

UNSUCCESSFUL RESOLUTION OF OEDIPAL CONFLICTS AT BAR MITZVAH

The affects mobilized by the experience of Bar Mitzvah may upset the equilibrium within the ego and make necessary new measure of defense. This may result in symptom formation and/or characterological changes.

For example, as Z approached Bar Mitzvah, an older cousin, who had preceded him by several months in this rite, introduced him into the practice of masturbation with the assurance, now that the patient was about to become a man, he should feel free to enjoy the pleasures of sex. In addition to masturbating together, the two cousins arranged to exchange younger sisters for the purpose of sexual play. This introduction to masturbation marked the beginning of a protracted struggle between temptation and guilt feelings concerning the practice. In later years when Z learned that the older cousin had grown into a sick-looking, emaciated adolescent, he was convinced that this was due to masturbation.

Throughout the period of the preparation and during the ceremony, Z felt great anxiety that he would fail to perform adequately by forgetting some portion of his speech. During the speech he was overcome by emotion. When thanking his mother for her devotion and tenderness, he began to cry and had difficulty in finishing his address. He was also acutely aware of missing his grandfather who had died some time before.

Following Bar Mitzvah, for a period of six months, he became intensely religious.[11] He prayed with his phylacteries every morning and on Saturdays would walk several miles to the neighboring town in order to attend services in the synagogue. There was a synagogue in his own town, a town to which his parents had moved immediately following the Bar Mitzvah. The patient insisted, however, upon worshiping in the old synagogue, the one in which he had been initiated into his religion. This degree of religious observance was entirely out of keeping with the practices and the traditions of Z's family. When his father, who actually was mainly concerned with the weekly six-mile walk which his son had undertaken, questioned Z about this practice, the boy became indignant. He felt that his father was undermining his faith and he told him angrily, "You wouldn't understand anything about such matters."

Application of the phylacteries and devotion to synagogue attendance, Z felt, would help him overcome his temptation to masturbate. This temptation had by this time become an ever-present preoccupation. While walking to the synagogue on Saturday he would engage in obsessional rumination over the idea, "What if a big storm were to blow up now? Should I, or should I not, give in to temptation and take the trolley, thereby desecrating the Sabbath?"

This period of intense religious observance, entirely out of the familial context, was in effect the equivalent of a transitory obsessional neurosis. When this period came to an end, definite obsessional compulsive trends became manifest in regard to orderliness, punctuality, etc. He developed a remarkable ability to recall dates, names, places, and time, minutely. One aspect of this trend was linked in a striking way to examinations. At college Z kept a very detailed record of every quiz or examination together with the date and grade, in a subject in which he felt a very special need to achieve competitive success. Before examinations in this subject, he would feel especially anxious to the extent that he would route his roommates out in order to be alone to study. When alone he would often masturbate "in order to relieve anxiety," but if he did not get a perfect grade on the examination, he would blame it on the masturbation. His record, in general, and in this subject in particular, was very superior, but the circumstances surrounding this particular course were such that it could be directly connected with guilt concerned with competitive victory over his father.

Clinical studies of examination phobias demonstrate how in competitive situations, where one is called upon to prove oneself, guilt arising out of hostility toward the examiners (or competitors) and the fear of retaliation and punishment may inhibit the candidate and prevent his optimal performance. In the presence of strong self-punitive or masochistic trends, the examination situation may unconsciously present the individual with a tempting opportunity to fail (1, 3, 4).[12] Failing an examination, together with the humiliation which the student experiences, is often unconsciously equated with being castrated. In the analyses of such patients, it has been shown how the examiners are unconsciously identified with the father image of the oedipal phase. The privileges to which one is entitled upon passing the test are equated with paternal license and as such come to be linked with incestuous wishes. Since succeeding in an examination may come to represent equaling or triumphing over the father, passing an examination may be fraught with the danger of castration.

These conflicts, which among primitive peoples are frequently discharged in a massive, cathartic way during the initiation period, play a role in the psychology of certain Bar Mitzvah boys, especially those with examination phobias.

For a patient of this kind, the Bar Mitzvah experience epitomized the essence of his neurosis. The day before he was to take an examination for a professional license, Y slashed both his wrists and cut his throat. His life long complaint and self-reproach was, "Why can't I be a man?" He endured the agonies of the Bar Mitzvah initiation many times every day. In school, in business, in love, in every competitive endeavor, he saw himself on trial to succeed and prove his worthiness, or to fail and be condemned to eternal inferiority. Actually, the unconscious wish to fail was very great due to an unresolved ambivalent attachment to his father, an attachment which expressed itself in the course of the analysis in a fantasy of identification with Jesus being crucified.

Two elements which figure importantly in the Bar Mitzvah rite were of special significance to this patient; namely, facility in declamation and intellectual prowess. The patient was the first son born to an unlettered immigrant pushcart peddler. Five daughters had preceded him. When the patient showed very early that he possessed exceptional intellectual endowment, his father prophesied proudly, "This will be my Doctor of Philosophy." The adulation which he received from his father also made him feel guilty. On a summer evening during his seventeenth year, for example, while leaving for a date immaculately dressed in a cool linen suit, the patient met his father returning from work, grimy with sweat and dirt. The father surveyed his son with tired but adoring eyes and exclaimed, "Hello, Sport." The patient could hardly restrain his tears and the evening's fun was ruined by a gnawing sense of guilt.

The patient turned out to be a self-defeating, miserable failure, who disappointed everyone's hopes, especially his own. He had been unable to master the guilt and anxiety arising out of his oedipal wish to kill and castrate the father and to identify himself with the father and his penis through an act of cannibalistic incorporation. A defensive regression to pregenital libidinal levels and an unconscious passive feminine identification proved inadequate to master his castration anxiety. The conflicts and defensive attitudes which originated in relation to the father were repeated in almost any rivalry situation, especially those involving authority figures.

When the analysis reached the point where it was possible to show the patient that he was subverting his own success in his business, intellectual activities, and love life, in order to avoid taking an active masculine role, the patient had the following dream:

> It is the day of my Bar Mitzvah. I run away from the synagogue, throwing off my talith [prayer shawl] as I do so. My rabbi is chasing me. He tries to get me to go to the platform and read from the Torah [the Law] but I won't do it.

This dream depicted the patient's reaction to the anxiety aroused in him by what he construed to be the analyst's attempts to force him into an active masculine role; that is, to make a man of him. From the associations the following pertinent material will be quoted:

His Bar Mitzvah was a very special occasion for his family as well as for himself. Since he had a fine style and a good delivery, he looked forward to making the Bar Mitzvah speech he had written. His ability to recite poetry used to delight his admiring older sisters. A fantasy which he frequently entertained was to see himself as a university professor (the Doctor of Philosophy), lecturing from the platform before a group of adoring women.[13] When the time came for him to make his Bar Mitzvah speech, he suddenly felt weak and anxious. He said, "I botched up the speech. I skipped whole paragraphs and stumbled over important passages. My father was sitting in the front row staring up at me. He got me all unnerved."

The talith (prayer shawl) he associated with a penis because of its dangling fringes. The casting off of the prayer shawl, therefore, equaled castration which he connected with his slashed wrists and his "botched up" professional career. He said he would never be admitted to the profession; he would never become a father; he would never be a man. He had previously identified himself with a character in a novel, a weakling scion of an illustrious family who surveyed his genealogical chart and realized that he was the sole male through whom the family's name could be perpetuated. With dramatic deliberation, this weakling drew a double line under his name to indicate that with him the family would come to an end. He would have no children.

From the symbolism of this dream it is clear that for this patient at least, the Bar Mitzvah privilege of access to the Torah (Law) is unconsciously equated with access to a woman. Certain traditional attitudes would suggest that this equation may have a more general application. It will be recalled that the Bar Mitzvah boy is ceremoniously called to the Torah as a bridegroom and that in orthodox communities a bridegroom customarily went through the ritual of being called to the Torah before his wedding. The association between Bar Mitzvah and marriage recurs repeatedly in popular as well as religious writing and thinking. At the festival which marks the termination of the reading of the Torah and its immediate reinauguration, the last person called to the Law is referred to as the bridegroom of the Torah. In talmudic, midrashic and cabbalistic literature are to be found many references to the Torah as a bride or a beloved woman.[14] In the dream mentioned above, the patient repudiated his right to ascend to the Torah as vigorously as he had renounced his rights to fatherhood and professional success, all of these having come to represent, for him, the fulfillment of unconscious incestuous as well as parricidal wishes.

SIBLING RIVALRY IN BAR MITZVAH PSYCHOLOGY

Those who prepare for a professional career experience the crossing of critical boundaries repeatedly. In these instances the unconscious rivalry with the father may be fused with conflicts relating to older siblings and colleagues. The reaction to the Bar Mitzvah may constitute for such individuals the prototype for subsequent crucial initiation experiences.

Such was clearly the case with patient X who transferred into the realm of intellectual endeavor the rivalry which he had earlier experienced in the field of sexual competition. As the youngest sibling, he felt hopelessly outclassed by his father and brother. He was completely overawed by his father whom he saw rather infrequently. His older brother and sister excluded him from participating in their sexual games although they did permit him to watch their activities. As he did so he sensed very keenly his inferior status. A screen memory connnected with this theme was the recollection of observing his older brother lift a heavy bronze lamp with his teeth to the admiration of his sister and the envy of the patient. His tendency to withdraw from situations which he could not master was reinforced by his castration anxiety as well as by the fear of his aggressive mother and sister. Until his analysis he retained a false recollection of having been injured seriously during childhood. Unable to assert his masculinity effectively in reality, he harbored heroic rescue fantasies in which he killed his rivals and won the love of a gracious woman. Because of his guilt and fear, however, he turned toward his older brother in a protective dependent attachment. When he realized that he could compete successfully with "siblings" scholastically, he wanted desperately to surpass his brother. The unconscious implications of this rivalry made him feel very guilty. This feeling was aggravated by the hostile attitude of the older brother who rejected him, charging, with justice, that the patient, the mother's favorite, had usurped his place in their mother's affections. As a measure of revenge the older brother persistently undermined the patient's confidence by calling attention to his immaturity. X, even in his adult life, could never feel secure in his manhood.

Although X was five years younger than his brother, he was keenly interested in his sibling's school books, perusing them avidly when he got an opportunity to do so. The brother retaliated by forbidding him repeatedly to look at the books and by placing under lock and key the many fascinating books which he had received as gifts on the occasion of his Bar Mitzvah. The key to his brother's bookcase was a much sought-after prize. When he found it, X would enjoy the surreptitious delight of poaching on his brother's intellectual domain.

For a few months during his eleventh year, X changed from a compliant youngster to a reactively defiant one. He stopped doing his school work and in the company of a somewhat older playmate embarked upon a series of petty thefts. He barely escaped being caught when he stole the fountain pen of the "captain" of his class, a boy whom he envied greatly. These thefts culminated in the patient's stealing of a book belonging to a boy several years ahead of him in school. X's brother found him reading the book and knew immediately that it could not be the patient's. He concluded correctly how X had come by the book and made him return it to its rightful owner. With this event the stealing period came to an abrupt end. Shortly after this, X became very interested in his Hebrew school work and began to observe religious practices very strictly although his home was not at all a religious one. Soon after Bar Mitzvah, the older brother had stopped going to Hebrew school. Since his rival had withdrawn, X was determined to shine in this field. This was a characteristic pattern which resulted in X being inhibited in any studies with which his brother remained identified. As a result of this tendency, it was discovered in the analysis, X would unconsciously spoil his grade in final examinations in these subjects through careless oversights. The stories of Cain and Abel and Jacob and Esau were recurrent themes in his analysis.

The Bar Mitzvah initiation was experienced by X in terms of rivalry with his brother. The ceremony was celebrated on a grander and more ostentatious scale than had his brother's. For X, the Bar Mitzvah ceremony served as an exhibitionistic foray against his brother, demonstrating among other things how much more he had achieved in his studies. He read several additional portions of the Torah and composed a long speech which made a great impression upon the guests. In recalling these events, X had no recollection of his brother having been at the celebration, although it was obvious that he must have been there.

Certain events in connection with the actual celebration are noteworthy. During his reading of the Torah, this very religious boy kept mispronouncing—of all things—the name of God. After the services the rabbi congratulated the boy and they drank a toast together. X took the liquor into his mouth but could not swallow it. He had never had any whisky before and he lacked the courage to try it now.

His older brother helped him celebrate the Bar Mitzvah by taking X to his first Broadway show. X passed the station and came late for the performance. In the theater, in a spirit of fraternal permissiveness, the brother called X's attention to the fact that the girl in the row behind them in the balcony was sitting in such a way that one could see way up under her skirt.

The experience of the Bar Mitzvah was the patient's first clear-cut competitive victory over his brother. The conflict between his exultant victory and his guilt feelings characterized almost every other transition experience. At his graduation from high school, for example, the patient felt very depressed. He had had a very superior record and had achieved rewards and recognition which his brother had not. X went to the same college to which his brother had gone. When he completed an important set of qualifying examinations he celebrated the event much as his brother had helped him celebrate his Bar Mitzvah. He went for the first time to a burlesque show. In the company of the mother and his brother's fiancée, X attended his brother's graduation. This was the first academic degree bestowed upon a member of the family and the exercises left a great impression upon the patient. At his own commencement from the same university two years later, when X was being graduated with honors, he turned in his cap and gown immediately after the ceremonies and before his mother and sister had an opportunity to admire him in his academic attire. Subsequently, in an important professional examination, because of his guilt feelings, X meticulously, but unconsciously, arranged his own failure. To X, Bar Mitzvah and every subsequent graduation situation represented a guilt-laden usurpation of his brother's prerogatives. As in the case of the previous patient, this was related to unconscious fantasies of killing and castrating the rival and of enjoying unchallenged the fruits of victory; namely, the mother's love.

For all the male patients who have been presented the fact that Bar Mitzvah represents an ordeal by examination was particularly pointed because they were all professional men who experienced so much of their competitive life in terms of intellectual rivalry.

It is by no means unusual for sons of irreligious or antireligious parents to insist upon being Bar Mitzvah, contrary to the wishes of their parents. Unfortunately, no clinical data on such a situation have been available to me. One patient in analysis, however, did reproach his dead father for not having had him go through the Bar Mitzvah ceremony. He interpreted his father's failure to do so as evidence of hostility toward the son's maturing prowess. This fear of paternal retaliation for competitive success contributed to the patient's symptoms of impotence and examination phobia. Although he had been graduated from professional school with the highest record in the history of the institution, the patient, before analysis, had been unable to extricate himself from the self-defeating habit of attaching himself in a second-rate position to professional father figures. He sought in the analysis what he felt Bar Mitzvah might have given him—permission to repudiate the authority of the father, assurance of being accepted as an equal.

CONCLUSIONS

In the Bar Mitzvah ritual two elements are fused, a conscious religious component of induction into Judaism and a more general unconscious component of transition to sexual maturity. Because of the powerful affects connected with it, this latter, biological event can be utilized as the occasion for strengthening the affiliation of the developing young man to the historic traditions and values of the group or community; that is, to the values of the father generation and those which preceded it. Bar Mitzvah therefore represents an institutionalized experience, tending toward the resolution of ambivalent feelings derived from the oedipus conflict in a manner compatible with the demands of the social order. During the ceremony, communal sanction is given the initiate to repudiate the authority of his father. This could help the boy overcome the guilt and fear connected with becoming a man, a necessary step in the development of psychological maturity and independence. But where the authority of the father leaves off, obligation to the community and its ideals takes over. Thus the father image, so recently cast off, re-emerges on a new and more elevated plane. This is often represented in the person of the rabbi who at the Bar Mitzvah ceremony welcomes the boy into manhood but at the same time thunders at him the obligations to the Jewish community.

In actual practice, the Bar Mitzvah initiation is not nearly as effective as its counterpart among primitive peoples. What the experience actually accomplishes for the individual boy depends primarily upon his previous development. Bar Mitzvah is really only one of the turning points, albeit an exceedingly important one, in the vicissitudes of the oedipal conflict. Generally speaking, in our cultural context in which religious observance is minimal, the most common reaction is for the boy to adhere to some of the rituals, notably praying in the morning with phylacteries, for a period of weeks or perhaps months. At the end of this time in a spirit of rebellion he proclaims that he is fed up with this burdensome task and puts aside his phylacteries forever, thus becoming the equal of his father in the nonobservance of the commandments. As his father had defied the authority of his elders, the boy now does the same. In the exceptional situation where the father adheres strictly to religious practice, this act of repudiation on the part of the boy is much more dramatic and weighty in its significance.

From the material presented it is possible to observe several different attempts to resolve the ambivalent conflicts which Bar Mitzvah epitomizes. In one instance, a temporary allegiance to an idealized substitute father image, the rabbi, served as a transitional figure in the process of detachment from the authority of the father—a rather common phenomenon in the psychology of adolescents. For those individuals whose anxiety over casting off the authority of the father is very great, the Bar Mitzvah experience may suggest a way out in the form of renewed submission to an exalted father image—God. In one case, this religious observance was an intensely ambivalent one, fraught with anxiety and hardly distinguishable from an obsessive-compulsive neurosis. In another instance, a prolonged period of religious adherence which followed Bar Mitzvah signified a passive masochistic character formation. The unconscious substitution of the right to acquire knowledge for the prerogative of sexual practice indicates an additional solution which Bar Mitzvah suggests.[15] Sexual and aggressive energies may be channelized into study and the acquisition of power through knowledge. This is a particularly favorable way out consistent with the demands of a society in which there is a considerable time lag between sexual maturity and sanctioned heterosexuality. Certain authors have demonstrated how book learning may have either masculine or feminine meaning to the individual (11), but in the context of the Bar Mitzvah initiation the prestige of learning as a masculine attribute is clearly pre-eminent, reinforced by, and at the same time re-enforcing, a tradition of esteem for learning in which the heroes are the heroes of the intellect.

The dawning manhood of the primitive youth was signalized by the gift of a spear; the Jewish boy at his Bar Mitzvah gets a fountain pen. While the unconscious phallic significance of these gifts remains unchanged, their application in the social setting is quite different. That the same affect-arousing situation, namely, the transition to sexual maturity, should be celebrated with such different symbols is a measure of the change in social values.

The dual aspect of Bar Mitzvah—the fusion of a religious component of induction into Judaism with an unconscious but more general component epitomizing the ambivalent attitude which holds true in the relations between the generations—may perhaps provide the solution of a number of puzzling sociological problems posed by religious educators and rabbis. Despite the progressive deterioration of the religious significance of the Bar Mitzvah ceremony, the demand of Jewish parents to have their sons undergo Bar Mitzvah has abated only slightly (2, 20). This phenomenon is all the more striking when one considers the fact that most of these parents are not at all religious and not particularly interested in Jewish learning. Reformed Judaism attempted to eliminate Bar Mitzvah entirely and to substitute for it a more meaningful confirmation service open to both sexes and taking place at a somewhat later age than thirteen. Reformed rabbis report nevertheless that requests for the Bar Mitzvah ceremony continue as numerous as before. Bar Mitzvah furthermore is celebrated in radical labor and Zionist circles with an elaborate ceremony which omits reference to God or religion entirely (17, p. 72). It seems plausible to suppose that we must attribute the persistent vitality of the institution of Bar Mitzvah to this sexual element, to the representatives of the conflicts connected with arriving at sexual maturity. These conflicts are universal and are experienced from one generation to another with undiminished intensity.

For psychoanalysts the study of the reactions to the Bar Mitzvah experience may furnish valuable insight into the dynamic interplay of the feelings growing out of the oedipal conflicts as they appear during the crucial years of puberty. There seems to be a special affinity between significant Bar Mitzvah conflicts and the later or concurrent appearance of examination anxiety.

Finally, clinical material demonstrates that the Bar Mitzvah assertion of religious manhood is unconsciously understood by the Bar Mitzvah boy and the members of the community in terms of physical, sexual maturity. From the metapsychological point of view, libidinal and aggressive energies of the id are neutralized and placed at the disposal of the superego. The initiate renounces remnants of his oedipal wishes for the demands of the developing superego, namely, group loyalty and studiousness.

REFERENCES

1. Blum, E. "The Psychology of Study and Examination," *Int. J. Psa.*, VII, 1926.
2. Edidin, B. L. *Jewish Customs and Ceremonies*, Hebrew Publishing Co., New York, 1941.
3. Feldmann, S. "On Blushing," *Psa. Quart.*, XV, 1941.
4. Fenichel, O. *The Psychoanalytic Theory of Neurosis*, Norton, New York, 1945.
5. Flugel, J. C. "The Examination as Initiation Rite and Anxiety Situation," *Int. J. Psa.*, XX, 1939.
6. Flugel, J. C. *Man, Morals and Society*, Int. Univ. Press, New York, 1945.
7. Freud, A. "Types of Homosexuality," Address before the New York Psychoanalytic Society, May 1950.
8. Freud, S. "Totem and Taboo," *The Basic Writings of Sigmund Freud*, Modern Library, New York, 1938.
9. Jones, E. "The Significance of the Grandfather for the Fate of the Individual," *Papers on Psychoanalysis*, Wood and Co., New York, 1913.
10. Jones, E. "Religion and Psychoanalysis," in Lorand, S. (ed.), *Psychoanalysis Today*, Int. Univ. Press, New York, 1944.
11. Klein, E. "Psychoanalytic Aspects of School Problems," *Psychoanalytic Study of the Child*, III/IV, 1949.
12. Lewin, B. D. "The Body as Phallus," *Psa. Quart.*, II, 1933.
13. Low, L. *Die Lebensalter in der jüdischen Literatur*, Szegedin, 1875, quoted by Rivkind (see ref. 17).
14. Nunberg, H. "Homosexuality, Magic and Aggression," *Int. J. Psa.*, XIX, 1938.
15. Nunberg, H. "Circumcision and Problems of Bi-Sexuality," *Int. J. Psa.*, XVIII, 1947.
16. Reik, T. "The Puberty Rites of Savages," *Ritual*, Farrar, Straus, New York, 1946.
17. Rivkind, I. *Bar Mitzvah: A Study in Jewish Cultural History*, Shulsinger Brothers, New York, 1942.
18. Róheim, G. "Transition Rites," *Psa. Quart.*, XI, 1942.
19. Sachs, H. "The Community of Daydreams," *The Creative Unconscious*, Sci-Art Publishing Company, Cambridge, Mass., 1942.
20. Schauss, H. *Lifetime of a Jew*, Union of American Hebrew Congregations, 1950.
21. Schechter, S. *Studies in Judaism*, I, Jewish Publication Society of America, Philadelphia, 1924.
22. Scholem, G. G. (ed.) *Zohar—The Book of Splendor*, Schocken Library, New York, 1949.
23. Wice, D. H. "Bar Mitzvah," *The Universal Jewish Encyclopedia*, II, 1940.

NOTES

[1] By restricting conclusions to data drawn from clinical psychoanalytic experience, it is hoped that some of the methodological difficulties inherent in the application of psychoanalytic thinking to cultural processes may be avoided. A number of qualifications concerning the sampling of the patients must be introduced. The data cited in this study were obtained on patients in psychoanalytic treatment. There were eleven such patients drawn from the New York Metropolitan area. Of these patients, nine were men and two were women. All of the patients were native-born Jews but the parents of eight of the eleven were foreign-born. In only one case was a patient raised in a devoutly observant, orthodox Jewish home. For the rest, religious observance was never a matter of compulsion. Both women were housewives and college graduates. One of the women did some teaching in a Sunday School. Of the nine men, six were professionals, two were businessmen, and one was an advertising executive. Four of the patients, including both women, had hardly any religious instruction. Two had less than three years of religious schooling and five had more.

The method of approach delineated above differs in many aspects from the more common applications of psychoanalysis to religion in so far as no attempt is made to confine religious experience within the framework of any nosological entity, as, for example, Freud and others after him did when they considered religion as "the universal, obsessional neurosis of mankind." Psychoanalysis permits us to observe what affects are aroused in an individual who participates in any communal experience—religious, artistic, political, or otherwise. What the religious experience signifies to the particular patient, its connection with other elements in the patient's psychic life, and the fantasies which it provokes in him, can be understood during psychoanalytic therapy. In this respect, the interplay of psychological forces resembles more closely the affective situation one observes in communal participation in a work of art. Many elements in religious observance are of the nature of a "shared daydream" which enables the participants to discharge various tensions after the fashion which Sachs has described (19).

I am indebted to Dr. Irving M. Clyne for some of the clinical material.

[2] The literature on initiation rites is of considerable import for psychoanalytic theory in general. The main ideas concerning initiation rites which pertain to the problems discussed in this paper follow the work of Reik (16), Freud (8), Flugel (6) and Róheim (18).

[3] In some communities the privilege of wearing the prayer shawl was granted a man only when he married (20). The symbolic representation of masculine sexual prerogative by the prayer shawl is made all the more clear by this example.

[4] The time and manner in which this ceremony originated is completely obscure since there is no reference to Bar Mitzvah as such in either the Law of Moses or Talmud. For a historical survey cf. Wice (23), Low (13), Rivkind (17) and Schechter (21).

The ceremony of Bar Mitzvah is by no means absolutely necessary in the religious life of the Jew. In spite of this, the ceremony has spread throughout the world. Many of the semiautonomous Jewish communities of the late Middle Ages and early Modern Times passed ordinances which provided fines and other penalties for fathers of eligible boys who were not presented for Bar Mitzvah at the appropriate time. It is striking to notice the ceremony being observed quite regularly in families who are not at all religious or God-fearing.

[5] In the past the "examination" aspect of the initiation was even more manifest. In many Jewish communities in Europe it was customary for the initiate to be quizzed by a rabbi on the day of his Bar Mitzvah or to engage in talmudic disputation with his elders.

[6] The content of these speeches is fairly uniform and the speech itself has usually been borrowed *in toto* from a standard textbook collection of speeches. This is no recent innovation. Books of this sort dating back more than one hundred and fifty years have been preserved.

[7]He is the center of congratulations and celebration and the recipient of many gifts. If the grandfather is alive he most likely will present the boy with a set of phylacteries and a prayer shawl. In this respect the grandfather fulfills the function which Ernest Jones (9) described. In our society certain gifts have become characteristic for this occasion, namely, a fountain pen, a watch, books or jewelry. The grave proclamation of "Today I am a man" and the fountain pen gift have been linked humorously but tellingly to the Bar Mitzvah celebration.

[8]In European communities of the past, occasionally engagement and even marriage followed Bar Mitzvah almost immediately, but this was by no means the rule. The traditionally accepted age for marriage was eighteen.

[9]Israel, Joseph Benjamin II, *Eight Years in Asia and Africa*, Hanover, 1858, cited by Rivkind (17).

[10]This form of assault is a variation of a rather common form of "initiation" practice among pubescent boys in the New York Metropolitan area. The full initiation practice consists of pulling down the victim's trousers and spitting upon his penis. Other similar practices have in common some element of humiliation to masculinity, symbolizing castration.

[11]This is a very common development. In a certain sense, the debt of guilt upon achieving manhood is not paid off in full at the time of Bar Mitzvah but is amortized in small doses over a period of several months following the Bar Mitzvah.

[12]Cf. also E. Bergler, quoted by Flugel (5, 6).

[13]The material of the analysis had demonstrated the connection between his interest in writing and declamation to phallic exhibitionism and to the concept of the whole body as a phallus (12).

[14]"She [the Torah] may be compared to a beautiful and stately maiden who is secluded in an isolated chamber of a palace and has a lover of whose existence she alone knows. For love of her he passes by her gate unceasingly and turns his eyes in all directions to discover her. She is aware that he is forever hovering about the palace, and what does she do? She thrusts open a small door in her secret chamber, for a moment reveals her face to her lover, then quickly withdraws it. He alone, none else, notices it; but he is aware it is from love of him that she has revealed herself to him for that moment and his heart and his soul and everything within him are drawn to her. So it is with the Torah which discloses her innermost secrets only to them who love her. . . . When finally he is on near terms with her, she stands disclosed face to face with him and holds converse with him concerning all of her secret mysteries and all of the secret ways which have been hidden in her heart from immemorial time. Then is such a man a true adept in the Torah, a 'master of the house,' for to him she has uncovered all her mysteries, neither keeping back nor hiding any single one. . . . Hence should men pursue the Torah with all their might so as to come to be her lovers as we have shown" (22). One of the main arguments advanced by the rabbis for the inclusion of the sensuous poetry of the Song of Songs in the Holy Canon was that the poetry was allegorical. The beloved and beautiful Shulamith, they said, was the Torah, and her lover represented Israel. Literally, the Torah means learning and it stands for knowledge in general.

[15]Another element represented in Bar Mitzvah is the separation of the young boy from his mother and the rupture of the passive attachment to her. This was richly borne out by clinical material which could not be included in this study. Róheim (18) and Nunberg (15) have both stressed this element in the psychology of circumcision and puberty rites. The Bar Mitzvah initiation into the masculine prerogatives of religious study and ritual would indicate how Torah is used not only as a substitute for, but also as a diversion from, women and sexuality.

The Hypomanic Personality

MORTIMER OSTOW

EDITOR'S COMMENT

This essay, the third clinical study in this volume, was prepared for inclusion in a book about manic illness, *Mania: An Evolving Concept* by Robert H. Belmaker and H. M. van Praag (New York: Spectrum Publications, 1980). It expresses a psychiatric rather than a psychoanalytic point of view: it describes the phenomena of illness rather than its mechanisms.

It is included in this volume because it casts some small light on two of the major figures of the Sabbatean movement, that strange and damaging madness of seventeenth-century Jewry. Since the definitive biography of Shabbatai Zvi was provided by Gershom Scholem (*Shabbetai Zevi and the Shabbetian Movement During His Lifetime* [in Hebrew] [Tel Aviv: Am Oved, 1957], translated by R. J. Zwi Werblowsky as *Sabbatai Sevi, the Mystical Messiah*, Bollingen Series XCIII [Princeton: Princeton University Press, 1973]), it has become possible to examine this phenomenon and to analyze some aspects of it in modern times. Scholem believes that Zvi suffered from manic-depressive illness, and he supports this hypothesis with convincing data. He also makes it clear that the organizing genius of the movement was Nathan of Gaza.

I attempt to establish in this essay that Nathan may have exhibited the qualities of a normal variant of manic-depressive illness, namely, hypomanic personality, which is not only not disabling, but which actually confers supernormal capacities that often make for success and leadership. Nathan used Zvi as a fascinating figurehead, and through him, gave expression to his own antinomian tendencies.

The more interesting and important problem of why so very many Jews followed this unholy pair is not accessible to this type of clinical analysis.

Hypomanic personality differs from other states of mind in the manic-depressive group in that it is not only not pathologic, but in many instances seems to confer an advantage. The psychiatrist encounters it as the interim personality of many patients whom he relieves of manic or depressive episodes. He also encounters it among relatives of his manic-depressive patients. He encounters it too among the more successful of his friends and acquaintances.

An early description of the hypomanic personality was given, I believe, in the Book of Genesis. Joseph is recognized by his father as aspiring to dominate his siblings and parents. (It is interesting that the first two dreams of the Joseph cycle are interpreted by his father Jacob, and are the only two dreams that are interpreted as unconscious—or at least unacknowledged—wish fulfillments of the dreamer, rather than supernaturally inspired prophecies. In fact they were fulfilled.) He had already become his father's favorite.

In the biblical story there followed a number of vicissitudes, literally ups and downs. He was his father's favorite. Then he was abandoned in the pit. Then he became the steward of the house of Potiphar. Then he was incarcerated in the dungeon. And finally he became the vizier of Pharaoh. I should like to suggest that what in the biblical story are given as ups and downs in life experience, represented symbolically episodes of depression separated by intervals of hypomanically tinged success. The Bible says of him that he was a successful man. Finally, by virtue of his industry, intelligence and charm, in a society in which mobility was severely limited, if non-existent, he became second only to Pharaoh. In the end, his brothers did bow down to him as he had anticipated in his childhood dreams.

It is the hypomanic's consistently high level of activity which impresses his friends. His work occupies him during most of his waking hours. He takes few vacations, and when he does, he manages to use them to further his endeavors. Hypomanics, despite their busyness with their principal activity, seem to be able to participate in a number of peripheral endeavors. One finds them often at the forefront of community activities. While the energy of the hypomanic personality is usually reflected in physical action, it can often find major expression in intellectual or artistic work.

The individual with hypomanic personality can appear relatively youthful for his age. Not only does he look youthful, but he actually gives the impression of indefatigable busyness.

While at times such individuals can become angry, they usually present a cheerful and pleasant appearance. Moreover they convey an air of self-confidence and courage, expressed at least partly by an erect carriage. In fact they are both confident and courageous. They look optimistically toward the future, and if their judgment is biased, it is biased in the direction of assuming that success will be achieved more easily than most people would think. Despite their optimistic bias, they are able to form realistic assessments.

There is probably no significant correlation between the hypomanic quality and intelligence. However an impression of good intelligence is usually created by the combination of busyness, courage, optimism and pleasantness. When the individual with hypomanic personality also possesses good intelligence, he is likely to achieve unusual success.

The hypomanic personality exhibits problems primarily in the area of object relations. While his charm and success often attract people to him, and while he enjoys being admired and desired, he generally cannot return the love that is offered to him. In most instances, he understands the meaning of fidelity and can remain faithful to spouse and to friends. However he seems to lack the capacity for intimacy so that despite his attractiveness, generosity and popularity, he is seldom a good parent or spouse.

He has a need to have his impression of omnipotence and omniscience confirmed by others. Therefore he may attempt to please them as well as to impress them. Moreover he does not tolerate criticism well. Although he may attempt to conceal it, he does have the need to triumph over and to control others. Often therefore, he finds himself competing for leadership with others, and attracting followers. His self-confidence, attractiveness, his need for followers and their admiration, taken together create the potential for leadership. When a leader possesses these special qualities that attract followers to him he is said to be a charismatic leader. The term charism in theological language refers to a special gift or grace.

Among the changes most pronounced in the swings between mania and depression is the scope of the imagination. The truly depressed patient is imprisoned in current reality, which he sees as frustrating, uncongenial and unchangeable. He will frequently say that he sees the future stretching before him in an unrelieved, monotonous sameness. It reminds him of the eternal sameness of death. The same individual, when euphoric, finds the here and now not in the least restricting. His imagination sees possibilities of change and improvement and ultimate gratification. As contrasted with the individual who is neither manic nor depressed, the depressive individual will be unable to see the obvious potential in a situation, while the truly manic will see possibilities which are utterly unrealistic. The individual with hypomanic personality will see potentialities beyond those that are visible to the non-hypomanic; yet they will be sufficiently realistic to warrant being taken seriously. This perceptiveness and imaginativeness relates to problem solving in whatever area of interest. They may also lead to the creation of imaginative images of reality which will possess esthetic appeal for others. It is this ability which the creative individual cherishes and which is taken from him by a tranquilizing drug. He misses it and in many instances is willing to risk relapse into psychosis by omitting the therapeutic drug, rather than to accept the deprivation of his ability to imagine. Reality after all does hem us in, and while it offers opportunities for gratification, it more effectively frustrates the fulfillment of most of our wishes. Realistic fantasy, that is, imagination, can suggest ways of overcoming realistic frustration in some instances, and can permit the enjoyment of escape into the magical world of the arts in others. Depression and the tranquilizing drugs which facilitate depression, both suppress this capacity for imagination, while the manic tendency, of whatever extent, normal or abnormal, as well as the anti-depression drugs which facilitate that tendency, promote imagination and fantasy. Schizophrenia and the hallucinogenic drugs make fantasy replace reality, and even usurp the sense of reality.

The individual with hypomanic personality contributes much to society by virtue of his industriousness and his creativity. In addition, because he possesses so many attributes of leadership, he is often accepted as a leader. Problems arise however when the hypomanic personality is recurrently interrupted by episodes of mania or depression or both. The more serious problem is mania. The reason is that the leader is taken seriously simply by virtue of his leadership. Strange ideas which manic relapse induces, might at first be interpreted as the result of greater perspicacity and wisdom. It may take some time before the public realizes that their leader is ill. For a while they struggle to accommodate themselves to his illusions and delusions, so that they will not have to repudiate him.

When the hypomanic leader becomes depressed, the consequences are not so serious. He merely becomes less active, or completely inactive for a while, but seldom does anything that might injure others, unless the manic-depressive tendency is accompanied by a schizophrenic or paranoid quality. In that case the leader may perceive his own depression as an incipient universal apocalypse just as the schizophrenic does. If that is the case, he may lead his followers into some self-destructive struggle, failing to distinguish between his personal catastrophe and that of his community.

The history of the Sabbatian movement of the seventeenth century provides us with an instructive contrast between the individual with hypomanic personality and the individual in an episode of hypomanic illness or manic psychosis.

In 1665 and 1666 a large proportion of the members of the Jewish communities of Europe, the Middle East, and North Africa acknowledged the arrival of a "Messiah" in the person of a Turkish Jew, Shabbatai Zvi. The episode followed and brought to a climax 150 years of mystical, religious study and philosophy. It shifted the scene of anticipated redemption from the individual spirit to external political reality. Why so many Jews of diverse cultures, occupations, and of widely differing social and economic status were so ready to disrupt daily life and to prepare to depart for Palestine in order to participate in messianic redemption is difficult to understand. In any case it is clear that the moving force lay in the readiness of the responders, rather than in any external compulsion, or in any attraction exerted by the leaders of the movement that would be found irresistible by reasonable people in normal times. What is interesting from our point of view is the fact that the movement was led by two men. Shabbatai Zvi himself, and a younger man who has come to be known as Nathan of Gaza.

Shabbatai Zvi, the Messiah, was a rabbinic scholar, born in 1626, in Smyrna (Izmir), to a well-to-do family, probably Ashkenazic in origin. He occupied himself with religious and mystical studies, and led a life of asceticism, as did many others at that time and place. The biographical details that we possess leave little doubt that he suffered manic-depressive illness. Contemporaries describe what we recognize as classical episodes of both mania and depression. During melancholic episodes, he would withdraw into solitude, and his behavior did not occasion much comment. However, during his manic episodes, he engaged in characteristically grandiose and unconventional behavior.

Since he lived within a totally religious milieu, his delusions and provocations took religious form. He violated religious customs and laws publicly and noisily, and introduced bizarre and forbidden variations of ritual practice. He justified these innovations by characteristic manic word play on classical texts. It is not known whether he actually declared himself a Messiah before 1665.

At first his behavior was tolerated in his community because it was regarded as some sort of deviance, perhaps a manifestation of illness, and also because his interval behavior was characterized by dignity, asceticism, and studiousness. Ultimately, he was banished from his native Smyrna, then from Salonika, and then from Constantinople.

Shabbatai Zvi might have lived and died unrecorded in history had it not been for the efforts of another rabbinic scholar, about seventeen years younger, Nathan of Gaza. Nathan was celebrated as a brilliant scholar and a "prophet" who could understand people's problems, and prescribe kabbalistic remedies. In February 1665, Nathan, who was then twenty, described an ecstatic vision of Shabbatai Zvi, whom he had not yet met, as the Messiah. In April of the same year, having heard of Nathan's ability to provide remedies for the troubled, Shabbatai Zvi consulted him, hoping to find some relief for his illness. The two men spent many days together, conversing and exchanging views. Ultimately Nathan persuaded Shabbatai that not only did he not require a remedy, but that he was truly the long-awaited Messiah. At the end of May, in a state of manic elation, Shabbatai publicly proclaimed himself the Messiah, and he acted the role whenever he was manic. At other times he was diffident but did not disavow his claim. The latter was accepted by amazingly large numbers of people, including some who knew him, but also many who had merely heard of him by letter. It was Nathan rather than Shabbatai who instigated diffusion of the messianic claim, who called upon all Jews to initiate a preparatory effort of repentance, who created new prayers and liturgical recitations appropriate to the event, and who provided a revision of kabbalistic theory to accommodate the new situation created by the arrival of the Messiah.

To complete the story, Jews all over the world responded to the proclamation by preparing to leave their homes for Palestine, once the Messiah had assumed political powers, as he promised he would. Shabbatai Zvi was arrested by the Turkish authorities in February 1666. He was held in prison, first in Constantinople and then in the fortress of Gallipoli. Here he continued to play the role of Messiah whenever he was in a state of manic elation, and continued to impress many of his followers who visited him there. Because the messianic furor continued to unsettle the Jews of Turkey, Shabbatai Zvi was removed to Adrianople, and there he was induced to apostasize to Islam by threats and promises. It is interesting that the messianic movement was not damaged by the incarceration of the Messiah; it lost only some of its adherents after his apostasy; and retained a faithful few even after his death in exile in 1675. Just as Paul transformed a crucified Messiah into a more powerful symbol than a living one, so Nathan transformed an incarcerated and then an apostasized Messiah into a powerful symbol with a similar promise of redemption upon his reappearance.

What is of interest from our point of view is the contrast between the two men, Shabbatai Zvi and Nathan. Shabbatai Zvi was the Messiah, but he was passive and ineffective. During the intervals of freedom from illness, he was inactive. When manic, he was so psychotic and disorganized that he could accomplish nothing. Nathan, on the other hand, was the leader, guiding light, and theoretician of the messianic movement, who, if Shabbatai Zvi had not been available, might have organized the same movement around the person of someone else.

When not elated, Shabbatai was described as possessed of personal charm, conveying an impression of nobility, kind, dignified, and tactful. Yet he failed on his own to establish a coterie of followers. At times he gave the impression of being ascetic and saintly. Even when not depressed, he preferred solitude. But he was passive, lacking in initiative, and unable to form and execute long-range plans. When he was neither manic nor depressed, he did not retain enough of the manic drive or imagination to achieve anything remarkable.

Nathan, on the other hand, exhibited none of the manic or depressive swings. He is described (by Scholem) as possessor of "visionary power, intellectual capacity, and untiring energy." His qualities include "tireless activity, unwavering perseverance without manic depressive ups and downs, originality of theological thought, and considerable literary ability." One of those who visited Nathan after the proclamation of Shabbatai Zvi as Messiah, recorded his experience as follows (Scholem, 1973: p. 260): "When I stood before Nathan the prophet all my bones shook, although I had known him before, for his countenance was completely changed. The radiance of his face was like that of a burning torch, the color of his beard was like gold, and his mouth which (formerly) would not utter even the most ordinary things, now spoke words that made the listeners tremble. His tongue speaks great things . . . and the ear can hardly take in that which comes out of his mouth with a wonderful eloquence. And verily, every moment he tells new things, the like of which have not been heard since the day that the Law was given on Mount Sinai." Allowing for the enthusiasm of the believer, the contagious excitement of the situation, and the hyperbole of the then current literary fashion, Nathan's impressiveness nevertheless comes through. This combination of a consistently high level of activity, imaginativeness, creativity, charisma, ambition, an interest in accomplishing things in the world, concern with community, an ability to convert misfortune into advantage, leadership, consistently high morale, strongly suggests that Nathan's was what we have been calling a "hypomanic personality."

Nathan and Shabbatai Zvi shared the same antinomian tendency. Shabbatai expressed his only during states of manic elation, at least at first. Even after he announced himself as Messiah, his posturing was greatly diminished during non-psychotic intervals, and there were some hints that in melancholic episodes, he detached himself from the whole project. Nathan's antinomianism expressed itself in his sponsoring Shabbatai's claims and in leadership of the movement which in many respects violated normal Jewish practice. However he was not so uninhibited as to follow Shabbatai into apostasy. In other words, Shabbatai, in his manic episodes, personified Nathan's antinomianism, and Nathan used Shabbatai to give vicarious expression to this tendency without going to the same extremes. It is interesting that when led—or rather misled—by a charismatic hypomanic, large numbers of thoughtful and reasonable people can take seriously the delusional behavior of a psychotic. Evidently the qualities of the hypomanic personality compel the ordinary person to respect and defer to him, and to accept his influence.

What we learn from the comparison of these two men is that the same psychic process which in pathologic degree creates gross and disabling psychosis, when limited, can give rise to superior psychic function and a potential for leadership.

REFERENCE

Scholem, Gershom, 1973. *Sabbatai Sevi, The Mystical Messiah*. Princeton University Press, Bollingen Series XCIII.

Applied Psychoanalytic Studies

The Jewish Response to Crisis

Mortimer Ostow

EDITOR'S COMMENT

The final three essays illustrate what is called "applied psychoanalysis." This rubric comprises studies of individual and group behavior by the application of psychoanalytic principles to the data of history, of biography, of social phenomena, and to artistic and intellectual creations. Bergmann's and Rubenstein's papers both illustrate applied psychoanalysis, the former employing psychoanalytic principles to elucidate Freud's attitude toward his Jewishness, and the latter, to elucidate the concerns of the Jewish community at the time the Midrash was composed.

This essay summarizes very briefly the findings of an interdisciplinary study group. The group included experienced analysts who were knowledgeable in Judaica, and serious scholars of Judaism who were sophisticated in psychodynamic thinking. Original texts were considered and were studied for both their explicit and implicit meanings. While no striking new insights were obtained, the observations here recorded achieved varying degrees of consensus and therefore deserve to be taken seriously.

A number of the serious crises of Jewish history were examined. In each case attention was given to the nature of the trauma that created the crisis, the immediate response of the Jewish community, the manifestations of demoralization when resistance failed, and a number of activities that, taken together, could be called "working through."

Most of the subjects discussed here deserve more intensive study and elaboration. The contribution of this essay is the demonstration that many of the well-known religious, cultural, behavioral, and attitudinal characteristics of Jews and of Judaism can be seen in psychodynamic terms as responses to past and current crises of Jewish history.

This paper was read before the Wisconsin Society for Jewish Learning and the Mount Sinai Medical Center of Milwaukee on the occasion of the presentation of the Maimonides Award of Wisconsin to the author, 15 September 1979. It was published in *Conservative Judaism*, Volume 33, Number 4, pages 3–25, Summer 1980.

INTRODUCTION

This essay is based upon and derives from the deliberations of an interdisciplinary seminar organized to study "The Response of Jews to Crisis."* The group included members of the Jewish Theological Seminary's faculties of history, Talmud, and theology; historians, sociologists, and philosophers affiliated with other academic institutions; observers of the Jewish scene; and seven psychoanalysts, four of them from the Department of Pastoral Psychiatry of the Seminary.† This seminar met about once a month during the academic year, that is, about eight sessions a year, for about five years.

It was the intention of the group to attempt to learn something about the "nature" of the Jewish people—if such a thing exists—by studying the way Jews have responded to the many crises and tragedies of their history.

The participants were selected on the basis of their interest in this problem, some professional expertise that they could contribute, their openness to new ideas, their demonstrated originality, and also their ability to work cooperatively in a group. One more

---

*The project was sponsored by the Ostow Family Fund for the promotion of psychoanalytic studies in Judaism, established at the Jewish Theological Seminary by Kalman I. Ostow.

†The membership of the group increased as it became evident that a greater variety of information and expertise was required. Those who participated over a significant period of time included the following: Dr. Gerson D. Cohen, Chancellor of the Jewish Theological Seminary, who served as co-chairman along with the author of this essay; Jacob A. Arlow, Professor of Psychiatry, Downstate Medical Center, State University of New York; Samuel Abrams, Professor of Psychiatry, Downstate Medical Center, State University of New York; Samuel Atkin, psychoanalyst, private practice; Martin Bergmann, psychoanalyst, private practice; Mortimer Blumenthal, Professor of Psychiatry, Mount Sinai Medical School, City University of New York; Lucy Dawidowicz, Professor of History, Stern College; Chaim Zalman Dimitrovsky, Professor of Talmud, Jewish Theological Seminary; Henry Friedlander, Professor of History, Brooklyn College, City University of New York; Sidney S. Furst, Department of Pastoral Psychiatry, Jewish Theological Seminary; Milton Himmelfarb, editor American Jewish Yearbook; Wolfe Kelman, executive vice-president, Rabbinical Assembly; Milton Malev, Department of Pastoral Psychiatry, Jewish Theological Seminary; Ivan Marcus, Professor of History, Jewish Theological Seminary; Ismar Schorsch, Professor of History, Jewish Theological Seminary; David Sidorsky, Professor of Philosophy, Columbia University; Seymour Siegel, Professor of Theology, Jewish Theological Seminary; and Allan Silver, Professor of Sociology, Columbia University.

requirement was imposed. Since the Holocaust was uppermost in everyone's mind, and since we wished to minimize the kind of commitment to positions that personal suffering in the Holocaust might have induced, we did not consider for membership in the group anyone who had experienced the Holocaust personally.

In order to attempt to understand internal motivation of behavior in addition to external pressures and constraints, we examined primary sources rather than secondary accounts, wherever we could. When we dealt with accounts which were composed some time after the event, we studied them as reactions of their authors to contemporaneous circumstances.

Because the largest amount of primary source material derived from the Holocaust, and because of the uniqueness of the Holocaust and its immediacy, we studied it first and at considerably greater length than any other historical period. Professor Dawidowicz selected a number of published and unpublished journals, and these formed the basis for the group's discussion. We then turned our attention to the period of the Roman conquest of Jerusalem, using Josephus and some selections from Talmud and Midrash as our study material. We also considered the sectarian heresies of two thousand years ago on the basis of Dead Sea texts and the Christian Bible. Thereafter we studied the periods of the Crusades, the Spanish and Portuguese expulsions, the Chmielnicki massacres, and finally the rise of Zionism against the background of the Russian pogroms.[1]

During the course of the deliberations some subjects which were not associated with any specific historical incident came under consideration. For example, there was a good deal of discussion of the question of whether masochism in particular and passivity in general is especially characteristic of Jews. The nature of the ties holding the Jewish community together and the conflicts of the forces within the Jewish community were also considered. Such subjects as guilt, journal writing, myths and myth making, self-esteem, morale and demoralization, universalism versus particularism, messianism, apocalyptic, and mysticism were given attention by the group.

This essay is not intended as a definitive report of the transactions of the seminar. It is, rather, a synopsis of some of the arguments together with my own elaborations, and some original contributions which did not come up for discussion in the group. While most of the ideas presented were contributed by the seminar, I take responsibility for the presentation and elaboration. A full report of the transactions of the seminar is being prepared for publication.

It was not possible in such a study to compare Jewish behavior with the behavior of non-Jews, for there could be no meaningful comparison experiences and no comparison groups to serve as controls. Therefore we can only describe the Jewish experience and the Jewish response. It is not easy to discern which components of the response were determined by the Jewishness of the group being studied, which were determined by the nature of the trauma and by the resources available to cope with it, and which were conditioned by the culture in which the Jews lived.

We still do not possess an adequate theory to understand group behavior, nor to relate individual behavior to group behavior. Our efforts, then, were exploratory. We considered theory of individual behavior, extrapolations from that to the group, and some tentative hypotheses about group theory. Obviously, the first step was to define the nature of the trauma.

TRAUMA

Trauma is an experience which, by its quality or intensity, causes injury to an individual or a group, in such a way or to such a degree that the subject's ordinary coping mechanisms are overcome. A problem arises in applying the concept to such a wide range of historical events. While there are certain similarities, the various crises that the Jews have encountered have differed in many ways—so that the specific traumata that we attempted to study were far from uniform. Not only is it often difficult to determine the specific nature of the trauma, but there are usually many traumata involved. For example, what was the trauma which affected Judea two thousand years ago, to which the Jewish community responded by spawning a plethora of heretical sects? Was it Roman military oppression, economic oppression, social disorganization or demoralization? What was the trauma associated with the destruction of the Temple? It is obvious that there were military defeat, loss of many lives, miseries of the siege of Jerusalem, vast financial loss, and of course, loss of the Temple with a concomitant loss of a way of life. But there were other effects of a nonmaterial nature. The loss of the Temple deprived the Jews of their principal channel of communication with God. In fact it deprived them of the sense of having a special relation with God, and of being protected by Him. If God could not, or would not, protect His Temple, how could one believe that He would protect Israel? And if one lost one's view of a familiar universe, how then was one to maintain any orientation in life? In the aftermath of the defeat, there was a good deal of concern with its cause and with placing the blame. While various forms of misbehavior and immorality were adduced, perhaps one of the most painful facts that had to be acknowledged was that internecine strife contributed heavily. It would probably be correct to say that the military defeat, the siege that preceded it, and the enslavement, exile, and expropriation that followed, traumatized the Jews in many ways. It is probably also true that a study of any of the serious traumata to which Jewish communities have been subjected in historical times would demonstrate a complex set of painful and injurious experiences.

As painful as all the physical and material effects of persecution were, an important, and probably more persistent effect was a profound diminution in self-esteem.

Among the many parameters of psychic function, self-esteem is one of the most influential. It determines where one places oneself among the other members of one's social group. It determines one's ambitions and goals, and one's style of living. It plays a significant role in determining one's degree of success or failure in life.

Self-esteem in turn is determined by a number of influences, external and internal, group and individual. Clinical experience suggests that each individual is born with a degree of self-confidence and courage that appears even in childhood, and that serves as a baseline for perhaps the rest of his life. External influences elicit deviations from this baseline, either positive or negative, enduring or transient.

Self-esteem may be influenced seriously and permanently by intense childhood experiences. Current data and theory inform us that to elicit a child's maximum potential, parents should provide the care and love, protection and tenderness which the child requires at each stage in his development, while at the same time, relinquishing surveillance and control gradually, and to the degree that the child's maturation dictates. When parents reject the child, or treat him with hostility or derision, the child's need for protection induces him to attempt more and more vigorously to elicit this protection by subordinating and degrading himself. He may grow up with a degree of self-contempt which he will carry for the rest of his life. Conversely, if a parent overwhelms the child with protection and love, discouraging his attempts to become independent, his continuing and excessive dependence upon his parents will also limit his self-esteem.

Self-esteem is influenced by current experience, but such influence will persist for relatively short periods of time as current experience changes. Self-esteem will be increased by affection returned, by admiration, by success, and by the experience of living up to one's ideals. Self-esteem will be diminished by affection rejected, by the contempt of others, by failure, especially in relation to one's ideals.

The social group, the community among whom one lives also influences self-esteem—in two ways: The individual and the group together establish a position for the individual within the group, a position vis-à-vis other members of the group, a status. This status influences self-esteem. It is also true that the individual's self-esteem influences the station that he strives to achieve within the group. To the degree that he achieves that station, or transcends it, his self-esteem is reinforced. To the degree that he falls short, his self-esteem is diminished. Secondly, the community itself is assigned a status by surrounding communities. That status adheres also to its members. In a surrounding community in which the Jewish community is assigned low status, the self-esteem of the individual Jew will be diminished. Where the Jewish community is respected, individual Jews will acquire reinforcement of their self-respect.

I have taken this time to discuss self-esteem because it is my impression that one traumatic influence common to perhaps all of the various traumatic experiences which have affected the Jewish community, is a sharp diminution in self-esteem. Diminution in self-esteem is both a result of trauma, and a trauma in its own right. The diminution may have been caused by military defeat, persecution of individuals, exile, various forms of expression of hostility by surrounding communities, by loss of lives and loss of wealth. That the painful humiliation was not the least of the components of the trauma is suggested by the vivid and poignant references to it in Lamentations, and in several warnings and prophecies in other portions of the Scriptures. (Some citations are included in the semi-weekly Tahanun prayer.)[2]

But challenges to Jewish self-esteem have characterized even tranquil intervals in the many centuries of exile. The very word "tolerance" implies a difference in status between the host community and the Jewish guests. I should like to suggest that the assault on Jewish self-esteem by external tolerance or intolerance has played a shaping role in the determination of the character and personality of the individual Jew, as well as the behavior of the Jewish community and the culture it has created. Specifically, I believe that we can attribute to some extent, to the need to overcome Jewish low self-esteem: Jewish ambition and success, Jewish cohesiveness and divisiveness, Jewish loyalty and disloyalty, Jewish self-effacement and Jewish ostentation.

RESISTANCE

In each instance Jews resisted the trauma to which they were subjected.

In recent considerations of the Holocaust, much effort has gone into attempts to establish that Jews actively resisted rather than passively accepted the systematic efforts to destroy them. Accusations that the Jews were too passive have been voiced within the Jewish community itself. If we try to look at the controversy we realize that what is at issue is whether or not Jewish behavior complied with the generally accepted notions of a heroic ideal. In other words, did we Jews conduct ourselves in a manner we can be proud of? Again the issue is self-esteem.

If we study the history of Jewish resistance we find that modes of resistance were determined primarily by the nature of the danger, the resources available to the Jewish community, the opportunity for resistance, the availability of actual or potential allies, cultural modes which the Jews had absorbed from their environment, and the history of past persecutions and Jewish responses to them. Therefore the question arises: Are there any modes of resistance exclusively Jewish, or characteristically Jewish? It is doubtful that one could find social behavior responses that are exclusively Jewish. It would even be difficult to establish that any behavior response is characteristically Jewish. All we can do is catalogue what the Jews did in response to the various crises that they encountered.

Consider for example the simple response of unification of the Jewish community. The efforts to mobilize the Jewish community under attack, and its surrounding Jewish communities, do not always succeed as one would hope and expect. It was only in the past 140 years that Jews in different parts of the world have attempted to protect each other.[3] In the Roman campaign against Judea, only a fraction of the Jewish inhabitants of Palestine participated in the struggle. In medieval times, there is no evidence that the Ashkenazic and Sephardic communities responded to or even took notice of each other in good times or bad. Ibn Daud, for example, in 1161 gave no evidence of knowing about the 1096 massacres in the Rhineland. It is true that Jews are instructed in the Talmud to rescue each other when the opportunity presents itself. It is also true that many Jewish communities around the Mediterranean accepted exiles from Spain and Portugal. However, the kind of active mutual assistance reaching all around the world that we expect today, does not antedate the middle of the nineteenth century. Certainly the availability of communication influenced the ability of Jews in different parts of the world to be aware of each other and to request and offer assistance. Yet even such geographically close communities as those of Southern France and

Northern Spain seem to have had little contact, and what contact there was seems to have been hostile. Furthermore, assertions of mutual responsibility in the case of the Damascus Affair in 1840 preceded the era of modern communication. Perhaps, more than anything else, it was the emancipation that facilitated international Jewish mutual concern and assistance. It was the Jewries of England and France, the most emancipated groups of European Jewry, that responded to the Damascus Affair.[4]

While we now take for granted mutual assistance and Jewish unity under attack, that unity has seldom been impressive. One of the best known aspects of the tragedy of the conquest of Jerusalem (in 70) is the costly internecine strife. In most of the tragedies of Jewish history, we learn about individual dissidents and traitors. Even with respect to the Holocaust, we continue to learn of disreputable and disloyal behavior, many reports of which are probably true. The Jews of the United States today could probably be considered one of the most activist groups in terms of self-defense and defense of Jews in other parts of the world. Yet fewer than one-third contribute anything to the United Jewish Appeal.

One fairly common Jewish response to catastrophe is recording the events. There are two kinds of recording: that done by the victims of their experiences, and recording done by the community considerably later, of a preceding trauma.

Why do victims keep journals? Inspection of some Holocaust journals suggests a number of answers. Some victims see the journals as witnesses that at some time in the future will testify against their persecutors. To a certain extent such an expectation is realistic. The journals that have survived the Holocaust do bear eloquent witness against the Nazis and their collaborators. On a conscious level, the diary is addressed only to human survivors, but on an unconscious or perhaps only a minimally acknowledged level, it is addressed to God, in whatever religious or secular form He may be perceived. The hope is that God will take vengeance. Other journal writers felt that the journal is a form of communication with God, not only for the purpose of obtaining revenge, but also as a way of feeling close to, and feeling loved, protected and cared for. Many journals were produced by individuals who were incarcerated alone or in relative isolation. These journals created the illusion of contact with a companion. Writing such a journal combatted the feeling of isolation and the anxiety and the hopelessness that isolation itself brings about. Even in normal times, lonely individuals write diaries to create the illusion of companionship. Writing a journal recreated to some degree the ambience of normal life and permitted the writer to reaffirm his commitment to ideals. We find these last two motivations in the diaries of Anne Frank and Moshe Flinker.[5]

How Jewish is it to write a journal in the face of persecution? The journals we have date mostly from the past two centuries. While we have written records of previous persecutions, they were mostly created after the event, and in retrospect. Certainly journal-producing is not an exclusively Jewish activity. We possess journals written during the Holocaust by non-Jews (e.g., Peter Moen).[5] However, the concern with maintaining moral standards in adversity, with remodeling reality by mental creativity, with reaching out to a protecting, transcendent Deity—these are Jewish, if not exclusively Jewish, concerns.

This leads us to ask what the explicitly religious response of Jews has been to catastrophe. It is generally thought that in times of crisis, people become religious. The cliché is "There are no atheists in foxholes." This is not really true in individual life. Faced with crisis, religious individuals become more intense in their observance; secular individuals continue to ignore religion; and those partly committed may first renew their interest, but later they may become angry and deliberately flout religion. It is also common to see superstitious behavior, often in religious form, expressed by individuals not ordinarily superstitious. In the history of Jewish response to crisis, there is no religious behavior that appears consistently, at all times and all places. Again it is true that Jewish experience has left changes in religious doctrine and observance, but these lasting changes are adopted only years after the fact.[6] In the recent past, at least within the Jewish community, the religious have become more religious, the secular have developed no interest in religion, and those not wholeheartedly committed have gone either way, or first one way and then the other.

Within the religious community, the crisis poses four problems: How can one continue to observe religious law in the presence of external obstacles? How can religious values be used for guidance in making moral decisions? What assistance can be expected from religion? And how can one understand current events within the framework of a religious *Weltanschauung?*

To those who are committed to a religious life, the existence of a crisis makes observance even more necessary. It is vital to retain the forms of observance and worship that have signified continuity with the past, and that protect against discontinuity. Maintaining one's way of life under hostile attack serves also to sustain one's self-esteem, which is always at risk under pressure. Some of the most moving documents we possess about Jewish suffering deal with the determination to adhere to religious precepts.[7] Our history, of course, records the instances of determined resistance, but the many instances of capitulation are seldom recorded. (With respect to the latter, Rashi, for example, in his Responsa, refers to Crusade apostates.[8]) The major exception is the willingness of some Sephardic Jews, tolerated by Maimonides, to adopt the Moslem religion.[9] The difference between this behavior and the martyrdom of the Ashkenazim of about the same period requires explanation. It has been suggested that the difference may be attributed to the fact that Christianity was unacceptable because it requires belief in a Messiah and a new Divinity, whereas conversion to the Moslem religion seemed less heinous because it requires acceptance merely of a new prophet. It has also been suggested by Gerson D. Cohen that the medieval Ashkenazi Jews accepted the other-worldliness of the medieval Christians, whereas the Jews living in the Moslem world were influenced by the this-worldliness of their hosts, and were therefore more willing to make compromises.

Persecution invariably generates conflict among various loyalties and commitments. There are selfish interests, the interests of one's family, the interests of one's community, and then there are moral and religious commitments. Life-and-death decisions are often demanded which require a choice among these commitments. They are always heartbreaking, and inevitably they give rise to guilt. If one can look to the priorities established and sanctified by religion,

and accept its guidance, one can minimize the guilt, though often at
the cost of sustaining painful personal loss.

Inevitably one wishes for magical rescue within the religious
context. These wishes are seldom voiced, for fear that their non-
fulfillment might give rise to blasphemous thoughts. Generally,
too, one finds in the classical and medieval sources more or less
disguised expressions of anger with God. The anger may be
expressed still within the context of the tradition or it may result in
frank and open repudiation of the tradition.

At some point there is an attempt to understand the reason for
the catastrophe. The demand to understand it in terms of the
philosophy of the religion arises from two sources. It is characteristic of the human psychic apparatus that it requires an understanding of cause-and-effect relations. Psychoanalysts speak of a "need
for causality."[10] When one's physical, social, and familial moorings
are being broken abruptly and violently, one strives to retain at
least the sense that one lives in a comprehensible world. Normally
one can tolerate a degree of ambiguity and uncertainty. Under
stress the need for consistency grows greater. For example, in the
case of organic brain disease, which interrupts the patient's conceptual contact with his familiar universe, he becomes panicky in
the presence of almost any change. That is why old people resist
moving from the homes in which they have lived for decades. The
need to understand arises also from a second source, that is, the
need to justify God, in order to overcome the temptation to
repudiate God because misfortune has occurred without a valid
religious reason.

When an individual finds himself confronted with an intolerable
and unyielding reality, he resorts to intrapsychic defensive maneuvers which do not change the reality, or prepare him to deal with it,
but which spare him pain. Such defensive maneuvers include
denial, which is simply refusing to acknowledge that the distressing
reality exists, ignoring the facts and their implications and suppressing one's own emotional response; hysterical detachment, which is
a more profound disengagement in which not only the unpleasant
reality, but the entire area of concern is rejected, the affect is
blunted, and the individual busies himself with some substitute

activity; and psychotic detachment, which is detachment from reality complemented by commitment to a fantasy in which the world is presented in distorted form, a form which complies with the individual's conscious or unconscious wishes. While these defensive maneuvers protect the individual from the pain of confronting his unacceptable reality, they do so at the cost of impairing mental function, so that he cannot assess reality objectively, and more realistic endeavors, if any are possible, are delayed or prevented. Therefore we consider their use pathologic.

There is a similar though somewhat different maneuver, sanctioned in our society and many others, in which consensually recognized reality is acknowledged, but it is seen alongside a wish fantasy which is also designated reality and is in fact labeled an "ultimate" and "transcendent" reality. This transcendent reality outweighs material reality but does not obliterate it, so that affective commitment to it can blunt the pain of material reality, and yet permit appropriate response to it.

We know of three types of transcendentalism: mysticism, apocalyptic, and messianism. Of these, messianism is closest to normative Judaism, apocalyptic most remote, and mysticism between. These manifestations of transcendentalism exhibit themselves in two forms: personal belief and commitment, and a social movement. The evolution of a transcendental movement requires a period of time. It does not therefore occur in the midst of an acute crisis. It is seen more commonly during the process of recovery from tragedy, or during a protracted period of oppression, for example during the period of the Roman rule of Palestine.

All such transcendental phenomena are based upon psychologic regressions from normal, reality-oriented function, and correspond to the dynamics of certain clinical syndromes. The mystical orientation toward a fantasy world, constructed to accommodate conscious or unconscious needs, resembles the delusional phase of schizophrenia. But there are important differences. The schizophrenic regression occurs automatically, beyond the control of the individual, while the mystical regression is optional. Similarly, the schizophrenic regression is fairly fixed, while the mystical regression is reversible. The schizophrenic cannot understand the fact that he has displaced the quality of reality from the material world to the fantasy world, while the mystic preconsciously understands that he has done violence to the reality principle, but sees that violence as a paradox. The schizophrenic regression prevents the individual from engaging in realistic affectionate relations with others, while mystics retain the capacity to cohere in groups and to work together. Schizophrenic delusions are usually accompanied by unpleasant affects because the schizophrenic retreat itself creates anxiety, and the conflict in schizophrenia is internal and therefore finds representation even within a problem-solving delusion. On the other hand, mystical fantasies convey pleasant affects, although even a mystical trance retreat can elicit anxiety.

Mysticism occurs in two forms: the mystical trance state or fantasy, and the mystical way of life. In the trance state, the individual enters into a state of altered consciousness, a personal retreat which can be called narcissistic because external reality is replaced by internal pseudo-reality. In the mystical way of life, the individual conducts his life in an unremarkable way, but experiences it subjectively flavored by the ecstasy and awe appropriate to the mystical fantasies with which he lives.

In the paradigmatic mystical fantasy, the individual approaches God. In the Jewish prophetic vision, only the approach is experienced. Other accounts describe proximity, *devekut* (adherence). In the Christian fantasy, there may be an illusion of actual union, i.e., *unio mystica*.[11]

The apocalyptic fantasy that the world will be reborn at "the end of days" following a final struggle between the forces of good and evil, resembles the acute, attack phase of the schizophrenic breakdown. This is characterized by what has been called the *Weltuntergang* fantasy, namely, the fantasy that the universe is being destroyed by some violent forces, and that thereafter it will be reborn. The fantasy indicates the existence of murderous fury in the subject, literally a wish first to destroy the world, and a wish then to remake it according to his own design.

The messianic fantasy corresponds to the belief among a few

schizophrenic patients that they will be rescued from their unhappy situation by some redeemer. It represents a fairly uncomplicated yearning for rescue by a parent or parent substitute.

The recurrence of these transcendental phenomena in individuals is of less significance than the organization of movements based upon them. There are times when large portions of the population organize themselves into groups based upon the adoption of such transcendental beliefs. We know of mystical movements, messianic movements, and apocalyptic movements (e.g., the Dead Sea sects). What these movements have in common is a repudiation of reality, including the reality of the current organization of society, temporal and spiritual. That is, the movements are deviant, or rebellious, or heretical. Being derived from personal "revelation" rather than conventionally recognized tradition, they are essentially antinomian. They secede from, or attempt to take over, current social organization. Those that are more realistic may succeed; very few do. Those that are less realistic usually fail, so that we hear little or nothing of them in the annals of history.

Any of these movements can justify and motivate passive acquiescence to the march of history, attempts to strive only for personal righteousness, or political or even military activism. The outcome depends upon external factors, such as opportunities, allies, resources, and morale. While these movements usually begin as rebellions, if they endure, they are sooner or later incorporated by the establishment, and become part of it, giving up their original antinomian thrust; or, if they are successful, the revolutionary organization becomes the new "establishment."

In essence, transcendentalism attempts to deal with intolerable external reality by distorting one's view of it. When the readiness for transcendental commitment facilitates the organization of movements and sectarian heresies, these movements usually die because their entire basis is unrealistic. In the case of activist movements, the participants attempt to change external reality so as to make it conform to their subjective view. When the change is entirely subjective and internal, psychoanalysts speak of autoplastic efforts to accommodate to reality; when an attempt is made to change reality, we use the term alloplastic. Alloplastic movements, even though driven by commitment to a transcendental vision, may be sufficiently realistic to become successful in the real world. The transformation of a messianic Zionist vision into the reality of the State of Israel exemplifies such a process.

DEMORALIZATION

If the attack cannot be resisted effectively, as defeat becomes likely, morale becomes impaired and then destroyed. At that point courage and idealism vanish and give way to primitively conceived self-interest.

What are the conditions for demoralization? The disappearance of any reasonable chance of survival; isolation, that is, separation from the group; starvation; illness; loss of leaders; and systematic and consistent degradation.

What are the consequences of demoralization? Abandonment of commitment to the group; deflection of hostility from the enemy to group members; defection from standards of personal and group behavior; pessimism; and ultimately, panic.

We read relatively little about demoralization in historical documents. We have some material from Holocaust sources. Josephus describes demoralization during the siege of Jerusalem. Vivid and accurate descriptions are provided by Scripture: for example, Leviticus 26 and Deuteronomy 28, which are presumably warnings, may well be based on eyewitness accounts of catastrophe. Lamentations is construed as an actual account of the fall of Jerusalem in 586 B.C.E. What we see in all of this is murder and oppression of individuals by the enemy; poverty and starvation; hostility within the group and within the family; and humiliation.

The reason we possess so few documents describing demoralization is that most descriptions of catastrophe are written years later, in retrospect. They are written for specific purposes other than simply historical recording. A record of demoralization usually does not serve these specific purposes and so it is not provided. We have no reason to believe that Jews behaved differently in demoralization from others.

WORKING THROUGH

We use the term "working through" to designate a relatively long process by means of which the individual, and possibly the group psyche—if we may use such a term—accommodates to the traumatic disruption of its ordinary activities, and finds a new basis for functioning. Working through includes such activities as recollecting the traumatic events in detail so as to overcome the denial that was the initial response to overwhelming trauma; examining the implications of these events for the present and the future; recollecting similar events from the past and taking courage from the fact that they were overcome; reconstructing personal and group myths which provide a sense of origin, continuity, identity, and destiny; making practical plans for the future that will compensate for the losses of the trauma and that will promise a reasonable prospect of protection against similar trauma in the future. In a sense one constructs a new image of the universe to replace the one that has been lost. When the working-through process has been completed the individual experiences a sense of invigoration, remoralization and renewal, which in the unconscious is represented as a feeling of being reborn.

It is because one of the initial procedures of working through is the recollection of the traumatic events that we have the written accounts of past crises; that is, the events were recorded not for the purposes of history in its modern sense, but for the purpose of working through.

Gerson D. Cohen has observed that most of the written accounts of traumatization of the Jewish community were recorded no earlier than a generation after the event. The Holocaust is different in that recording started very soon after liberation, for the following reasons: journalism encourages the writing of history; modern historians record events for the purpose of history-making as a discipline; the creation of the State of Israel has accelerated the process of working through; and the availability of restitution payments was contingent upon the recording of injuries. And yet in the case of the Holocaust, too, we see even greater interest in recent years, that is, about a generation after the trauma.

The records of previous crises that we do have were probably prepared as part of the process of working through. They vividly recount the suffering of the victims. They were intended to influence Jewish thought and behavior of the time at which they were written. Many of these accounts were intended to be incorporated into the liturgy. They often associated the recent crisis with previous similar catastrophes of the Jewish past. This association reassures one of continuity with the past, and thereby encourages hope for the future. The author often presents the accounts with emphases and distortions which seem to validate and reinforce the central themes of Jewish history. For example, accounts of the persecutions by the Crusaders in the communities of the Rhine refer to the Akedah as a paradigm of Jewish suffering.[12] These retrospective, slanted accounts serve the purpose of encouraging a spirit of Jewish élan and courage to resist oppression, to attempt to forestall similar catastrophes, and to proceed hopefully with efforts to rebuild. In our own day, Holocaust material is presented early in the training program of the Israeli air force.

The assimilation of this material by the Jewish reader results in a sense of renewal and rebirth. The history of Jewish catastrophe is presented no more movingly or concentratedly than in the Yom Kippur service. The penitential service of Yom Kippur aims at creating a sense of renewal and rebirth, primarily by encouraging a recommitment to religious values, and abandonment of sensual pleasure as a means of seeking gratification. The recollection of Jewish tragedy seems intended to contribute to that feeling of renewal. I refer here not only to the *Eileh Ezkerah*, but also to the *piyyutim*, some authors of which were themselves *m'kadeshei hashem* (martyrs).[13] Personal losses are also commemorated in the Yizkor service, and the loss of the Temple is vividly dramatized. In this Yom Kippur service we see two things: Personal losses are brought together with historical tragedies, including both recent history and more remote legendary events, as though they were all congruent but separate manifestations of a recurrent process. The losses are recollected and commemorated as though they conveyed some special merit to us, the survivors.[14]

Perhaps the most compelling and complex religious concept that has allowed Jews to cope with history is that of sacrifice. Psychiatrists and psychoanalysts are frequently confronted with the seeming paradox that individuals often seem to act against their own best interests. Examples of such paradoxical behavior include recurrent behavior that is self-defeating and self-destructive; melancholic depression with its self-criticism, self-degradation, paralysis, and occasional suicide; personality disorder manifest chiefly by timidity, fearfulness, self-effacement, and diminished self-esteem; and masochism.

Various explanations have been suggested for all of these, the most common of which is that they are forms of expiation of guilt. The explanation which I favor is that to the small child, submission, self-effacement, self-degradation, and accepting abuse and hostility, all seem intended to secure mother's protection and love or to appease father. In mental illness the same mechanism probably obtains. Even in suicide, the individual cultivates the fantasy that in his death he will be rejoining mother. (In the Hebrew idiom, one rejoins *Avraham avinu*, Abraham the Patriarch, as in Josippon's account of Hannah and her seven sons.)[15] The normal adolescent and adult will be ready to make sacrifices for the welfare and protection of his family and community. This readiness I see as a normal instinct, related to and perhaps derived from the childhood readiness to submit. The same impulse may be regarded as the motivation for accepting a subordinate place in the social order and submitting to a leader.

Certainly society can function and in fact can exist only when nourished by the contributions, that is, the sacrifices, of its members. In the words of Thomas Jefferson, "The tree of liberty must be nourished from time to time with the blood of patriots and tyrants. It is its natural manure."[16] The mechanism that I am proposing may be the instinctual basis for social organization. The individual is motivated to submit and make his contribution. In return he obtains the feeling of being entitled to protection and beneficence. This instinctual and affective basis of social organization finds representation in the institutions of religion (from which civil government has only gradually and recently been differentiated). Religion involves submission to the authority of God, who is father and ruler.

In the religious context, however, the concept of sacrifice has been modified by the addition of the possibility of vicarious sacrifice. Thus "human sacrifice" means not that one gives up something of one's own, but that one murders another, and hopes thereby to obtain some religious advantage. If the victim is a stranger, such as an enemy, the "sacrifice" really means no loss to the sacrificer, but rather a gratification of hostile wishes. If the victim is someone whom one presumably loves, the sacrifice does represent a loss to the sacrificer, though an even greater loss to the victim. Animal sacrifice in Jewish practice included a number of separate elements. It was a personal gift, a giving-up of one's property for the maintenance of the institution by which one relates to God, and thereby of the relation with God. It was a replacement for human sacrifice, and therefore gave expression to a certain amount of murderous aggressiveness, in sublimated or purified form. It was a device for the support of the Temple establishment. Because it did discharge religious obligation, presumably it left the worshiper with a feeling of righteousness, of being entitled to and indeed of possessing God's favor.

But the concept of vicarious sacrifice applies not only to the ritual context, but to the social context as well. By virtue of a sacrifice offered by, or victimizing, any member of the group, the entire group feels entitled to special favor. The Hebrew word is *z'chut* (merit). We acquire *z'chut* by virtue of sacrifices of others, especially our predecessors. Every morning, in the Shacharith prayer, we remind God of the Akedah and ask him to treat us with compassion, in recognition of the obedience of Abraham. (It is interesting that we do not claim the virtue of Isaac, the intended victim, but that of the father, who was torn between duty to son and duty to father.) On Yom Kippur we recite the *Eileh Ezkerah* hoping to acquire merit on the basis of the sufferings of our predecessors. In the Goldschmidt Mahzor the *Eileh Ezkerah* is followed by the verse:

Chasidim eylu v'harigatam / Av harachamim z'chor otham
Z'chutham uz'chuth avotham / Ya'amdu l'vanecha b'eyth tsaratham

(Lord of Mercy remember/These righteous and their murder./May their merit and the merit of their fathers/Protect your children in time of need.)[17] The Christian religion is based upon the claim that salvation can be acquired by virtue of the sacrifice of Jesus. He is the "Sacrificial Lamb" whose blood purifies his adherents.

But what is the relevance of these considerations to the working through of trauma? It is reported that during the Crusades, the Jews of the Rhine valley, when their position became hopeless, slew each other by common consent. They compared their acts of mutual and self-slaughter to the Akedah, and to acts of animal sacrifice in the Temple.[18] We do not know whether the identification of the martyrs with the Akedah was literally theirs, or whether it was projected back to them by those who, a generation later, recorded the events, or whether there was some of each, that is, perhaps the idea existed at the time of the Crusades, but in recording, it was given a much larger role than it really had.

If it accompanied the event, what thoughts and feelings could it have reflected? A desperate plea for divine intervention? Repressed anger directed toward God, who now again seems to require human sacrifice? I suspect also that the idea that they were reenacting a completed Akedah gave expression to the hope that in death, they would be resurrected like Isaac and accepted into *olam haba*, the world to come.

But then what could the association of these events with the Akedah have meant to the recorders a generation later? If it expressed repressed anger, the anger could not have been the major issue. The writers themselves were not victims. They were probably attempting, by recollecting and recording past events, to deal with their current problems, including their need to come to terms with past generations, their own children, their own economic and political situation, and their own relation with God. We, a generation after the Holocaust, are puzzled, guilty, and ashamed, but not many of us are angry. I would assign greater importance to a need to come to terms with God, and to reinforce one's cosmology and theology. By establishing an identity between the Akedah and the catastrophe of the Crusades, the succeeding generation seeks to acquire credit with God. The community of Israel, having made this sacrifice, is now entitled to the *z'chut* of their forebears. Second, the same identity confirms the continuity of the community of Israel, and resssures the survivor of his future.

The theme of the Akedah and its relation to persecution is preserved in the often-repeated tale of the woman (Hannah) and her seven sons.[15] This tale was told (in later sources) of the Hasmonean persecution, and also of the Roman persecution. Yet the Akedah was not invoked by Josephus in his description of the contemporary mutual murder and suicide at Masada. This last seems consistent with my suggestion that the Akedah paradigm served a more useful purpose for succeeding generations than for the victims themselves. It can also be ascribed to the fact that the authors of the Crusade chronicles were writing for Jews, while Josephus was addressing himself to the Romans. (Possibly, the Akedah came to be used this way only after Josephus.)

The concept that the death of others acquires *z'chut* for us is demonstrated by the simple fact that we demand and expect special consideration by virtue of having been the victims of the Holocaust. On the most literal level, many Jews demand and expect financial restitution payments. On the political and social level, we expect that all non-Jews will understand that we are entitled to special consideration. We do not literally ask for special privilege. But nevertheless we expect it.

Our enemies too seem to agree that persecution purchases a right to special treatment. They argue that there was no Holocaust, and that Jews suffered no more than others during World War II. The purpose of this argument is to deprive the Jews of this credit. But the argument implies that they recognize that Holocaust experience does acquire credit.

I would infer that vicarious sacrifice is a central and cohesive feature of all religions. We have already observed that it is the central feature of Christianity. Judaism however differs in several respects. The sacrifices are not limited to a single historical occasion; they are recurrent—over millennia. They affected large numbers of ordinary people, rather than a single or a small number of legendary figures. They threaten each generation.

To return to the issue of working through, we can see that

persecutions of the past, however understood, are endowed with the power to protect the Jews now living.

Jews respond to catastrophe not only with the feeling of having acquired credit, but also with a feeling of guilt. The feeling of guilt as a response to misfortune is well known in individual psychopathology and psychology. It is encountered in almost every patient with melancholic depression. Psychodynamically it represents an attempt to become reconciled with a protecting parent, and to submit. What is implied is that the reconciliation and submission will purchase rescue and relief.

Self-blame occurs frequently in Jewish liturgy. The best-known formula is *mipnei hata'enu galinu me'artsenu* (Because of our sins we were exiled from our country). This statement is followed by the petition *shetashuv uterahem alenu* ([may it by Thy will] again to have mercy on us). The issue of guilt is often raised at the time of persecution, but it is overshadowed by the real need for self-defense. In the process of working through the trauma, accepting guilt implies that one has control over one's fate, and that God can be persuaded to favor the community.

Guilt appears not only in a religious context, but also in a personal and social context. In a paper written in 1961, Dr. William Niederland described what he called the "survivor syndrome," which includes as one of its major components, "survivor guilt."[19] This is a phenomenon which Dr. Niederland says he observed in almost all of the large number of concentration-camp survivors who consulted him and whom he examined with respect to their applications for restitution payments. These individuals expressed the feeling that they did not deserve to survive their relatives and friends who had perished. Dr. Niederland does not know how prevalent this feeling of guilt may be because he has seen it only among those individuals who have come to him for examination, that is, among individuals who present themselves with pathology. Feelings of guilt were expressed in journals by individuals facing imminent death. It is my impression that these sentiments really express a wish to be reunited with those who have been lost—in death, if not in life. I expect that the "survivor guilt" observed by

Dr. Niederland derived from an underlying state of depression. In conversations with me, he concedes that that might be true.

We know of a somewhat different type of guilt observed among many Jews, now alive, who lived through the period of the Holocaust. They feel guilty that they were not more active in combating it. This differs from survivor guilt in that it is not accompanied by clinical depression, it does not relate to the loss of someone personally known or loved, and it does not relate specifically to survival, but rather to inactivity in the presence of serious danger to fellow Jews.

Among the various kinds of guilt—religious and liturgical, depressive and personal, and social—which is most likely to be specifically Jewish? Perhaps the depressive and personal would occur universally. That guilt which is based upon the feeling of responsibility to *klal yisrael* can probably be considered most specifically Jewish. I have already observed that mutual defense had not been observed among Jews of different communities before the nineteenth century. In modern times, Jews of different communities have accepted responsibility for each other. Mutual defense has become far more aggressive since the Holocaust and the reconstruction of the State of Israel. I believe that we must include among the reasons for this greater aggressiveness, both the feeling of guilt which prevails among surviving Jews for having failed to rescue European Jews from the Holocaust, and the greater assertiveness of small peoples everywhere. While examples of mutual loyalty among segments of a people are encountered not infrequently, the degree of involvement of the various Jewish communities with each other far exceeds that seen among others. For example, Jews are astonished by the apparent lack of concern of the Christian religious establishment for the fate of Lebanese Christians. If we keep in mind the fact that "working through" the trauma at any given time means utilizing the memory of the trauma to meet current needs, then we understand that the relative ineffectuality of American Jews in saving European Jews from the Holocaust is recollected in the hope that the guilt which that memory induces will help to mobilize the Jews today to support the State of Israel, and to protect Jews living in countries in which they are in jeopardy.

Certainly the concept that Israel suffers because of its sins can be considered characteristically Jewish, though I do not know to what extent it prevails also among others. Although the Book of Job argues that suffering does not establish guilt, it expresses only a minority opinion. The doctrine of *mipnei hata'enu* continues to be held valid in accordance with the dominant view voiced in Deuteronomy 28 and the Book of Chronicles. What is its function in the working through of trauma? Primarily it reasserts the principle of God's justice in the face of events that might tend to question belief in it. If we have suffered it is because we have sinned, not because God is unjust. The doctrine of reward and punishment, so basic in Jewish thinking, must not be challenged. When it seems inconsistent with the facts, then our view must be questioned. In individual depressive illness, the feeling of guilt occurs almost universally. Clinical evidence demonstrates that the guilt arises from the conflict between resentment against the protecting parent image who failed, and a wish, notwithstanding, to attempt to maintain a loving relation. In effect the depressed individual says: "It isn't your fault, it's mine. Please take care of me." It seems reasonable to assume that a similar mechanism prevails with respect to the guilt which appears in the religious context. We repress anger directed toward God and redirect it against ourselves, in the hope of retaining or increasing God's protection. We do this because otherwise we should have to repudiate our entire understanding and view of the universe, to reject the cosmos as we have known it. Those who cannot do that try to reconcile the facts of the misfortune with religious theory by assuming blame.

Each society develops its own mythology. We have seen in our time how the Palestinian Arabs have quickly developed a mythology about a "Palestinian entity" which they energetically pass on to succeeding generations. The mythology functions to facilitate the cohesiveness of the group, and to mobilize the energies of the individual to the service of the group and its purposes.

The mythology usually includes myths of origin and myths of

crisis. Specifically, one set of myths will speak of the origins of the group: The group was created despite efforts to thwart its creation at the earliest stages. Another set of myths describes a series of critical adversities, each of which threatens to destroy the group. But the group weathers each storm, and survives nevertheless. These myths are usually based upon actual historical events, but they are molded and worked so as to comply with the current needs of the group.

They are offered as factual history to children, who respond to them by seeing themselves as integral parts of the group. Membership in the group becomes a major component of the core of their identity, their self-image. As they mature, and especially with the acquisition of education and some intellectual sophistication, they are able to replace mythological history with veridical history while still retaining the identity feelings and commitments which were elicited by the myths.

Why are children and even adults so ready to take these myths seriously? The myths appeal because they can apply to the individual too, i.e., we each entertain fantasies in which we combine actual memories and distortions. These fantasies serve specific purposes within the intrapsychic economy. In effect they become personal myths. Most of these myths deal with our own ideas about our origin, for example: whether we were wanted by our parents, and welcomed by them; how we were received by our siblings; whether we were in danger of serious injury or death at some early point in our lives; what adverse circumstances and influences we overcame. In other words, personal and group myths become congruent with each other. The individual then feels that his personal history and the group's history are the same, and therefore that their fate is identical.

I introduce the subject of myths here because as part of the working-through process, the crisis is mythologized. That is, the account of the events is crystallized in a form which lends itself to the current needs of the surviving community. For example, the community constantly requires encouragement of cohesiveness. Both at times of crisis and at times of ease, the Jewish community is troubled by factionalism and divisiveness. Recollection of mortal danger to the community does encourage commitment. Usually the form imposed upon the recent accounts of the last crisis, emphasizes its congruence with past crises, and so conveys a sense of timelessness and continuity with Jewish history. As we recite in the Haggadah every year: "In every generation tyrants have sought to destroy us, and the Holy One, blessed is He, has delivered us from their hands."

Yet there are specific features of each myth that make it seem particularly apposite to some crises rather than to others. For example, myths in which the Jews fought to defend themselves, as they did at Masada, or in the ghettos of Eastern Europe, are recalled now during periods of serious concern for the State of Israel. On the other hand, on occasions when flight and migration are called for, myths such as the Exodus, or ben Zakkai's establishment of the academy at Yavneh, or the story of the four captives become appropriate. (The latter, according to Gerson D. Cohen, sought to validate the transfer of authority from Babylonia to Spain.)[20] When passive resistance and surreptitious teaching of Judaism become necessary, myths of the Hadrianic period are recalled.

One would think that such crisis myths might discourage Jews from adhering to a community which seems inevitably to incur misfortune. Perhaps some or many Jews do defect under this influence. I know of at least one individual who, as a child of about ten, when he learned about the tragedies of Jewish history, decided that assimilation was the best course for the Jews and made an effort to assimilate. To be sure there were other motives, but this probably did play some significant role. On the other hand, many young Jews, perhaps most, under the influence of these myths, are encouraged to commit themselves to the community even more intensely. In fact, at a time when many adolescents are finding it difficult to emancipate themselves from their attachment to their parents, some find not the dangers to the Jewish community, but the compelling power of the myths, too constraining. The attempt to escape these constraints often lies behind the tendency to seek out companionship with non-Jews and to marry them.

Group myths also function to augment the self-esteem of the

community. When there has been an actual victory, its commemoration helps to overcome current humiliation by reminding one of past glories. When there has been an actual defeat, its commemoration may achieve a similar result by pointing up the nobility of the victims, the injustice, the bad character of the persecutors, and the virtue acquired by the community as a result of the sacrifices made by its members in the past, and as a result of expressions of guilt and contrition.

SUMMARY

It is difficult if not impossible to determine whether any specific pattern of behavior is exclusively Jewish.

Our study of the psychology of Jewish behavior must be limited by the absence of a good theory of the psychology of group behavior in general.

Traumas to the community are usually multiple and complex so that it is not always easy to know, in the case of any given historical event, what the various traumata were and how significant they were.

One of the major and consistent effects of persecution has always been serious impairment in Jewish self-esteem. This impairment in self-esteem has had important consequences both positive and negative for Jewish individual and group behavior.

Modes of Jewish resistance to crisis were determined by the realistic qualities of the nature of the persecution, the availability of external help, the condition of the Jewish community, and the history of past persecutions and responses to them.

Cohesiveness of the Jewish community under stress has not always occurred to the same extent as we have seen it in recent decades.

One of the most common responses to Jewish catastrophe has been the recording of the event. There have been both contemporary and retrospective records made. In each case the record has been made for the purposes of the recorder at the time of the recording.

Persecution of the Jews has caused some Jews to abandon Judaism and others to adhere more intensely.

In many instances where the trauma was a continuing rather than an acute crisis, the Jews developed commitment to a transcendental orientation.

The ultimate effect of trauma, namely demoralization and dissension, are described vividly in Scriptural sources, which emphasize not only murder, oppression, and starvation, but also humiliation.

The late response to crisis may be called "working through." The latter is a process of accommodating to the traumatic disruption of the group's life by taking proper cognizance of the facts, re-moralizing the group, and making appropriate plans for the future.

Recording serves the purposes of working through.

Viewing the past injury as a form of sacrifice helps the community to derive both a sense of comfort and a sense of credit and virtue *(z'chut)* from it.

Guilt in many forms usually appears among the survivors of Jewish catastrophe, and the process of working through must help the individual to come to terms with that guilt and responding to it.

In the process of working through, the crisis being dealt with is made to conform to the mythical history of the Jewish people, and in addition, the event itself becomes mythologized.

NOTES

[1]The texts studied include the following:

A. Holocaust Materials

Alton (Tauber), Ruth. *Litzmannstadt* [Lodz Ghetto]. From Memoir Collection Leo Baeck Institute, New York. Translated by M. Goldschmidt, 1971.

Atchildi, Asaf. "Rescue of Jews of Bukharan, Iranian and Afghan Origin in Occupied France (1940–1944)." *Yad Vashem Studies*, Vol. 6, 1967, pp. 257–281.

Berlinski, Hersh. "The Organization of the Jewish Resistance Movement in Warsaw." Translated by Lucy Dawidowicz, from: "Dray: Ondenbukh: Pola Elster, Hersh Berlinski, Elyohu Erlikh." (Tel-Aviv, Ringelblum Institute, 1966). Unpublished, in mimeograph form.

Flinker, Moshe. *Young Moshe's Diary*. Jerusalem: Yad Vashem, and New York: Board of Jewish Education, 1971.

Frank, Anne. *The Diary of a Young Girl*. Translated by B. M. Mooyaart. Garden City, N.Y.: Doubleday, 1952.

Goldstein, Charles. *The Bunker*. Philadelphia: Jewish Publication Society, 1970.

Kalmanovitch, Zelig. "A Diary of the Nazi Ghetto in Vilna." In the *Yivo Annual of Jewish Social Science*, Vol. 8 (*Studies on the Epoch of the Jewish Catastrophe, 1933–1945*). Edited by Koppel S. Pinson. New York: Yiddish Scientific Institute—YIVO, 1953.

Kaplan, Chaim A. *Scroll of Agony: The Warsaw Diary of Chaim A. Kaplan*. Translated and edited by A. I. Katsh. New York: Macmillan, and London: Collier-Macmillan, 1965. Selections.

Karski, Jan. *Story of a Secret State*. New York: Houghton Mifflin, 1944. Selections.

Katznelson, Yitzhak. *Vittel Diary*. Tel-Aviv: Ghetto Fighters House, 1964. Selections.

Korbonski, Stefan. *Fighting Warsaw*. New York: Funk and Wagnalls, 1968. Selections.

Kret, Jozef. "One Day in a Penal Company." In *Reminiscences of Former Auschwitz Prisoners*, translated by Krystyna Michalik. Panstwowe Muzeum, W Oswiecimiu, 1963.

Mechanicus, Philip. *Year of Fear*. Translated by Irene F. Gibbons. New York: Hawthorne Books, 1968. Selections.

Miedzyrzecki, Wladka. "The Underground." In *The Root and the Bough*. Edited by Leo W. Schwarz. New York: Rinehart, 1949.

Milejkowski, Israel. Interview (from Ringelblum Archives, Document 86). In *Bleter far Geshikhte*. Vol. 1, No. 3–4, August–December 1948, pp. 188–194. English translation by Lucy Dawidowicz in mimeograph.

Moen, Peter. *Peter Moen's Diary*. Translated by K. Austin-Lund. London: Faber & Faber, 1951. Selections.

Orska, Irena. *Silent Is the Vistula*. New York, London, and Toronto: Longmans, Green & Co., 1946. Selections.

Ringelblum, Emmanuel. *Notes from the Warsaw Ghetto: The Journal of Emmanuel Ringelblum*. Edited and translated by Jacob Sloan. New York, Toronto, and London: McGraw-Hill Book Co., 1958. Selections.

Schwarz-Bart, André. *The Last of the Just*. Translated from the French by Stephen Becker. New York: Atheneum Publishers, 1960.

Trembaczowski, Jan. "The Road to Death." In *Reminiscences of Former Auschwitz Prisoners*, translated by Krystyna Michalik. Panstwowe Muzeum, W Oswiecimiu, 1963.

Wells, Leon Weliczker. *The Janowska Road*. New York: Macmillan, 1963. Chapters 22 and 35.

Yoors, Jan. *Crossing*. New York: Simon & Schuster, 1971.

Zeitlin, Hillel. Interview. In *Bleter far Geshikhte*. Vol. 1, No. 2, April–June 1948, pp. 111–114. English translation by Lucy Dawidowicz in mimeograph.

Zywulska, Krystyna. *I Came Back*. New York: Roy, 1951. Selections.

B. *Classical Sources*

The Dead Sea Scriptures. Translated by T. H. Gaster. Garden City, N.Y.: Anchor Books, Doubleday & Co., 1964. pp. 46–70, 291–340.

Josephus. *The Jewish War*. Translated by J. A. Williamson. England: Penguin Books, 1970.

The New English Bible. The New Testament. Oxford University Press, 1971. Matthew, Mark, John, The Revelation of John, Letters to Romans, Corinthians I & II, Ephesians.

"Second Esdras." In *The Oxford Annotated Bible with the Apocrypha*, Revised Standard Version. Edited by H. G. May and B. M. Metzger. New York: Oxford University Press, 1965.

The Fathers According to Rabbi Nathan. Chapter 4, pp. 32–38. Translated by Judah Goldin. Yale Judaica Series. New Haven: Yale University Press, and London: Oxford University Press, 1955.

Babylonian Talmud. Gittin, folios 55b–58a. Translated by M. Simon. Edited by I. Epstein. London: Soncino Press, 1963.

Midrash Rabbah. Translated and edited by H. Freedman and M. Simon. London: Soncino Press, 1961. Lamentations s.a.

C. *Medieval Sources and Materials*

Solomon bar Simeon. "Massacres in the Rhineland." In *Ideas of Jewish History*. Edited by Michael A. Meyer. New York: Behrman House, 1974. Pp. 93–102.

Lewisohn, Ludwig. *The Island Within*. Philadelphia: Jewish Publication Society, 1968. Selections.

Spiegel, Shalom. *The Last Trial*. Translated by Judah Goldin. New York: Pantheon Books, Random House, 1967.

Maimonides, Moses. *Epistle to Yemen*. Edited by A. S. Halkin. Translated by B. Cohen. New York: American Academy for Jewish Research, 1952.

Maimonides, Moses. "Letters of Maimonides." In *A Maimonides Reader*. Edited by I. Twersky. New York: Behrman House, 1974. Pp. 179–182.

Maimonides, Moses. *Mishneh Torah*, Book I, *Hilkhot Yesoday ha-Torah*, Chapter 5. Edited and translated by Moses Hyamson, New York: Bloch Publishing, 1937.

Maimonides, Moses. "Letter to Obadiah the Proselyte." In *A Treasury of Jewish Letters*. Edited by F. Kobler. New York: Farrar, Straus & Young, 1953. I, pp. 475–476.

Cohen, Gerson D. "Messianic Postures of Ashkenazim and Sephardim (prior to Sabbethai Zevi)." In *Memorial Lecture No. 9*. Leo Baeck Institute. New York: Frederick Ungar Publishing Co., 1967. Pp. 117–156.

Joseph ben Joshua, ha-Kohen. *The Vale of Tears* (Emek Habacha), by Joseph Hacohen and the anonymous corrector. Translated from the Hebrew plus critical commentary, by Harry S. May. The Hague: Nijhoff, 1971.

Usque, Samuel. *Consolation for the Tribulations of Israel.* Translated by M. A. Cohn. Philadelphia: Jewish Publication Society, 1977.

Ibn Verga, Solomon. *Shebet Yehudah.* Edited by A. Shohet and A. Baer. Jerusalem, 1946–47.

Hanover, Nathan. *Abyss of Despair* (Yeven Metzulah). Translated by A. J. Mesch. New York: Bloch Publishing, 1950.

D. Modern Sources and Materials

Pinsker, Leo. "Auto-Emancipation: An Appeal to His People by a Russian Jew" (1882). In *The Zionist Idea.* Edited by Arthur Hertzberg. Garden City, N.Y.: Doubleday and Herzl Press, 1959.

Herzl, Theodor. "The Jewish State" (1896). In *The Zionist Idea.* Edited by Arthur Hertzberg. Garden City, N.Y.: Doubleday and Herzl Press, 1959.

[2]See *Weekday Prayer Book* (Rabbinical Assembly of America, 1961), pp. 71–79. For annotations see also *Avodat Yisrael*, edited by Isaac Baer (1868), pp. 112–118, reprinted Tel Aviv, 1957.

[3]For the Damascus blood libel and its impact, cf. Howard M. Sachar, *The Course of Modern Jewish History* (New York, 1963), pp. 134 ff. On the Mortara affair and its impact, cf. I. Elbogen, *A Century of Jewish Life*, trans. M. Hadas (Philadelphia, 1945), pp. 30 ff., 34 ff.; Sachar, *op. cit.*, pp. 178 ff. On Kishinev, cf. Elbogen, pp. 378 f., Sachar, pp. 249 ff.

[4]See Sachar, pp. 134 ff.

[5]See Note 1 for references.

[6]See Gershom G. Scholem, "Jewish Mysticism and Kabbalah." *Jewish People Past and Present* (New York: Jewish Encyclopedic Handbooks, Central Yiddish Culture Organization, 1946), Vol. I, pp. 322 f.; idem, *Major Trends in Jewish Mysticism*, 3d ed. (New York: Schocken Books, 1961), pp. 244 f., where the chronology of kabbalistic expression after the expulsion of Spain provides the evidence of our assertion.

[7]Irving J. Rosenbaum, *The Holocaust and Halakhah* (New York: Ktav Publishing House, 1976). Hirsch Jacob Zimmels, *The Echo of the Nazi Holocaust in Rabbinic Literature* (London: Marla, 1976).

[8]On Jewish apostasy in the face of medieval persecutions, see Jacob Katz, *Beyn Yehudim legoyim* (Jerusalem, 1960), chap. 6.

[9]Moses ben Maimon, "Iggeret haShemad," *Iggarot.* Edited and translated by Joseph Kafih (Jerusalem, 1972), pp. 107–120.

[10]See H. Nunberg, *Principles of Psychoanalysis* (New York: International Universities Press, 1955), pp. 151–152.

[11]See Evelyn Underhill, *Mysticism* (London, 1930), pp. 413–443; and Gershom G. Scholem, *Major Trends in Jewish Mysticism* (New York, 1971), p. 123.

[12]See Shalom, Spiegel *The Last Trial*, full reference in bibliography, Note 1.

[13]For *Eileh Ezkerah*, see reference Note 17, pp. 568 ff. *The Book of Memoirs*, Penitential Prayer and Lamentations of Rabbi Ephraim Bar Jacob of Bonn, edited by A. M. Haberman, (Jerusalem, 1970); Shimon Bernstein, *Al Naharot Sfarad* (Tel Aviv, 1956).

[14]In contemporary High Holy Day prayerbooks, a special commemorative service on the Holocaust has been added. See, for example, the *Mahzor for Rosh Hashanah and Yom Kippur*, edited by Jules Harlow (New Yor, 1972), pp. 566–569. There, the Mourner's Kaddish is interwoven with the names of the death camps and of other centers of atrocity.

[15]See Gerson D. Cohen, "Hannah and Her Seven Sons (in Hebrew literature)," in *The Mordecai M. Kaplan Jubilee Volume*, Hebrew section (New York, 1953), p. 109.

[16]Thomas Jefferson, Letter to William Stevens Smith, November 13, 1787.

[17]Daniel Goldschmidt, editor, *Mahzor LeYamim haNoraim lefi Minhag Bnei Ashkenaz* (Jerusalem, 1970), II, p. 574.

[18]Spiegel, *op. cit.*

[19]William G. Niederland. "The Problem of the Survivor," in *Massive Psychic Trauma*, edited by Henry Krystal (New York: International Universities Press, 1968), pp. 8–22.

[20]See Gerson D. Cohen, "The Story of the Four Captives," *Proceedings of the American Academy for Jewish Research*, 29, 1960–1961.

Unconscious Fantasy and Political Movements

Jacob A. Arlow

While this essay considers the role of myths in integrating internal motivation and social need, the illustrative case and the historical examples deal with specifically Jewish themes and make the essay appropriate for this volume.

It is Arlow's argument that the shared myth carries the common projections of the members of the society that entertains it, and permits, by its retelling, the indirect expression of projected, unconscious wishes. At the same time, the social sharing of the myth dissipates individual guilt.

Society, he argues further, encourages those myths that give expression to personal qualities or ideals of behavior desirable for society's needs at the time. Since such qualities change from time to time, the myths encouraged by society also change.

It is interesting to observe how the child in the illustrative case at first identified with the mythic character of Dracula, a projection of his Oedipal wishes (Oedipus was after all, himself, a mythic character), and subsequently with legendary ideal characters from American and Jewish history. The earliest figure resembled the deities of the pagan religions, supernatural and representing personal wishes, and the subsequent figures resembled the heroes of monotheistic religions, human, and representing ego ideals sanctioned by the superego.

What we learn from this essay, of practical utility, is which issues to consider in selecting curriculum materials for children, interpreting Jewish holidays for them, in changing the emphases of synagogue service, and in teaching Judaism at home.

History, we have been informed, is constantly being rewritten. The record of the past is treated in such a way as to conform with the viewpoint and interests of the victors of great historic struggles. Historians may write to justify the exploits of conquerors or to glorify their memory. The study of history, however, serves other purposes than to record and explicate events of the past. How history is interpreted, passed on and taught to the mass has profound implications for the present and may be used to alter the course of events in the future. The manner in which a people comes to conceptualize the meaning of its history may correspond to the function which the personal myth serves for the individual (Kris, 1956). In addition to integrating the fears and aspirations of the past, the abiding myths, vehicles for unconscious fantasies shared in common (Sachs, 1942) may become an instrument to be used to turn the course of history in a particular direction. This will be the central theme of this presentation.

Intuitively, statesmen, political and religious leaders long have apprehended and appreciated the powerful force of mythology in history. Important historical happenings, like dramatic personal events, affect the individual and the mass in a metaphorical way. Beyond the pressing practical needs of the moment, people respond to certain of the grand themes suggested by the unfolding of events in history. Because these themes have become incorporated into the mythology of the community, they take the role of political metaphors that may be used to instruct the community and in times of crisis these myths have the power to galvanize the mass into action (Arlow, 1951).

What, we may ask, is the source of this enormous power of the myth? How does it come about, and in what form does it operate? Much has been written from the psychoanalytic point of view in answer to these questions (for summary, see Arlow, 1961). As will shortly be demonstrated through clinical material, myths, like dreams, symptoms, artistic creations and other products of mental life have their origin in private daydreams, in the secret fantasies, conscious or unconscious, that are the earliest organized purveyors of our childhood wishes. The private world of our daydreams is characteristic for each individual and is, in fact, even idiosyncratic for him (Arlow, 1969*a*, 1969*b*). It represents the individual's secret rebellion against the need to grow up, to renounce the wishes he cherishes, a rebellion against reality and, therefore, in a very specific sense, a rebellion against society and the strictures of civilization. The world of private daydreams is a world of protest against the need to renounce the self-centered, antisocial, pleasure-seeking wishes of childhood. The world of daydreams is like a preserve of nature in its original form, set apart and untouched by the progress of civilization, or in the case of the individual, by the progress of maturation and development (Freud, 1911). It is possible that human beings could not really bear the strictures civilized life imposes upon the primitive drives if it were not for the ability to abrogate these prohibitions in dreams by night and in daydreams during waking hours.

Because daydreams are derivatives of powerful wishes, there is constant pressure on the mind to transform such fantasies into action. This inevitably leads the individual into conflict within himself and with the society around him. This eventuates in a fear of retaliation and ultimately in guilt, as the child incorporates the prohibiting, inhibiting attitude of the human environment. There are many pathways out of conflict, some leading to normal development, others to unresolved conflict and neurotic illness. The individual may modify his private daydreams into sublimated forms which are acceptable both to him and to the world of objects around him. With the beginning of the process of socialization, he may share this modified version of his private dreams with his fellows. The advantages of this latter process are numerous. Dreams and daydreams are private, guilt-laden experiences. They separate the individual from the group. The shared fantasy, on the other hand, is a step toward socialization and group formation. What the poet does is to transform his private daydreams into a creation which is compatible with the ideals of the community, capable of giving pleasure and conveying, at the same time, like a dream, a disguised, transformed expression of a basic set of wishes shared in common by other members of the community. The poet presents his audience with a preformed fantasy onto which they may project their own unconscious fantasy wishes and elaborate them in keeping with their own psychological needs. A bond of mutual exculpation operates between the artist and his audience. By participating in the work of art, the audience relieves the poet of his private guilt. By sharing with other members of the group disguised indulgence in forbidden impulses, each member experiences a sense of exculpation, if not catharsis. Everybody's guilt is nobody's guilt (Sachs, 1942).

The members of the audience become a temporary group brought together by sharing a common set of wishes, expressed in the form of a modified, unconscious fantasy. This type of group formation corresponds to what Freud described as mutual identification based upon common needs or wishes (Freud, 1921). By identifying with the main character of the work of art, the individual members of the group can obtain vicarious gratification of impulses ordinarily forbidden and repressed. Group formation serves to relieve individual guilt and to unite the individuals on a basis of common need.

The myth is a special form of daydream. The childhood wishes that have to be repressed are projected onto some heroic figure, usually from the past history of the nation. What is forgotten in the life of the individual is remembered and repeated in the experience of the myth. The myth is a special way in which a private daydream becomes a shared public experience on condition that the basic wishes are repudiated by the individuals and projected onto some ideal object.

Before passing on to the dynamics of group formation based upon unconscious fantasies shared in common, it will be useful to observe how the basic process operates in the case of the individual. In the clinical vignette about to be presented, I hope to demonstrate the following: (1) the influence of a daydream upon the development and the symptomatology of a young child with moderate neurotic conflicts; (2) the transformation and substitution of myths in place of the daydream; (3) the role of mythology in fostering progressive development and socialization.

This presentation is organized around the typical daydream or fantasy known as the rescue fantasy. It derives its name from the central theme which has the following features in the case of a young boy, namely, to rescue a woman in need of saving by destroying the intruding or opposing villainous male rival. The culmination of this basic plot is a typical one: the hero and the rescued woman unite in loving union in marriage, presumably to become parents to a large and happy family. The theme of rescuing is perhaps the commonest one in literature and mythology. It has its origin in the fact that unconsciously rescuing is equated with giving new life, therefore creating a life, that is, giving a child. In its conscious form the rescue fantasy is a disguised representation of the classic oedipal wish of childhood to displace the father in relation to the mother and become in turn the progenitor and creator of life. Detached from its childhood sexual moorings, the wish to rescue may be transformed and expressed in later life in the noblest achievements of dedication and self-sacrifice (Freud, 1910).

CASE PRESENTATION

This clinical material is taken from the record of the treatment of a young boy during two periods in his life, one between the ages of four-and-a-half and six, the second between the ages of eight and twelve. This little patient, whom we shall call Morris, suffered from a tic in one eye, insomnia, nightmares and enuresis. He was afraid of dying and expressed concern that his body, particularly his genitals, might be damaged. In his fantasy and play activity with the therapist, he was fascinated by weapons. When he entered school, he was disobedient, hyperactive and the ringleader in all mischief. He considered himself as at war against the authorities. His parents were refugees, deeply religious. They differed, however, in their attitude concerning the boy's education, the mother favoring a more liberal American education, the father insisting upon old-fashioned, strict, religious upbringing. Morris appreciated the differences between his parents and took the opportunity to establish an alliance with his mother against his father.

In the opening phase of his treatment, he spoke of his fear of monsters who might attack him during the night. He dreamed of horrible animals emerging from the water. He produced his first daydream in treatment in which he imagined himself as Dracula killing men and sucking blood from the necks of beautiful women. In the next phase of treatment, he was no longer identified with Dracula but remained intensely interested in stories about Dracula and in watching Dracula on TV. After his fears subsided somewhat during treatment, his daydream began to change. Dracula now became the enemy from whom he was rescuing the beautiful woman and in his daydreams, he saw himself as opposing the monster who came out of the sea; he no longer identified with the monster who killed men.

Morris soon began to describe his war against the school authorities. Treatment demonstrated the connection between his enuresis and fantasies of killing with a gun. In dreams, as in play activity, he would shoot down the enemy with a water pistol. When he did so, he would wet the bed. Ideas of warfare were paramount in his fantasy and play activity. When he saw the movie, *The Bridge over the River Kwai*, he identified with the general, a model soldier and decent man devoted to his men and honoring his responsibilities. From his studies in religious school, however, Morris began to question the idea of having a soldier as a hero. He had been taught that the model to emulate was Aaron, the brother of Moses, who, in the religious teaching, represents the leader of those who love peace and pursue peace. This mythic figure of Aaron now became the patient's new ideal after whom he decided to model himself. He began to give up his aggressiveness, lost interest in knives, began to make peace with his teachers and discovered to his satisfaction that he could be a very good student.

When he learned about Abraham Lincoln, he connected him with Moses—saw them both as liberators and rescuers of mankind—and, by way of identification, with the Biblical Abraham, the father of a numerous and mighty people. Since his own Hebrew name was Moses, he thought of himself as coupled with Abraham Lincoln and Moses in their role as liberators of mankind. In this way, he established a bridge of identification with the Biblical Abraham who was the father of his people. Thus, out of the original primitive rescue fantasy involving the mother figure and the monster, the themes of saving life and creating life reemerged in a more grown-up setting. The dynamic charge of what was originally an incestuous wish in childhood was now used to identify with Lincoln and Moses, heroic figures from two traditions, propelling the young patient to find a new set of ideals, to reshape his character, modify his behavior, and consolidate his identity.

Toward the end of the second period of treatment, when the patient had been doing very well in school and had discovered that he was unusually proficient in mathematics, a new figure began to occupy his fantasy life and to take its place in the growing world of his values. This was the figure of Einstein who epitomized to the patient how to use the intellect as an expression of power, a power, however that is turned not towards war but to advancement of science and to the betterment of mankind. The patient said that he did not quite expect to be another Einstein, but he expected to follow in his footsteps.

In this story of the reformed warrior turned intellectual liberator, one can observe how the primitive daydreams of childhood are transformed into myth. Under the influence of certain dominating mythic themes, this little patient's wild spirits were domesticated and his development was guided towards integration with the moral values of his community. In the course of its history, each society selects from the heroes of the past certain figures whose qualities of character are idealized and who are then transformed into the heroes of its mythology. These personalities come to represent ego ideals. They are held up as models for the younger generation to emulate. In this way, through its mythology a society tries to influence the formation of the character structure of the next generation, character structure that will be in consonance with the goals and values that the community cherishes. The images of the heroes of mythology thus become the transmitters and carriers of the accumulated experience and ideals of the larger group. They serve as examples of how to behave in particular situations as well as in periods of national crisis. Accordingly, we pass from the subject of character building in the individual to the ego ideal of the group, the historic figures whose personality traits and guidance point the way to the solution of political and historic dilemmas at times of national crisis. Depending upon the goals and the preferred solution of the political choices facing a particular group, differing mythic images of the past may be put forward in teaching history and in political exhortation in order to suggest what is conceived to be the proper solution of the political crisis. The material which follows will serve to illustrate this process in history.

During the siege of Jerusalem by the Roman general Vespasian, Rabbi ben Zakkai perceived that the fall of the city was imminent. He foresaw the dissolution of the national state, the destruction of the Temple and how the inevitable dispersion would threaten the historical continuity of religious tradition and moral identity. He arranged to have his students smuggle him out of the besieged city in a coffin past the picket line of the Zealots. Brought before the future emperor, he prophesied the victory of Rome and for these good tidings was rewarded with permission to found an academy where he might continue to study the law and to teach it. Modern commentators might regard this behavior as an act of collaboration with the enemy, but this is not the image of ben Zakkai which came down in Jewish history. Through this myth transmitted by rabbinic tradition and culture, Rabbi ben Zakkai came to epitomize the qualities of devotion to tradition by submission to and abnegation of temporal authority, by renunciation of force as a solution to national problems and by the surrendering of aspirations for a political state in favor of idealizing learning and religious observance. Historically his solution may be regarded as extremely fortuitous and adaptive, and he became the mythic model, the ego ideal for generations of young Jews. The incorporation of ben Zakkai's idealized character traits into the personality structure of succeeding generations of Jews helped to preserve the national identity in the unfavorable historical circumstances of living in dispersion, powerless and unprotected in the ghetto.

At the same time that ben Zakkai was being received in the camp of the future emperor of Rome, no more than fifty miles away on a prow-shaped fortress overlooking the Dead Sea and the tawny, sun-drenched sands of the Negev Desert, a group of Judean soldiers and their families determined to defy the power of Rome to the very end. Totally besieged and surrounded, with no prospect of victory or relief, they continued to struggle for three more years, ultimately choosing to kill their women and children and die by their own hand rather than submit to the Roman yoke. This story of the heroes of Masada we learn from the accounts of Josephus Flavius. The story played no role in the rabbinic tradition; there is hardly any mention of it in the Talmud.

For almost two thousand years Masada had little or no impact on the ideology, imagination, education or character formation of the descendants of the principals of that drama. In the late nineteenth and the beginning of the twentieth century, however, new forces were at work in European history. Europe was swept by a rising tide of nationalism. In place of numerous duchies, Italy and Germany became unified states. Among the Jews a new political movement began to develop—Zionism, a movement which saw the solution of the Jewish problem in terms of reconstituting a national state. To achieve this goal, a generation of militant, active individuals had to be developed, a generation which would not shrink from seizing temporal power or joining in battle. For such a generation, a character structure vastly different from that modeled after the image of ben Zakkai was needed. The old model would hardly meet the necessities dictated by the new political solution proposed by the Zionists. Accordingly, like all societies, the Zionist movement reinterpreted its past, sought out and mythologized heroes in terms of what current history required. The Zealots of Masada were resurrected from their historical sepulchers to become the central figures of a new mythology, a mythology that could create a psychological climate fostering character structure consonant with new ideals and with changed political objectives. The commanding position which the Zealots of Masada now occupy in current Israeli and Jewish mythology could hardly have been predicted as recently as fifty years ago.

In the transformation of character ideals for the purpose of new political objectives, there are a number of associated psychological problems that must be solved. These problems face all revolutionary leaders. To activate the mass, it is essential for the current generation to be alienated from the preceding generation and particularly from the traditional habits of thought and behavior. It is essential to break the process of automatic identification with the parent generation and, accordingly, with its political and social choices. Of the many psychological factors that enter into this process, one that is introduced intuitively involves the elaboration and utilization of a set of myths based upon a very common unconscious fantasy.

The fantasy is known as the family romance, a daydream that originates a bit later than the rescue fantasy. According to this fantasy, the young child comes to believe that the parents whom he knows and who raised him are not his real parents, that is, they are not the biological parents. He feels that he is a foundling or an adopted child, who some day will be reclaimed by his nobler, more elevated biological parents. Of all the fantasies of childhood nourished in the hearts of members of our society, this is the easiest one to demonstrate. Several studies have established that upwards of seventy to eighty percent of the people interviewed recalled having entertained this fantasy at some time in their lives.

The family romance fantasy derives from many sources in the individual's life and serves several functions. It is an alienating fantasy of revenge against the parents who have disappointed and thereby disillusioned the young child. It feeds on the inevitable frustration of the child's growing up and learning that he is not the center of the universe, that his parents are devoted to each other as well as to him, that he cannot have whatever and whomever his heart desires. The disappointed child, feeling lowly and humiliated, repudiates his parents as being inferior to him, disowns them as he feels they have disowned him, and dreams of some day being reunited with the true and worthy parents, coming into his rightful elevated status and putting his disappointing parents to shame.

In the mythology of practically every culture on earth, this private daydream has been transformed into a pre-eminent myth, a general configuration that has been called the myth of the birth of the hero. In this myth, the scion of a royal family, for various reasons, has to be separated from his parents. He is placed in a container, usually a basket, in the open, usually on a river, and abandoned, only to be found by shepherds, peasants, or even animals who raise the child as their own. Finally, after a series of mighty deeds, it comes to pass that the hero of the myth wins the kingship or some other victory in his own right and then learns of his true, his noble origin. The story has been told about Moses, Oedipus, Romulus and Remus, Lohengrin, Sargon, and a host of other figures from the mythology of all nations (Rank, 1952). In the popular mind, because the family romance fantasy is so universal, the image of the hero is inevitably associated with the notion of secret noble lineage. For example, within hours after the first cosmonaut completed his epochal flight into space in his carefully sealed capsule, a rumor raced around the world, a rumor subsequently proven false, that Yuri Gagarin, this first hero of the space age, was not really the son of a humble Soviet carpenter, as he was known to be, but actually the son of a czarist aristocrat, a member of the nobility living incognito since the Revolution. It seems that, given the opportunity, mankind awaits only the appropriate occasion to set in motion the process of mythopoesis, of creating myth, so that it can find in the real world actualized projections of its inner daydreams (Arlow, 1961).

Harnessed to a communally shared myth, this propensity on the part of each individual to interpret experience metaphorically can supply the driving power for group action. An instructive example was furnished by certain features of the Black Revolution. Intuitively and unconsciously, the movement utilized the psychology inherent in the fantasy of the family romance. By the clothes they wore, the language they used, the speech they affected, the songs they sang, the interest and studies they furthered, the followers of the movement proclaimed, however unwittingly, a new and nobler lineage. They traced their descent from the ancient kingdoms of Africa where blacks had been independent and creative. They rediscovered the inventions black people have contributed to mankind. They ritualized their allegiance to this proud past in their dress, speech, hairdo, etc., in order to accomplish their historic task of liberation, a task that could not be fulfilled with a self-debased image. The Uncle-Tomism of the immediate past generations, with its implications of submission, passivity, cowardice and second-rate status, was repudiated and black pride was reconstituted by identifying oneself as the descendant of an older, more elevated, nobler ancestry. To unfriendly or uninformed observers, these developments may have seemed like the excesses or aberrations typical of revolutionary movements, but actually what we witnessed was the outcome of historic necessity, the intuitive recasting of a mythology consonant with the political responsibilities of a new generation.

The manner in which great leaders—political, religious, or otherwise—intuitively resurrect or create myths and, with them, manipulate the masses resembles the effectiveness and the power of great poets. They appeal to powerful, deep-seated primitive wishes, ready to be unleashed in the soul of each person. The political leaders bend these forces to the immediate purposes of the hour, to the solution of problems or crises that they, the leaders, believe in, to goals that they wish to realize in practice. In the end, the practical consequences of such programs may indeed be disastrous, as Hitler's daydreams for the Third Reich proved to be, or they may be contrary to the interests of the group. The exploitation of mythology is a powerful instrument but a dangerous one as well. In the sphere of politics, such exploitation plays upon deep emotions and intensifies dreads that derive from irrational, oft-time uncontrolled feelings. In times of crisis political leaders may refurbish the image of national heroes of the past and reinterpret the history of the group along mythological lines, in order to harness in the mass the emotional dynamism so powerful in the private daydream of the individual. By evoking derivatives of an unconscious fantasy shared in common and giving it concrete representation in the form of an appealing mythic configuration, the political or religious leader is able to potentiate the powerful emotional drives latent in the individual members of the group. When added to other motivating forces, whether rational or irrational, economic, political or social, the unleashed power of the unconscious fantasy channeled into mass action becomes a formidable factor in any political movement.

REFERENCES

Arlow, Jacob A. (1951). "The Consecration of the Prophet." *Psychoanalytic Quarterly*, Vol. 20, pp. 374–397.

———— (1961). "Ego Psychology and the Study of Mythology." *Journal of the American Psychoanalytic Association*, Vol. 9, pp. 371–393.

———— (1969*a*). "Fantasy, Memory and Reality Testing." *Psychoanalytic Quarterly*, Vol. 38, pp. 28–51.

———— (1969*b*). "Unconscious Fantasy and Disturbances of Conscious Experience." *Psychoanalytic Quarterly*, Vol. 38, pp. 1–27.

Freud, S. (1910). "A Special Type of Choice of Object Made by Men." *Complete Psychological Works of Sigmund Freud*, Vol. 11, pp. 163–176.

———— (1911). "Formulations on the Two Principles of Mental Functioning." *Complete Works*, Vol. 12, pp. 218–226.

———— (1921). "Group Psychology and the Analysis of the Ego." *Complete Works*, Vol. 18, pp. 67–143.

Kris, Ernst (1956). "The Personal Myth: A Problem in Psychoanalytic Technique." *Journal of the American Psychoanalytic Association*, Vol. 4, pp. 653–681.

Rank, Otto (1952). *The Myth of the Birth of a Hero*. New York: Robert Brunner, Inc.

Sachs, Hanns (1942). "The Community of Daydreams." In *The Creative Unconscious*. Cambridge: Sci-Arts Publishers.

Monotheism and the Sense of Reality

Leonard R. Sillman

EDITOR'S COMMENT

Dr. Sillman, who died in 1976, was an analyst with wide-ranging interests in all aspects of human thought and behavior. He rejected Judaism as a religion early in life, and, as the reader will observe, associated himself with what Freud called the scientific *Weltanschauung* (Standard Edition, Vol. 22, pp. 181 f.) and its atheism. However, in later years, his intellectual interests, facilitated by his clinical psychoanalytic experience, brought him to study Judaism closely and to consider its influence on both the individual Jew and the Jewish people.

In this essay, written before Kaufmann's landmark study became available in English *(The Religion of Israel* [Chicago: University of Chicago Press, 1960]), the author observes that in many respects true monotheism is considerably more frustrating but also more useful than polytheistic paganism. It imposes on the subject a stringent discipline of morality in behavior, family cohesiveness, realism in dealing with the world, objectivity and logic in thought, and self-awareness. These qualities have contributed to the survival of the Jews and to their capacity to contribute heavily to Western culture.

This paper is reprinted from the *International Journal of Psycho-Analysis*, Volume 30, Part 2, pages 1–9, 1949.

One of the most striking phenomena in history has been the rise and spread of monotheistic cults since the fall of classical civilization. For almost two thousand years after its adoption by the Jews to the decline of the Roman Empire (*circa* 1400 B.C.–A.D. 300), the idea of a single abstract God held no general appeal for humanity except for the politically insignificant peoples of Israel. Then there would seem to have developed an urge for some concept of a single God, for within a period of seven hundred years, or from the conversion of Constantine to approximately A.D. 1000, monotheism spread all over Europe, North Africa and the Near East in Christian and Mohammedan forms. At present it is the religious faith of half the peoples of the world and of the politically and culturally advanced societies of Europe and the Americas.

When one considers the vast multitude of religions which the fertile imagination of man has created, one cannot help but wonder why this triumph should have occurred. In this as in so many later discoveries and changes in belief, a premonition of coming events may be found amid the Greeks. Gilbert Murray (11) points out: "It is curious how near to monotheism, and to monotheism of a very profound and impersonal type, the real religion of Greece came in the sixth and fifth centuries. Many of the philosophers, Xenophanes, Parmenides, and others, asserted it clearly or assumed it without hesitation. Æschylus, Euripides, Plato, in their deeper moments point the same road."

In the search for explanations for this remarkable change in the religiosity of half the human race, every possible motive has been explored. Freud (4) considers the emergence of a racial memory to be the factor that has made the idea of a single God so compelling. He states that monotheism represents the return of the repressed memory of the father's murder by the primal horde. Political and economic factors were pointed out by Kautsky (9) to explain the triumph of Christianity. His thesis is that this was an initially revolutionary movement which later became changed to reaction. In Josephus (8) from whence he derives most of his evidence there are to be found descriptions of various rebels and dissenting sects which, when fused together, bear a striking resemblance to the official version of the life and preachings of Jesus. In agreement with Kautsky, B. H. Streeter in the *Cambridge Ancient History* (16) states: "Of the first Christians, many, like the Communists of the present day, confidently expected themselves to live to see the mighty put down from their seats and the exaltation of the humble and meek—only this would happen, not as the result of political insurrection, but through the direct act of God in the hour of Judgement."

At the onset of any scientific consideration of religion, it should be recognized as a delusional system created by man because of his inability either to grasp or accept reality which in turn generally functions to estrange him from reality. Establishing and imposing false ideas to account for the facts of nature and the causes for human woe and weal, it inevitably displaces consciousness from discovering and accepting the often hard and bitter truths which are essential for the real solution of problems. Although most of the higher religions have fostered excellent moral ideals, by encouraging symbolic and magical methods for the fulfillment of the ideals, they have more often been used to rationalize the inhibition of human development than as inspirations for human advancement.

In terms of a specific guide to the understanding of and dealing with reality, religion has provided and continues to provide illusory solutions to problems encrusted by fascinating, often beautiful, always gratifying narcissistic solaces for the suffering and difficulties which ensue as a result of its false guidance. However, by means of establishing moral ideals and some sort of a causality, at various times religions have had a beneficial effect on the moral and intellectual development of man. A clear-cut instance was the Puritan revolution in England. An understanding of the intrapsychic effect of the monotheistic ideology will help in discovering how religion can assist the mental development of man by virtue of certain well-chosen ideals and by the establishment of an intellectual discipline.

One of the hidden factors in the value of monotheism can be discerned by an analysis and revaluation of the myth of its origin. According to Genesis, the Jews were differentiated from the rest of mankind by virtue of Abraham's pact with God. This pact was made because Abraham wanted a son by the woman he loved—Sarah, his half sister. In return for God's making Sarah fertile, Abraham accepted circumcision and dedicated his descendants to the worship of God and obedience to God's ordinances. Thus, according to the Bible, monotheism was instituted to fulfil Abraham's desire for a child by the woman he loved which he could thereby love completely.

By virtue of the Abraham myth the value of love between parents and the love between father and son was greatly exalted. Using insight gained from psycho-analytic studies, we know that it is the lack of this love in the family which has the most crippling effect on the mental development of the individual. The ideal of love between a man and his wife and a man and his son received among the Jews a religious sanctification, the value of which is completely confirmed by our scientific knowledge of human development. For the œdipus complex is only overcome through love and identification with the father and through the mother's returning her love to the husband after the child begins his independent development.

Freud (4) has pointed out a peculiar characteristic of the Jews in their continuing devotion to a pretended omnipotent God, impotent to prevent millennia of persecution and degradation. Nunberg (12) has clearly discerned the importance of the homosexual attachment in the Jews, acceptance of God, the father substitute. Both are derived from the loving father which the Old Testament glorifies. For it is from the love the father shows the son that the homosexual component develops and on the basis of the same fixation (in reality), the illusion of a God (or father) favouring (loving) the Jews could be maintained, despite the reality of their spoliation and degradation throughout most of their known history.

In this connection it should be remembered that in the ancient world the father was closer to the tyrannical horde leader than to-day; he held life and death powers over his children in early Rome, Greece, and among the Semitic tribes. Child exposure among the Greeks and Romans was common, reflecting an attitude of hostility towards the child which has become alien to our conscious ways of thinking. By seeking to establish the loving, protective father, the Jewish religion, as compared with other ancient sects, tended to provide its children with greater security for development and for mastering the instinctual problems the individual passes through in growing up.

A second factor in the strength of the idea of monotheism is the clear-cut atheism implied in claiming that one God rules the universe and is involved behind all natural phenomena. In stating that God is one, omnipotent and omnipresent, cannot be seen, with effects which are everywhere, the idea of God becomes merged with the realities of nature and God becomes Nature. This implication is seen clearly in Spinoza's Pantheism and the completely spiritualized conception of God among the Unitarians, Congregationalists and Reformed Jews. The Greeks were the first to point out the atheism of the Jews. For it was clear to these very keen observers that if you worshipped a God you could not see, you worshipped a God not there or no God at all.

It should be realized that absolute monotheism has never been practised by any people. The three major monotheistic religions all claim to worship a single God of the universe, but the very names all but the Jews have taken unto themselves reveal this to be untrue. For they are Christians or Mohammedans or worshippers of Christ and Mohammed. The Jews have been more deceptive in their use of names, and it took one of the greatest of them to demonstrate clearly that they, too, worshipped a human being, i.e. Moses (cf. Freud's *Moses and Monotheism*). An exclusive belief in one God of the universe constitutes clear-cut atheism because without demigods to act as intermediaries the believer can have no connection with such an omnipotence and therefore has no connection with God; and with demi-gods as intermediaries (saviour, prophet, saint) the believer is no longer an absolute monotheist. Not that any devout Jew, Christian or Mohammedan would admit any element of atheism in his or her worship. For the atheistic reality has been completely obscured by thought prohibitions, phobias, and illusions which prevent the true believer from recognizing the reality behind the unreality of his or her faith.

Freud (4, p. 178) has pointed out how the prohibition of making any image of God by the Jews facilitated the "subordination of sense perception to abstract idea." The turning away from worship of "things made by the hand" which the Bible enjoins may also be seen as suppression of man's narcissism or tendency to worship his own productions. As a matter of fact the Old Testament may be considered the first great enemy of man's omnipresent narcissism in its prohibition of onanism, sodomy, image worship, and magical practices. All of these are denied in favour of the value of procreation and moral and intellectual devotion to a deity outside the self. One's sexual instincts are directed to the opposite sex and one's intellect to moral behaviour rather than to the imagery of the unconscious. The turning away from mysticism with its crippling effect on the intellect through encouraging disassociation is another derivative of the insistence on "object relationships."

Of great importance in the mental moulding of monotheism was the belief in the omnipresence of God. In animistic and polytheistic cults various places and different types of human activity have their own presiding spirits or gods. The multiplicity and inconsistencies of the Greek pantheon, for example, offer a comforting reflection of the inconsistencies of man's unconscious. In monotheism there is no escape from one god to another in the event of one having transgressed. God is supposed to be everywhere, and thus there is no escape from his wrath. By thus enveloping all of nature with a highly moral God, ready to flame into righteous indignation at lapses from his commands, the devout monotheist projects around himself a rigid, inflexible reflection of his own sense of guilt.

The distinctive achievement of the ancient Jews in developing their sense of guilt beyond that seen in any other religion has been noted and commented upon by many observers. Some of the mechanisms behind this development may now be understood. As a "textbook for fathers" the Old Testament fostered the attachment of the son to the father with powerful latent homosexual feeling. This facilitates the replacement of the œdipus complex with the super-ego (5), and as Freud (2) further points out, it is on the basis of repressed homosexual feeling that the conscience of man is fed. By surrounding himself with an omnipresent, omniscient, and omnipotent God of righteousness, the Jew further consolidated and secured the strengthening of conscience brought about by the distinctive family constellation laid down for him in his holy books.

The above characteristics of the monotheism created by the ancient Jews possess profound and far-reaching significance for the mental development of the individual. In his *Totem and Taboo* (6, p. 876), Freud states, "We find that the animistic phase corresponds in time as well as in content with narcissism, the religious phase corresponds to the stage of object finding which is characterized by dependence on the parents, while the scientific stage has its full counterpart in the individual's state of maturity where, having renounced the pleasure principle and having adapted himself to reality, he seeks his object in the outer world." This is just what monotheism has unknowingly encouraged, i.e. repression of narcissism and the fulfilment of the parental longing, enabling the individual to find his way to the world of real objects.

In his *The Ego and the Id* (3) Freud points out the varied functions the ego is called upon to perform. He states, "The ego has the task of bringing the influence of the external world to bear upon the id and its tendencies, and endeavours to substitute the reality principle for the pleasure-principle which reigns supreme in the id . . . it arranges the processes of the mind in a temporal order and tests their correspondence with reality." He further states, "The ego develops from perceiving instincts to controlling them, from obeying instincts to curbing them." Finally he writes, "It is not only the ally of the id; it is also a submissive slave who courts the love of his master. . . . Its position midway between the id and reality tempts it only too often to become sycophantic, opportunist and false. . . ."

It is clear that the ego has, as Wälder points out (17), multiple functions. It might appear that its functions are contradictory, but in regard to mental phenomena one might say that contradiction is the rule and not the exception. Because of its position mediating between reality, super-ego, and id, the ego develops special features resulting from its dealings with each institution of the psychic apparatus. Historical, constitutional and familial factors will determine how much energy will be devoted to developing the reality-ego, the id-ego, or the guilt-ego (moral ego).

The mechanisms behind the development of the guilt-ego have been most thoroughly explored for the over-development of this mental function as most likely to cause the individual to seek help in psycho-analysis. The mechanics of repression and symptom formation have been exquisitely revealed to us by Freud. In this connection it should be recognized that the super-ego not only assists the formation of repressions, but, by virtue of its being heir to the parents and their ideals, it contributes to the sense of reality (13), particularly social realities. In guiding the curbing of instincts the super-ego blocks animistic and cannibalistic object cathexes, thus permitting the attributes and features of the outer world fuller and more objective consideration. Also, under the influence of the super-ego's function of self observation, self from object becomes differentiated, thus offering the basis for reality testing.

The growth of the id-ego (sycophantic, opportunistic and false) is largely based on skill in acting out rôles derived from facile identifications plus a capacity for sensing weaknesses in others and exploiting them. To fulfil instincts to dominate, to aggrandize the self, and to confuse, seduce, conquer, etc., it is necessary that the individual should play the various rôles called for in the society of which he is a part. One frequently sees individuals "grooming" themselves for the rôle of a great business man, Don Juan, doctor, psycho-analyst. Often they do it so well that the grooming brings high position in the complete absence of special skill in their field of endeavour. In this connection, the absence of guilt and responsibility towards others for their performance facilitates success because there is less interference with their histrionic abilities. The id-ego has been most definitively described by Shakespeare (*Merchant of Venice*, Act III, Scene 2) as follows:—

> "So may the outward shows be least themselves,
> The world is still deceiv'd with ornament.
> In law, what plea so tainted and corrupt
> But, being season'd with a gracious voice,
> Obscures the show of evil? In religion

What damned error but some sober brow
Will bless it, and approve it with a text,
Hiding the grossness with fair ornament?
There is no vice so simple but assumes
Some mark of virtue on his outward parts.
How many cowards, whose hearts are all as false
As stairs of sand, wear yet upon their chins
The beards of Hercules and frowning Mars;
Who, inward search'd, have livers white as milk!
And these assume but valour's excrement
To render them redoubted. Look on beauty,
And you shall see 'tis purchased by the weight,
Which therein works a miracle in nature,
Making them lightest that wear most of it . . .
Thus ornament is but the guiled shore
To a most dangerous sea; the beauteous scarf
Veiling an Indian beauty: in a word,
The seeming truth which cunning times put on
To entrap the wisest."

The reality-ego functions by means of the pre-conscious, which has been described by Freud (7) as having the following characteristics: an inhibition of the tendency of cathected ideas toward discharge; establishment of censorship or censorships; communication between ideational contents; exclusion or restriction of displacement and condensation; giving ideational contents a relation to time; reality principle; reality testing; conscious memory; and linking of object ideas with word ideas. The first two functions of the pre-conscious are of a general nature, deriving their characteristics from the effect of higher systems inhibiting lower systems and from the specific ways in which the other seven characteristics of the preconscious function.

In establishing the idea of an omnipresent God who watches and knows every thought and action of his believers, a scrutinizing and judging of mental processes was encouraged. God becomes omniscience and therefore omniscience becomes godly, encouraging in the believer all his efforts to know. This is largely directed at his thoughts and actions, for it is in this sphere that God demands correctness. Such a watching or self-observation can be seen to encourage communication between ideational contents, for this consists in bringing past ideas to bear on each other and on each new experience. The insistence that the believer patterns his thought and behaviour on high moral ideals gives rise to the urge for consistency in thought which in combination with the self-observation and self-critique of borrowed "omniscience" prevents the individual from accepting the gross inconsistencies and disassociations of ideation produced by the unconscious.

Thus monotheism helped to develop the pre-conscious function of communication between ideas and thereby acted to enhance the intelligence of the believer. For the ability to compare, contrast, differentiate and distinguish which forms such a large part of intelligence is achieved through communication between ideas. The imperative of consistency creates within the psyche of the individual an ever active force which seeks to organize and co-ordinate the experiences of the individual into an integrated whole strengthening the synthetic function of the ego. The elaborate all-embracing casuistry of the Talmudists and Scholastics is the theological expression of this imperative.

The Oneness of God ("Hear, O Israel, the Lord our God, the Lord is One") has had varied effects. Its main influence was to inculcate in the believer the conviction that there existed some great unity behind the diverse; some great dominating force behind the multiplicity of sensory experiences. The commonplace experience of life reveals varieties of perceptions, sensations, impulses without obvious connection. Monotheism implies a higher, single significance, and by its emphasis on an abstract unity, it assists the intellect in its development of relevance or that quality of the mind which enables consciousness to pursue a specified goal without being distracted and absorbed by lesser, associated perceptions, ideas, or images.

It is the power of relevance which is largely responsible for restricting and excluding condensation and displacement. The unconscious tends to focus and discharge its energies on to irrelevant words, acts, rituals, gestures on the basis of the logos of symbolism. This tendency is a basic source for magic and animistic thinking. The O.T. prohibition of magic constituted one factor in restricting this latter type of mentation, but a second and equally potent factor was the relevance-fostering effect of the idea of a single God. By strengthening relevance the individual became better able to pursue any intellectual or logical operation without becoming diverted into partial or symbolic conclusions or acts. The general quality of clarity and vividness which the Old Testament displays in its account of the vicissitudes of the ancient Jews is derived from this intellectual trait.

In his *Moses and Monotheism*, Freud points out the uniqueness amongst religious traditions of a God adopting a people. He relates this notion to the repressed memory of Moses adopting the Jews. A second significance of the story of Moses consists in the portrayal of a people submitting themselves to commandments and laws derived from a force outside, above and beyond themselves. In the Pentateuch, involved and elaborate regulations are set down which seek to pattern the thought, emotions and behaviour of the Jews into a formula derived from the external world of reality or from God. This submission to externally imposed necessity in preference to immediate gratification as symbolized by the worship of the golden calf, can be seen to represent a religious version of the exaltation of the reality principle over the pleasure principle.

It is a general characteristic of the Old Testament that its people were constantly being urged to renounce immediate pleasures such as were provided by the local cults (Astaroth and other sensuous deities) for social rectitude which would in the future produce well-being (the Promised Land, a Messiah, Zion). Further, mystical or hallucinatory gratifications, also a derivative of the pleasure principle, were eschewed for ethical reform or the desire to improve the realities of the social life of the Jews. By this means the prophets of Israel constantly sought to develop the reality principle among the Jews, struggling against immediate pleasure for the benefit of future well-being. The Old Testament thus became largely a source book for mankind's age-old struggle between immediate pleasure and profit on the one side and righteousness and future well-being on the other; with the disastrous effects of the triumph of the pleasure principle repeatedly and dramatically illustrated.

W. Robertson Smith (15) has described this aspect of Judaism as follows: "The evils that slowly sap society, the vices that at first sight seem too private to be matters of national concern, the disorders that accompany the increase and unequal distribution of wealth, the relaxation of moral fibre produced by luxury and sensuality, were things that religion hardly touched at all, and that the easy, indulgent god could hardly be thought to take note of. The God who could deal with such evils was the God of the prophets, no mere Oriental king raised to a throne in heaven, but the just and jealous God, whose eyes are in every place, beholding the evil and the good, who is of purer eyes than to behold evil, and cannot look upon iniquity (Prov. xv. 3; Hab. i. 13)."

In the hidden atheism of monotheism there exists the implication that the phenomena of the external world are largely unexplained and caused by forces and factors outside the easy comprehension of man. Knowledge, therefore, can only come about by study of the intrinsic qualities of things rather than by creating fantasies and theories. This hidden atheism has given the monotheistic peoples a training in reality testing unknown to any others. In suppressing a plurality of spirits, demons, and gods, it left the functioning of wide vistas of nature unexplained, performing for its believers the first, all-important step in the development of true science, i.e. the admission of ignorance. "I don't know" is the most difficult thing for mankind to accept fully and the first step towards discovering the truth.

The rare quality of objective thought is based upon the higher development of all pre-conscious functions. The universal, animistic mind thinks with words and fantasies. To think objectively it is necessary to suspend wishes, fears, and verbal formulæ and compare perception with undistorted memory. Magical word screens tend to become over-cathected by condensation-displacement to hide memory in individuals who become verbally fixated. Wishes and fears frequently dictate which memory trace will be stimulated by a perception rather than the degree of similarity to the intrinsic characteristics of the perception. Objectivity demands a respect for objects (here are borrowings from the guilt-ego) which enables the individual to subordinate himself to their intrinsic qualities. It also demands free imagery and communication between ideas, and here the guilt-ego can interfere because of its power in prohibiting experiences and ideas that are "bad."

The establishment of the power of objective thought has two important consequences. Firstly, consciousness becomes greatly empowered because conscious memory grows. This grants the individual more and more experience to work with. Because more realities can be brought to bear upon any problem or decision, conclusions and actions have a greater chance for correctness and success. Secondly, the result of preconscious thinking is enabled to gain ever greater control over the emotional life and behaviour of the individual. When objective realities are given full credence, there arises the desire that reason rather than prejudice, myth, or tradition should dominate human relationships and social affairs. Such a tendency is the basis for the desire for maturity, progress, and advancement and creates the urge for social improvement and reform.

From the above it can be seen how monotheism has unknowingly encouraged the development of the sense of reality of its believers. Even though it has propagated and still propagates delusions, the system it established has performed two great services for humanity. First by civilizing the father, repressing narcissism, and attaching the son to the father, it has significantly furthered the development of man's conscience. Secondly its intellectual discipline has fostered the growth of man's preconscious and intelligence. It has encouraged the development of those higher intellectual faculties (relevance, consistency, objectivity, reality principle) which, as has been pointed out in a previous publication (14), form the basis for the civilized intelligence as compared with the primitive and decadent. Thus it equipped its adherents with a more highly developed reality-ego and super-ego, enabling them to survive and/or dominate peoples with religions that did less to encourage the development of man's higher mental faculties.

From this, the strange survival of the Jew may be understood. Despite persecution, intimidation and discrimination over millennia of time, his religion so developed his intelligence and moral sense that he was able to outwit his persecutors and survive. The Jews have achieved a unique position among peoples of the higher cultures by possessing the longest known continuous survival record. The recent Jewish Renaissance or flowering into intellectual brilliance of European Jewry in the nineteenth and early twentieth centuries is further evidence that this people have been well trained intellectually and morally by the religion for which their ancestors suffered and died.

The Mohammedan adaptation of monotheism represents an effort to utilize the reality-ego development for the benefit of the id-ego. Mohammedanism, as revealed in the Koran, expresses the demand that the highest function of the believer is to dominate, conquer, loot and kill the unbeliever. Mohammed (10, p. 252) states: "And they that believe not shall have garments of fire fitted unto them; boiling water shall be poured on their heads; their bowels shall be dissolved thereby, and also their skins; and they shall be beaten with maces of iron." Throughout this book there is a continuous incitement to the holy war with the promise of paradise to those "killed in action," making the sudden and dramatic conquest of the Middle East by the Arabs understandable. The absence of powerful moral demands caused the political instability and subsequent rapid political degeneration of Islam.

The early Christian form of monotheism, as Freud (4) points out, must be recognized as an ethical regression from the position achieved by the earlier development. This regression became institutionalized into the Catholic Church during the Middle Ages. Under its domination belief in miracles and magic flourished, encouraged by such figures as Gregory the Great, the turning away from reality to mysticism and self-absorption was fostered, and the peoples of Europe suffered, under recurrent invasions and feudalism, the intellectual, moral, and material debasement which is inevitable when confusion and corruption dominate the minds of men. Finally, with the decline of the Papacy and the irreligiosity of the Renaissance, the opportunity arose for Europe of rediscovering the monotheism it was supposed to have been practising. This rediscovery inaugurated Protestantism and the modern era with its distinctive developments.

The significance of Protestantism, which must be recognized as a return to a more Judaic Christianity, in the intellectual and moral development of Europe, has been well formulated by Max Weber (18). He states, "The rationalization of the world, the elimination of magic as a means to salvation, the Catholics had not carried nearly so far as the Puritans (and before them the Jews) had done. To the Catholic the absolution of his Church was a compensation for his own imperfection. The priest was a magician who performed the miracle of transubstantiation, and who held the key to eternal life in his hand. One could turn to him in grief and penitence. He dispensed atonement, hope of grace, certainty of forgiveness, and thereby granted release from the tremendous tension to which the Calvinist was doomed by an inexorable fate, admitting of no mitigation. For him such friendly and human comforts did not exist. He could not hope to atone for hours of weakness or of thoughtlessness by increased good will at other times, as the Catholic or even the Lutheran could. The God of Calvinism demanded of his believers not single good works, but a life of good works combined into a unified system. There was no place for the very human Catholic cycle of sin, repentance, atonement, release, followed by renewed sin."

The uniquely great moral, political, and intellectual achievements which occurred in Europe up to the twentieth century arose largely as the fulfilment of the high ethical demands of Protestantism. The influence of the Reformation in creating political democracy has been noted by various scholars. This influence has been confirmed in recent years by the fact that this advanced political form has been secure only in nations where the Reformation was complete (Scandinavia, England, the United States of America) as well as by the fact that the profound political regression which just murdered one-third of the strict monotheists had its origin in Catholic countries, was led by men trained in the Catholic faith, and was condoned by the Papacy.

It is in the realm of the reality-ego that there occurred amid the Christian peoples a unique achievement in the history of man. This was the development of experimental science. Although prior trends in this direction occurred in the Classical, Arabic, and Scholastic periods, the first real and continuous growth of experimental science commenced with the Renaissance. When the men of

Europe found themselves free to look, listen and think, their religious heritage, as pointed out above, inspired their intellects in the direction of understanding and mastering reality. The Counter-Reformation cut off this growth amid the Latin peoples wherever it prevailed, and its further development occurred mainly among the Protestants until the nineteenth century.

The basic requirement of the scientific mind consists in suppressing animistic mentation in favour of the reality principle and reality testing. To be scientific about something, it is necessary to inhibit wishes and fears (pain-pleasure reactions) and allow the phenomena to register in the mind with full freedom. From the data registered in the memory, abstracts or hypotheses arise as to the relationships that exist between the data. These are accepted or rejected by referring the abstract back to reality to see if it enables one to predict or control the phenomena out of which it arises.

Thus the overthrow of the Ptolemaic cosmology by Copernicus was derived from the strict observation of the positions of the planets in the solar system, which could be more simply explained by the heliocentric theory. The abstraction, i.e. the heliocentric theory, enabled more simple and accurate predictions to be made. It was finally proved by the reality-testing of Galileo when he observed the planets through a telescope, particularly the relationship between Jupiter and its satellites which showed a solar system in miniature. Although the formula of allowing experience full freedom of registration in the mind, developing hypotheses, and testing them with reality, sounds simple, the primitive, unconscious forces of the mind make this a difficult procedure. Each phase of this process is constantly being impeded by man's fears, wishes, fantasies, narcissism, repressive forces.

The influence of monotheism in fostering objective thought and reality testing was pointed out above. Its development of relevance was of great assistance in directing men's minds to objective reality and strengthening their powers of application so that the data could be worked over until plausible hypotheses could be deduced. The imperative for consistency is also of great value for scientific thought. For correlations between experience which science attempts to establish, give coherence to perceptual experience. A regularity or consistency is deduced from phenomena by science when it has succeeded in understanding a part of nature.

The above religious and psycho-analytic correlations find historic confirmation in the fact that the earlier developments of experimental science occurred mainly in areas under monotheistic influence. The most important centre in the ancient world was Hellenistic Alexandria, which had a very large Jewish population and an advanced Jewish culture. The development of science among the Mohammedans is well known. It should be recognized that Christianity in itself contributed a special intellect moulding factor not contained in either Judaism or Mohammedanism, which accounts for the uniquely rich development of science amid the peoples of Europe.

This consists of its emphasis on submission and passivity which the New Testament fostered. In the preachings and life of Jesus, from "turning the other cheek" to the account of his easy acceptance of crucifixion, submission and passivity are glorified. In the Middle Ages this characteristic found its expression in the retreat and self-mortification of the religious. Its essential character consists in a negation of the more primitive, activist, way of dealing with external objects, by seeking their mastery through repeating on them that which they do to the self. The savage who is frightened by the forces of nature tries to frighten nature with ugly grimaces or loud noises just as children, as Freud points out in *Beyond the Pleasure Principle* (1), master the anxiety caused by medical examinations by examining other children.

The suppression of this tendency to an immediate repetition of experience is of profound value for developing the scientific mind. By suppressing the repetition compulsion, experience is permitted to register with full value and the jumping to conclusion and action inhibited. The immediate surface appearance of things, such as that the sun goes around the world or that an object of greater density falls faster than one of lesser density, becomes questioned. The repetition compulsion suppressed by Christianity became transformed in the scientific mind into the search for repetitions in nature. This gave further impetus for the search for abstracts, constants, or repetitions derived from the phenomena of nature.

The vast accumulation of knowledge which constitutes modern science is merely the sum of the observable and provable constants found in nature. This is most obvious in the sciences which have yielded to mathematical treatment wherein a formula such as the law of gravity provides a constant for the attraction between bodies. In the other branches of science knowledge consists of repetitive reactions and interactions between substances (as Chemistry) or regularly recurrent structures (as Anatomy) or regularly recurring functions (as Physiology).

Freud (1) has pointed out that the repetition compulsion is derived from the death instinct. Modern science, created by the intellects nurtured by the Old and New Testaments, was at its inception hailed as man's hope for security and peace. In the present era we would seem to be witnessing a "return of the repressed." For science under capitalism has become the tool of the instincts of self-aggrandizement which are largely derived from the death instinct's drive for domination. As the submissive tool of the military, its extensive use for mass death and destruction most clearly demonstrates its deepest origins. For from Freud we have learned how indestructible early ideas are. It now looms as a real possibility that the world-destruction wish of primitive Christianity, after two millennia, has found its way to real fulfilment in the atomic age.

Although science is in part a sublimation of the instinct of destruction, the problem of what mankind does with the fruits of its sense of reality has broader implications. The use man makes of the god-like powers and machines created for him by the scientific geniuses of the past is determined by his social conscience and his sense of social reality. Unfortunately, the rise in power granted by science and industry has not been followed by any increase in man's moral or intellectual stature. Recent and current events would seem to indicate that the opposite has occurred. The utilization of the powers of science by business men for completely egocentric ends has been elaborately rationalized by economic myths and justified by skilled propagandists. Control over a large part of this new omnipotence has passed into the hands of confused, corrupt and incompetent politicians. Religious fixations help to maintain this irresponsibility by symbolic discharge of guilt and the displacing of the sense of social responsibility on to some ephemeral being whose mysterious gyrations are on the private property of clerical corporations. Nationalistic chauvinism has more recently entered the arena of science and industrial power, seducing men to dedicate their scientific skills for the extermination of other men who labour under the monstrous crime of speaking another language, of having a different economic system, of being foreign, or alien.

In the past few centuries a new generator of humanity has taken its place alongside the old. Millions owe their very lives, their security, all their material welfare and possessions to science. Their refusal to meet their responsibility to this new power is threatening the existence of civilization and perhaps the species itself. Its surrender to economic greed and political ambition transforms this potential source for human welfare into a veritable Moloch devouring its children who refuse to make the required personal sacrifices for the great benefits it has bestowed on the human race.

As shown above, the Judeo-Christian ethic and intellectual discipline has developed the sense of reality which, in turn, has created the vast generator of human welfare or woe constituting science and industry. To prevent its becoming a veritable Frankenstein monster it is imperative that its use be guided by an ever stricter sense of moral responsibility and an ever keener sense of social realities. Any use of this sacred trust for other than economic security, peace, and the truth amid humanity represents a suicidal desecration of the moral and intellectual heritage of Western Man. Its irresponsible exploitation may provide pleasure, profit, and excitement for the infantile megalomania of politicians and publishers, generals and business men, but such surrender to the pleasure-principle constitutes a major force toward the destruction of Western Civilization.

REFERENCES

(1) Freud, Sigmund. *Beyond the Pleasure Principle*, 1922 (London: Hogarth Press).

(2)———— "Dostoevski and Parricide," *Int. J. Psycho-Anal.*, 26, 1945.

(3) ———— *The Ego and the Id*, 1927 (London: Hogarth Press).

(4) ———— *Moses and Monotheism*, 1939 (New York: Knopf).

(5) ———— "The Passing of the Œdipus Complex," *Collected Papers*, 2, 1933 (London: Hogarth Press).

(6) ————*Totem and Taboo*, 1938 (New York: Random House).

(7) ———— "The Unconscious," *Collected Papers*, 4, 1934 (London: Hogarth Press).

(8) Josephus. *The Wars of the Jews*, 1936 (London: J. M. Dent & Sons).

(9) Kautsky, Karl. *Foundations of Christianity*, 1925 (New York: International Publishers).

(10) Mohammed. *The Koran*, Sale's edition, 1890 (London: Frederick Warne & Co.).

(11) Murray, Gilbert. *Five Stages in Greek Religion* (p. 92), 1930 (New York: Columbia University Press).

(12) Nunberg, Herman. "Circumcision and Problems of Bisexuality," *Int. J. Psycho-Anal.*, 28, parts 3 and 4, 1947.

(13) ———— *Practice and Theory of Psychoanalysis*, 1948 (Nervous and Mental Disease Monographs).

(14) Sillman, Leonard R. "Psychiatric and Social Processes," *Int. J. Psycho-Anal.*, 29, part 2, 1948.

(15) Smith, W. Robertson. *Lectures on the Religion of the Semites* (p. 65), 1914 (London: A. and C. Black).

(16) Streeter, B. H. *The Cambridge Ancient History*, 11 (p. 276), 1936 (Cambridge University Press).

(17) Wälder, Robert. "The Principle of Multiple Function," *Psychoanal. Quart.*, 5, 1, 1936.

(18) Weber, Max. *The Protestant Ethic and the Spirit of Capitalism* (p. 117) (New York: Charles Scribner's Sons).